W9-CCD-304

LEARN Adobe Photoshop CC for Visual Communication

Adobe Certified Associate Exam Preparation

Rob Schwartz

ADOBE PRESS
Adobe

LEARN ADOBE PHOTOSHOP CC FOR VISUAL COMMUNICATION
ADOBE CERTIFIED ASSOCIATE EXAM PREPARATION
Rob Schwartz

Copyright © 2016 by Peachpit Press

Adobe Press books are published by Peachpit, a division of Pearson Education.
For the latest on Adobe Press books and videos, go to www.adobepress.com.
To report errors, please send a note to errata@peachpit.com

Adobe Press Editor: Victor Gavenda
Senior Editor, Video: Karyn Johnson
Development Editors: Bob Lindstrom, Margaret S. Anderson
Technical Reviewer: Rocky Berlier
Copyeditor: Kelly Anton
Proofreader: Liz Welch
Senior Production Editor: Tracey Croom
Compositor: Kim Scott, Bumpy Design
Cover & Interior Design: Mimi Heft
Cover Illustration: alexvv, Fotolia.com

NOTICE OF RIGHTS
All rights reserved. No part of this book with video training may be reproduced or transmitted in any form by any means, electronic, mechanical, photocopying, recording, or otherwise, without the prior written permission of the publisher. The images and media files provided for download are copyrighted by the authors and Peachpit. You have the non-exclusive right to use these programs and files. You may use them on one computer at a time. Adobe product screenshots reprinted with permission from Adobe Systems Incorporated. For information on getting permission for reprints and excerpts, contact permissions@peachpit.com.

NOTICE OF LIABILITY
The information in this book is distributed on an "As Is" basis, without warranty. While every precaution has been taken in the preparation of the book, neither the authors nor Peachpit shall have any liability to any person or entity with respect to any loss or damage caused or alleged to be caused directly or indirectly by the instructions contained in this book or by the computer software and hardware products described in it.

TRADEMARKS
Adobe, the Adobe logo, Adobe Certified Associate, Photoshop, Illustrator, Adobe Capture, and Bridge are registered trademarks of Adobe Systems Incorporated in the United States and/or other countries. All other trademarks are the property of their respective owners.

Many of the designations used by manufacturers and sellers to distinguish their products are claimed as trademarks. Where those designations appear in this book, and Peachpit was aware of a trademark claim, the designations appear as requested by the owner of the trademark. All other product names and services identified throughout this book are used in editorial fashion only and for the benefit of such companies with no intention of infringement of the trademark. No such use, or the use of any trade name, is intended to convey endorsement or other affiliation with this book.

ISBN-13: 978-0-13-439777-1
ISBN–10: 0-13-439777-0

9 8 7 6 5 4 3 2 1
Printed and bound in the United States of America

To Caleb and Danny, you guys are the reason I work so hard. Stoked we make the time to play even harder! I love you guys!

Acknowledgments

Huge thanks to my kids for making this book possible. First, the kids in my house, Caleb and Danny, for understanding the times I had to get to work so we could play a little later. Second, to the kids in my classes who challenge me, encourage me, and make it all worthwhile. Last, to the kids I meet online through Brainbuffet.com or ACATestPrep.com who reach out to say thanks. All you guys help make me who I am, and you guys are an inspiration to me.

Also a huge thanks to the BrainBuffet team—especially Joe "Skibum" Dockery and Joe "Vampire" Labrecque—you guys keep it rolling. My educational and design heroes Mike Skocko and Kevin McMahon for inspiration, friendship, and encouragement in the classroom to think outside the box and aim high—you guys are my teaching heroes. The Adobe Education Leaders and the Education team at Adobe for being the source of many of my stolen ideas! Special thanks to Lisa Deakes and Johann Zimmern at Adobe for making our community what it is, and being an amazing voice for education. Thanks to Jack Podell and Megan Stewart for seeing something in that Florida guy back in the Macromedia days and bringing me into the fold.

And this book wouldn't have been possible without Bob Lindstrom and Margaret Anderson, who helped guide a newbie writer and made me sound like I knew what I was doing. Big thanks to Victor Gavenda and the rest of the Peachpit team who made this whole thing possible and gave the new kid a shot at doing something really cool for kids outside my classroom.

About the Author

Rob Schwartz is an award-winning teacher (currently at Sheridan Technical College in Hollywood, FL) with over 15 years experience in technical education. He is a popular speaker at state, local, and national conferences, and often presents on teaching strategies for Adobe products such as Photoshop and Illustrator. His focus on industry certifications and problem-based learning strategies are the secrets to his success.

Rob holds several Adobe Certified Associate certifications and is also an Adobe Certified Instructor. As an Adobe Education Leader Rob won the prestigious Impact Award from Adobe, and in 2010 Rob was the first worldwide winner of the Certiport Adobe Certified Associate Championship. Find out more about Rob at his online curriculum website at brainbuffet.com.

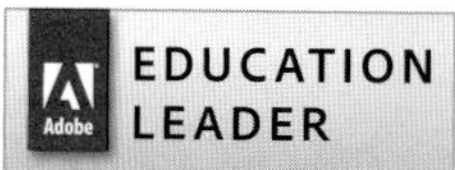

Contents

Getting Started

Welcome to *Learn Adobe Photoshop CC for Visual Communication!* We use a combination of text and video to help you learn the basics of working in Adobe Photoshop CC. We introduce you to each skill in the context of a hands-on project. Be sure to watch the video and download the lesson files to follow along. In addition, we cover other areas that you will need to master to work as a visual designer, including how to work with clients and how to approach design.

About This Product

Learn Adobe Photoshop CC for Visual Communication was created by a team of expert instructors, writers, and editors with years of experience in helping beginning learners get their start with the cool creative tools from Adobe. Our aim is not only to teach you the basics of the art of visual design with Photoshop, but to give you an introduction to the associated skills (like design principles and project management) that you'll need for your first job.

We've built the training around the objectives for the Visual Communication Using Adobe Photoshop CC (2015) Adobe Certified Associate Exam. If you master the topics covered in this book and video you'll be in good shape to take the exam. But even if certification isn't your goal, you'll still find this training will give you an excellent foundation for your future work in visual design. To that end, we've structured the material in the order that makes the most sense for beginning learners (as determined by experienced classroom teachers), rather than following the more arbitrary grouping of topics in the ACA Objectives.

To aid you in your quest, we've created a unique learning system that uses video and text in partnership. You'll experience this partnership in action in the Web Edition, which lives on your Account page at peachpit.com. The Web Edition contains 8 hours of video—the heart of the training—embedded in an online eBook that supports the video training and provides background material. The eBook material is also available separately for offline reading as a printed book or an eBook in a variety of formats. The Web Edition also includes hundreds of interactive review questions you can use to evaluate your progress. Purchase of the book in *any* format entitles you to free access to the Web Edition (instructions for accessing it follow later in this section).

Most chapters provide step-by-step instructions for creating a specific project or learning a specific technique. Other chapters acquaint you with other skills and concepts that you'll come to depend on as you use the software in your everyday work. Many chapters include several optional tasks that let you further explore the features you've already learned.

Each chapter opens with two lists of objectives. One list lays out the learning objectives: the specific tasks you'll learn in the chapter. The second list shows the ACA exam objectives that are covered in the chapter. A table at the end of the book guides you to coverage of all of the exam objectives in the book or video.

Most chapters provide step-by-step instructions for creating a specific project or learning a specific technique. Many chapters include several optional tasks that let you further explore the features you've already learned. Chapters 9 and 10 acquaint you with other skills and concepts that you'll come to depend on as you use the software in your everyday work. Here is where you'll find coverage of Domains 1 and 2 of the ACA Objectives, which don't specifically relate to features of Photoshop but are important components of the complete skill set that the ACA exam seeks to evaluate.

Conventions Used in This Book

This book uses several elements styled in ways to help you as you work through the exercises.

Text that you should enter appears in bold, such as enter **110** in the field.

Links to videos that cover the topics in depth appear in the margins.

Video 5.1 *Myths and Monsters*

The ACA Objectives covered in the chapters are called out in the margins beside the sections that address them.

★ *ACA Objective 2.1*

Notes give additional information about a topic. The information they contain is not essential to accomplishing a task but provides a more in-depth understanding of the topic.

NOTE *In time notation, the numbers after the last colon are frames. For video you read time as hours, minutes, seconds, and frames.*

Operating System Differences

In most cases, Photoshop works the same in both Windows and Mac OS X. Minor differences exist between the two versions, mostly due to platform-specific issues. Most of these are simply differences in keyboard shortcuts, how dialogs are displayed, and how buttons are named. In most cases, screenshots were made in the Mac OS version of Photoshop and may appear somewhat differently from your own screen.

Where specific commands differ, they are noted within the text as follows:

> Save your progress by pressing Ctrl+S (Windows) or Command+S (Mac OS).

In general, the Windows Ctrl key is equivalent to the Command key in Mac OS and the Windows Alt key is equivalent to the Option key in Mac OS.

As lessons proceed, instructions may be truncated or shortened to save space, with the assumption that you picked up the essential concepts earlier in the lesson. For example, at the beginning of a lesson you may be instructed to "press Ctrl+C (Windows) or Command+C (Mac OS)." Later, you may be told to "copy" text or a code element. These should be considered identical instructions.

If you find you have difficulties in any particular task, review earlier steps or exercises in that lesson. In some cases if an exercise is based on concepts covered earlier, you will be referred back to the specific lesson.

Installing the Software

Before you begin using *Learn Adobe Photoshop CC for Visual Communication*, make sure that your system is set up correctly and that you've installed the proper software and hardware. This material is based on the original 2015 release of Adobe Photoshop CC (version 16) and is designed to cover the objectives of the Adobe Certified Associate Exam for that version of the software.

The Adobe Photoshop CC software is not included with this book; it is available only with an Adobe Creative Cloud membership which you must purchase or it must be supplied by your school or other organization. In addition to Adobe Photoshop CC, some lessons in this book have steps that can be performed with Adobe Bridge and other Adobe applications. You must install these applications from Adobe Creative Cloud onto your computer. Follow the instructions provided at *helpx.adobe.com/creative-cloud/help/download-install-app.html*.

ADOBE CREATIVE CLOUD DESKTOP APP

In addition to Adobe Photoshop CC, this training also requires the Adobe Creative Cloud desktop application, which provides a central location for managing the dozens of apps and services that are included in a Creative Cloud membership. You can use the Creative Cloud desktop application to sync and share files, manage fonts, access libraries of stock photography and design assets, and showcase and discover creative work in the design community.

The Creative Cloud desktop application is installed automatically when you download your first Creative Cloud product. If you have Adobe Application Manager installed, it auto-updates to the Creative Cloud desktop application.

If the Creative Cloud desktop application is not installed on your computer, you can download it from the Download Creative Cloud page on the Adobe website (*creative.adobe.com/products/creative-cloud*) or the Adobe Creative Cloud desktop apps page (*www.adobe.com/creativecloud/catalog/desktop.html*). If you are using software on classroom machines, be sure to check with your instructor before making any changes to the installed software or system configuration.

CHECKING FOR UPDATES

Adobe periodically provides updates to software. You can easily obtain these updates through the Creative Cloud. If these updates include new features that affect the content of this training or the objectives of the ACA exam in any way, we will post updated material to peachpit.com.

Accessing the Free Web Edition and Lesson Files

Your purchase of this product in any format includes access to the corresponding Web Edition hosted on peachpit.com. The Web Edition contains the complete text of the book augmented with hours of video and interactive quizzes.

To work through the projects in this product, you will first need to download the lesson files from peachpit.com. You can download the files for individual lessons or download them all in a single file.

If you purchased an eBook from peachpit.com or adobepress.com, the Web Edition will automatically appear on the Digital Purchases tab on your Account page. Continue reading to learn how to register your product to get access to the lesson files.

If you purchased an eBook from a different vendor or you bought a print book, you must register your purchase on peachpit.com:

1. Go to *www.peachpit.com/register*.
2. Sign in or create a new account.
3. Enter ISBN: **978-0-13-439777-1**.
4. Answer the questions as proof of purchase.
5. The **Web Edition** will appear under the Digital Purchases tab on your Account page. Click the Launch link to access the product.

   The **Lesson Files** can be accessed through the Registered Products tab on your Account page. Click the Access Bonus Content link below the title of your product to proceed to the download page. Click the lesson file links to download them to your computer.

Project Fonts

All fonts used in these projects are either part of standard system installs or can be downloaded from Typekit, an Adobe service that is included with your Creative Cloud membership.

Additional Resources

Learn Adobe Photoshop CC for Visual Communication is not meant to replace documentation that comes with the program or to be a comprehensive reference for every feature. For comprehensive information about program features and tutorials, refer to these resources:

- **Adobe Photoshop Learn & Support:** *helpx.adobe.com/photoshop* is where you can find and browse Help and Support content on Adobe.com. Adobe Photoshop Help and Adobe Photoshop Support Center are accessible from the Help menu in Photoshop. Help is also available as a printable PDF document. Download the document at *https://helpx.adobe.com/pdf/photoshop_reference.pdf*.
- **Adobe Forums:** *forums.adobe.com/community/photoshop* lets you tap into peer-to-peer discussions, questions, and answers on Adobe products.
- **Adobe Photoshop CC product home page:** *adobe.com/products/photoshop* provides information about new features and intuitive ways to create professional-quality videos that play back on a wide range of devices.

- **Adobe Add-ons:** *creative.adobe.com/addons* is a central resource for finding tools, services, extensions, code samples, and more to supplement and extend your Adobe products.
- **Resources for educators:** *adobe.com/education* and *edex.adobe.com* offer a treasure trove of information for instructors who teach classes on Adobe software at all levels.

In addition we've set up some resources for you at Brainbuffet.com:

- Find resources for the series of books including ways to connect with authors and other readers on social media at *brainbuffet.com/peachpit*
- Find Photoshop resources at *brainbuffet.com/adobe/photoshop*

Adobe Certification

The Adobe training and certification programs are designed to help video editors, designers, and other creative professionals improve and promote their product-proficiency skills. The Adobe Certified Associate (ACA) is an industry-recognized credential that demonstrates proficiency in Adobe digital skills. Whether you're just starting out in your career, looking to switch jobs, or interested in preparing students for success in the job market, the Adobe Certified Associate program is for you! For more information visit *edex.adobe.com/aca*.

Resetting Preferences to Their Default Settings

Photoshop lets you determine how the program looks and behaves (like tool settings and the default unit of measurement) using the extensive options in Edit > Preferences (Windows) or Photoshop CC > Preferences (Mac OS). To ensure that the preferences and default settings of your Adobe Photoshop program match those used in this book, you can reset your preference settings to their defaults. If you are using software installed on computers in a classroom, don't make any changes to the system configuration without first checking with your instructor.

To reset your preferences to their default settings, follow these steps:

1. Quit Photoshop.
2. Hold down the Alt key (Windows) or Option key (Mac OS).
3. Continue to hold the key and start Photoshop.
4. When the program's splash screen appears, release the key.

CHAPTER OBJECTIVES

Chapter Learning Objectives

- Learn about the goals of the book and our style of teaching and learning.
- Get familiar with the Photoshop Welcome screen tabs and user interface.
- Learn to navigate and customize Photoshop.
- Learn to save custom workspaces and set workspaces for multiple users.
- Learn strategies to organize data and maximize efficiency.
- Learn to customize data display.
- Understand Creative Cloud features and benefits.

Chapter ACA Objectives

DOMAIN 3.0
UNDERSTANDING ADOBE PHOTOSHOP

3.1 Identify elements of the Photoshop CC user interface and demonstrate knowledge of their functions.

3.4 Navigate, organize, and customize the workspace.

CHAPTER 1

Meet Photoshop

Adobe Photoshop CC is one of the best-known pieces of software in the world, and—possibly even more impressive—it's also the first commercial software to be turned into a verb. (As in, "I *photoshopped* myself riding a fire-breathing shark!") Unless you've had your eyes shut for the last decade or two, you've certainly seen images there were edited with Photoshop.

In this combination of videos and chapters, you'll work on some awesome projects that will introduce you to Photoshop and help you establish some good workflow practices. We'll also share tips and resources that you can use to learn more on your own.

This book is intentionally different than most Photoshop books. It is designed to use project-based learning methods. This means that we won't teach you something that's out of context. When you need to use a tool, we teach it. This makes the learning much more engaging and practical. Your time is valuable and Photoshop is fun—so let's dig in fast.

Another thing that is really different about this book is that we intentionally avoid the monkey-see, monkey-do approach of many tutorials. We encourage you to use your own images, explore your own settings, and be sure to watch the videos where there is more time to explain the *reason* for using a certain setting. When using Photoshop, there are rarely settings that work in all circumstances on all images. We'll explain what you're looking at and why to use certain settings. This should help you understand how to venture out on your own.

Why We're Here

▶ *Video 1.1* Why We're Here

Let's take just a second to explain what we're trying to accomplish so we're all on the same page (pun intended!).

Have Fun

Seriously. This is a goal for us, and we hope for you too! When you're having fun, you're learning more, you're more likely to remember what you're learning, and it's easier to focus and stick with it. Every project might not naturally be your style, but we're going to try to make it as entertaining and rewarding for you as possible.

Just roll with it, and you'll find the time spent with the book and videos more enjoyable. Feel free to explore and customize the projects in the book to suit your own likes and interests. When we encourage you to explore an idea or concept, feel free to experiment. Have fun, make jokes, and enjoy your new superpowers.

Learn Adobe Photoshop Your Way

When you're doing the projects in the book, we really hope you feel the freedom to explore and make the projects your own. Of course, we welcome you to follow along with us precisely, but if we give you something to edit, feel free to change text or styles to fit your own interests. Make sure you understand the concepts we're discussing but also take time to explore and customize. There's much more to Photoshop than meets the eye (**Figure 1.1**).

Figure 1.1 The Photoshop splash screen

Prepare for Industry Exams

In this book, we'll cover every objective for the Adobe Certified Associate (ACA) exams. Passing this exam will allow you to display this cool badge (**Figure 1.2**). However, you won't learn the objectives in order or concentrate on "acing the test." We're teachers and trainers, and we've been doing this for a long time. So, we're going to take you through Photoshop in the way that makes the most sense for best *learning* and *retaining* your skills. We promise that you'll explore everything you need to pass the test and later take on an entry-level Photoshop job. But don't concentrate on testing or future work right now. Just focus on having a blast learning Photoshop!

Figure 1.2 Display this proudly after you pass your ACA exams.

Develop Your Creative, Communication, and Cooperative Skills

In addition to the hands-on work of learning Photoshop, we want you to develop the skills that you need to become a more creative and cooperative artist. Although these skills are tested on the Adobe Certified Associate exams, they're also critical skills for success. Every employer values creative people who can work and communicate well with others. This is especially true in graphic design and other creative areas. As a result, we will also take you through some basics of creativity, designing for others, working with others, and project management.

Getting to Know Photoshop

Before we get going with the application, let's just make sure you know how to launch Photoshop and work with its interface. This short section will introduce you to the interface, show you how to customize the configuration to arrange your work area exactly the way you want it, and then save that screen layout. It's a lot like adjusting the driver's seat preset in a luxury car. Once you configure Photoshop exactly as you like it, selecting one option sets up the entire application perfectly for your workflow.

Video 1.2 *Keep Photoshop Ready for Mac and Windows*

TIP *Do you need help launching your application or making it readily available on your desktop? Search online for videos on how to find and launch your Mac or Windows applications.*

A NOTE ON CREATIVITY

"An essential aspect of creativity is not being afraid to fail."—Edwin Land

The purpose of all the technical genuis behind Photoshop software is to allow you to be creative. There is a terrible misunderstanding that creativity is something you're born with. That is, some people have it and some don't. *Not true!* While some people might naturally be better at creative tasks, all of us can become more creative people (**Figure 1.3**). Like any other activity, creativity simply takes practice. The only way to get better at it is to experiment, explore, and even fail.

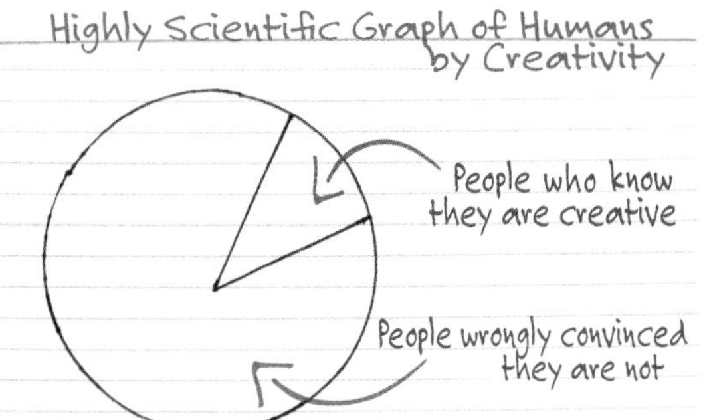

Figure 1.3 You might challenge the accuracy of these percentages, but please do so creatively.

In fact, failure is a *huge* part of creativity and an essential part of the creative process. So, celebrate and enjoy your failures! Art is a very experimental activity. Even the best artists make a bunch of junk. One difference between a capable artist and a newbie is that the pros learn to get comfortable with failure as part of the process. Everyone has 100,000 crummy ideas. A truly experienced artist has just used up (and set aside) more of them than the rest of us!

And don't worry if you feel like you aren't yet a strong artist. At the end of this book, we will explore ways to further build up your creativity and strengthen your creative muscles. It just takes spending some time in the creative gym!

The Welcome Screen

When you first launch Photoshop and after every software update, you will see a Welcome screen (**Figure 1.4**). This screen is divided into four tabs, which each provide information straight from Adobe about new features and tips:

▶ ***Video 1.3*** *The Photoshop Welcome Screen*

- **Create:** The Create tab enables you to create new documents using specific document presets for print, web, video, and so on. In this area, you can also find a list of your recent documents to easily open your current projects.
- **New Features:** The New Features tab introduces you to the newest functionality in this version of Photoshop.
- **Getting Started:** The Getting Started tab displays tutorials that offer great tips for beginners. Feel free to take a break from this book and check those out for a sneak peek at some basic, but critical concepts.
- **Tips & Techniques:** The Tips & Techniques tab includes videos that reveal insider tips and techniques.

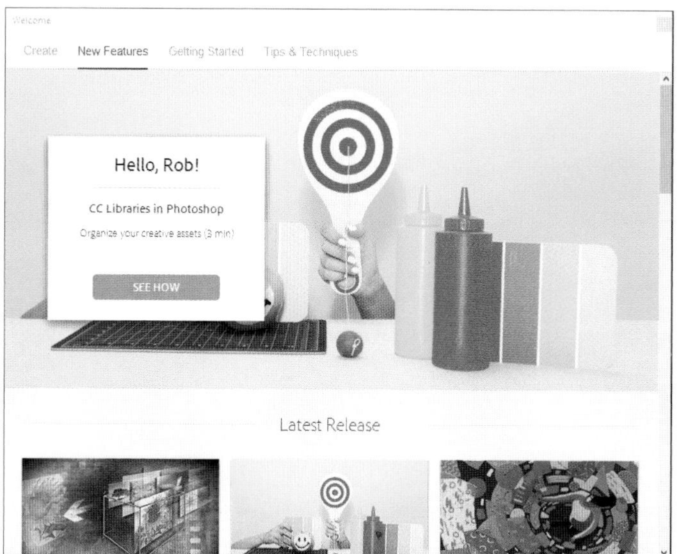

Figure 1.4 The Adobe Photoshop Welcome Screen

The videos and tips accessible in this Welcome screen are often very helpful, especially for discovering the latest features when Photoshop is updated. However, once you've seen it, you may prefer to disable this screen. No problem! Photoshop is highly customizable, and the Welcome screen can easily be disabled or activated by following these steps:

To disable or display the Welcome screen:

1 Scroll to the bottom of the New Features section.

2 In the lower right, select Don't Show Welcome Screen Again.

To display the Welcome screen again:

3 Choose Help > Welcome.

The Photoshop Interface

★ *ACA Objective 3.1*

The Photoshop interface is normally configured as in **Figure 1.5**, but it is highly customizable. Let's start with this default arrangement (called Essentials) to discuss the features of the workspace.

▶ ***Video 1.4*** *Tour the Photoshop Workspace*

- **Tools panel**: Contains all of the tools that you can use in Photoshop. It's important to know that each icon on the toolbar represents a stack of tools that you can access by clicking and holding down the mouse button over the tool's icon.
- **Options bar**: This is a context-sensitive area in which you can select options for your current tool. These options can be tricky when you're starting out with Photoshop and following tutorials. If you don't see the options that you want in this area, double-check to verify you have selected the correct tool.

Figure 1.5 The Photoshop interface in its default arrangement

- **Menu bar**: This is the standard application menu bar that displays all the menus for Photoshop.
- **Workspace switcher**: This menu on the Options bar enables you to choose preset workspaces and save the layout of your customized Photoshop interface.
- **Panels**: This highly customizable area includes the default panels for the application. These can be easily customized, moved, rearranged, or resized according to your needs. We'll get into the way to do that in just a bit.
- **Document window**: This area contains your work area and canvas.

Working with the Workspace

The Photoshop interface has multiple preset **workspaces** that quickly configure the interface to streamline specific tasks (**Figure 1.6**). You can also customize the workspace to meet your needs and save those configurations as your own workspace presets.

Video 1.5 Changing and Resetting Workspaces

- **Essentials**: This is the default workspace, which includes most of the commonly used tools.
- **3D**: This workspace includes the tools for working with 3D images.
- **Motion**: This workspace features the tools for video and animation.
- **Painting**: Use this workspace when you intend to create digital paintings and want your color and brush settings handy.
- **Typography**: This workspace is helpful for developing text and logo designs as it features the options for perfecting character and paragraph settings.
- **Photography**: Editing photographs is an important part of the Photoshop workload, and this workspace brings the appropriate tools to the forefront.

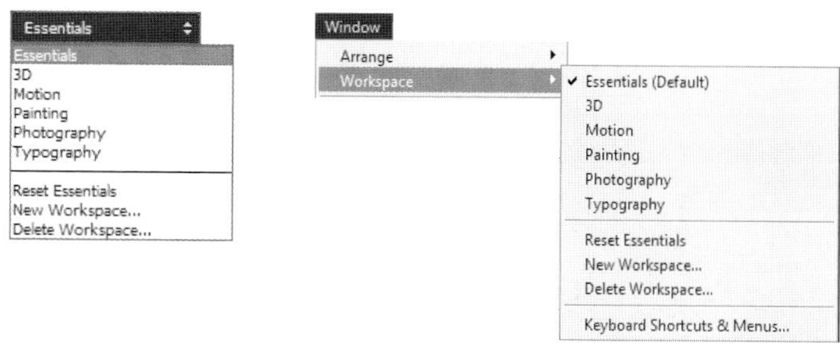

Figure 1.6 To find the Workspace menu presets, choose Window > Workspace or click the Workspace switcher in the Options bar. The Workspace switcher will be labeled with your current workspace (in this case, "Essentials").

To open a workspace and reset it to the default layout:

1. From the Workspace switcher, select the workspace preset you want to use.
2. Choose Window > Workspace, and choose the workspace preset you want to use.
3. To reset to default, select the workspace preset you want to reset.
4. Choose Reset *current workspace name* from the Workspace switcher, or choose Window > Workspace > Reset *current workspace name*. (The current workspace will appear as the menu option.)

In addition to the preset workspaces, Photoshop enables you to build and save custom workspaces based on your personal preferences and workflows.

★ *ACA Objective 3.4*

Creating Custom Workspaces

Video 1.6 *Creating Custom Workspaces*

Custom workspaces enable you to quickly configure that interface for specific users, jobs, and workflows. You simply set up the interface exactly as you want and then save the configuration as a new workspace (**Figure 1.7**).

To create a custom workspace:

1. Choose Window > Workspace > New Workspace, or from the Workspace switcher, select New Workspace.
2. Enter a name for the workspace. If you want to save any customizations you've made to the menus (Edit > Menus) or keyboard shortcuts (Edit > Keyboard Shortcuts), select those options as well.
3. Click Save.
4. Arrange your panels as you desire. The workspace will automatically update with every change.

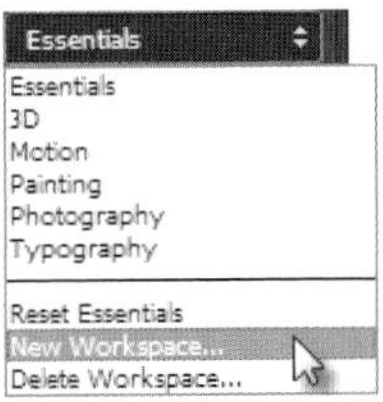

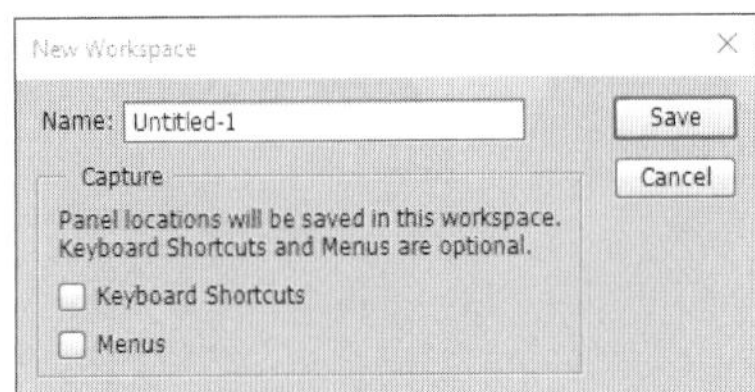

Figure 1.7 Create a new workspace and give it a name.

Rearranging the Workspace

Once you have created your own workspace, you can easily move the panels and panel groups to customize the interface configuration exactly as you desire. A **panel group** is the tabbed grouping of multiple panels.

To rearrange a panel in the same group, drag the panel tab and release the mouse button when the panels display in your desired order (**Figure 1.8**).

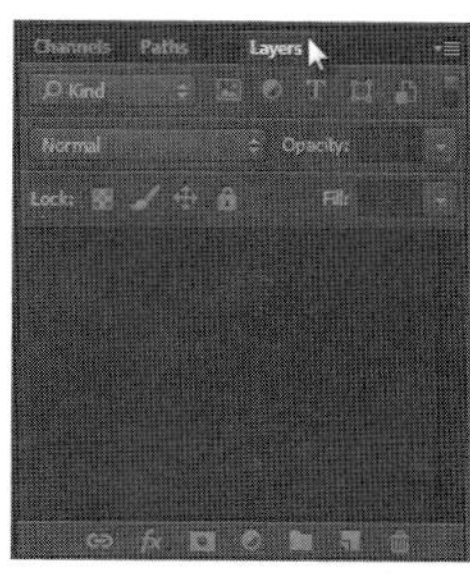

Figure 1.8 Drag to rearrange panels.

To create a new group, drag a panel tab and release the mouse button when a horizontal blue highlight bar appears (**Figure 1.9**).

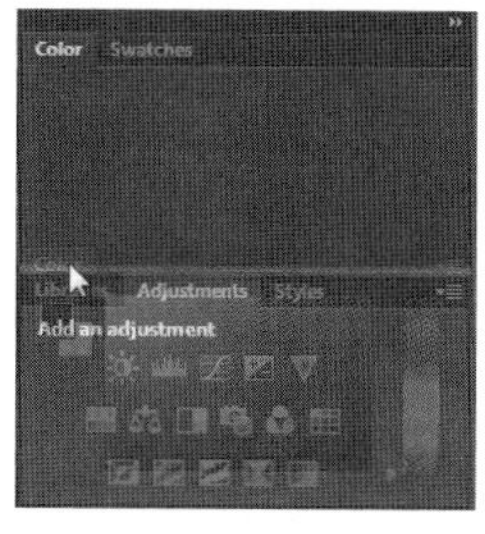

Figure 1.9 Create a new panel group.

To combine a panel with another group, drag the panel's tab into another panel group and release the mouse button when a blue highlight bar appears around the group (**Figure 1.10**).

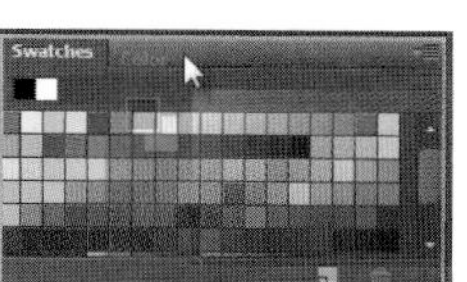

Figure 1.10 Combine a panel with another group.

To move panels and groups, drag the tab of that panel. To drag an entire group, drag the group by its title bar on the right, where the tabs end (**Figure 1.11**).

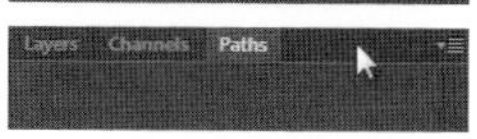

Figure 1.11 Drag a tab to move it to another group.

To resize panels, move the mouse pointer between the dividers of the panels until you see a double-headed arrow and then drag to resize (**Figure 1.12**).

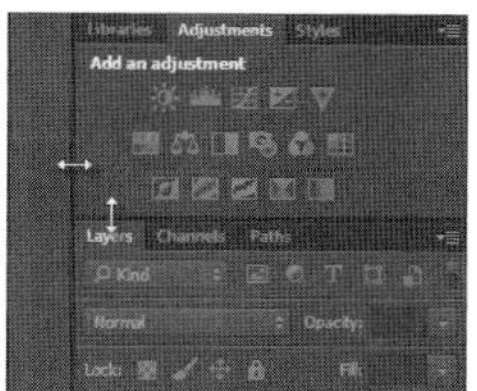

Figure 1.12 Resize panels to suit your needs.

You can organize your workspace any way you want. A properly configured workspace can really help you work more efficiently.

Organizing Your Data

Video 1.7
Organizing Your Data

As a digital artist, you will generate and work with many documents on your computer. It's a good habit to develop a system of organization that ensures you can keep track of all of those projects and files. Although I'm not going to get into detail here, let's talk briefly about a couple of good organizational habits that you can use while going through this book.

A Place for Everything

One of the most important tips I can share is to simply have a designated location for your Photoshop work. I also suggest that you make it easily accessible and just a click or two away from the Save dialog box. If you create a folder called `Photoshop` in that location, you can quickly access your documents when opening or saving work. Generally, the `Documents` folder is a great place to save your work as all operating systems have a quick link to this location within the Save dialog box, and you can customize its location in system settings.

If you have many files in this location, a well-known trick of computer users is to force folders to the top of the list by placing exclamation points in the beginning of the filename (**Figure 1.13**). For example, naming your folder `Photoshop` will place it in alphabetical order with the rest of your folders. On a PC, naming your folder `!!Photoshop` will make it jump to the top of the list. You can use the same trick to force folders to the bottom of the list by placing the letter "z" at the beginning of the name. For Mac OS, you can use underscores to force folders to the top.

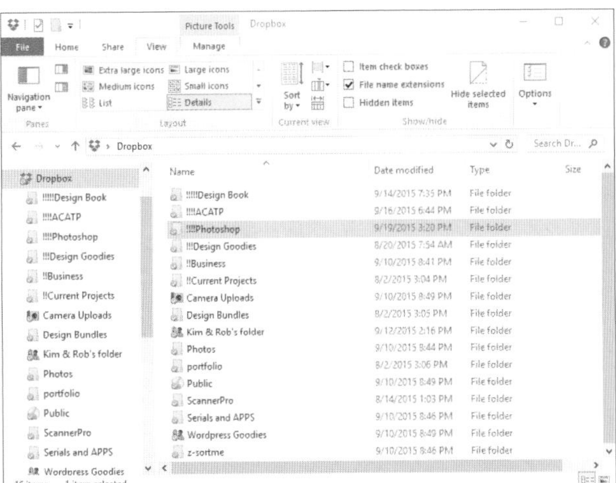

Figure 1.13 An organized file structure on your computer can save hours of file searching.

Back Up Often

Another important tip is to have a good system in place for backing up your work. You can do so manually by copying your work to a portable external hard drive by scheduling regular backups using backup software, or by automatically backing up your work using free services available online.

With your free Creative Cloud account, you receive two free gigabytes of online storage (as well as many other benefits). When developing this book, I saved all of my documents to my Creative Cloud folder, which automatically backed up my data as soon as I saved it to that folder (as long as I was connected to the Internet).

A Quick Word on Creative Cloud

When you sign up for a free Creative Cloud account, you can download free 30-day trials of Adobe applications (**Figure 1.14**). What's more, every time Adobe updates an app, you can get another free month of use to try the new features. You'll also get a free membership to the Behance community, which is a community for creative professionals where you can share your portfolio. Be sure to connect with us on Behance at *www.behance.net/brainbuffet* so we can see the amazing work you're doing as you learn!

***Video 1.7** About Creative Cloud*

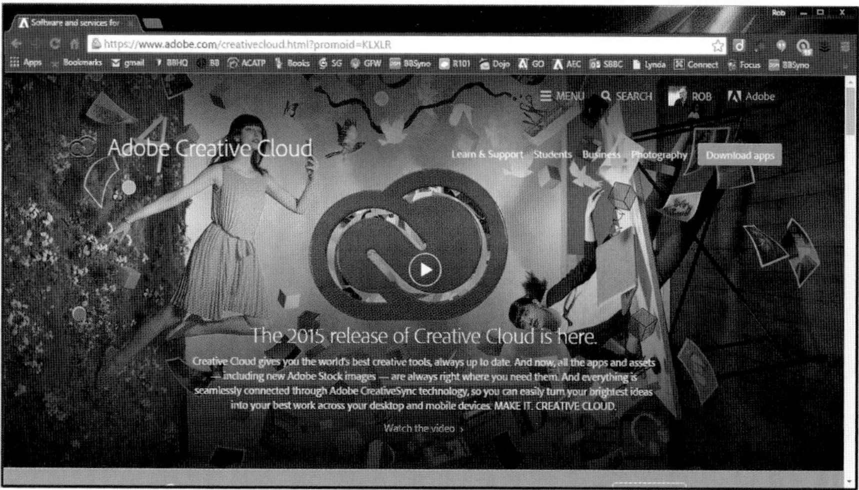

Figure 1.14 Adobe Creative Cloud guarantees you always have the newest version of the software and grants access to extra benefits.

After your 30-day free trial, you'll need a Creative Cloud subscription to continue to use the software. Adobe has actually offered subscriptions to their software for years, but not everyone could benefit from this program. It did provide substantial savings for program members and also allowed more frequent updates.

It's never been more affordable to get going with Photoshop—students can get a subscription for about $10 a month. With everything you'll be learning in this book, you should easily be able to generate enough work to pay for the subscription. For another $10 a month ($20 total), students can subscribe to the entire Adobe suite—a collection of 30 computer apps and 14 mobile apps. This is a spectacular deal and gives you every creative app you need for about the same price as a combo meal a week! Find out more at *www.adobe.com*.

Let's Get Going!

Okay—that's everything you need to know going in. You will be completing several projects in this book to cover all the basics of using Photoshop to edit photos and design images. The creative possibilities with Photoshop are astonishing. You won't believe what you'll be creating in just a handful of short projects.

CHAPTER OBJECTIVES

Chapter Learning Objectives

- Learn how to import and open images into Photoshop.
- Fix common problems in photographs from improper camera settings.
- Fix old photographs damaged with age and restore colors.
- Resize, sharpen, and save images for sharing on social media or the web.
- Convert images to Black and White with the ability to emphasize certain tones.
- Learn how to use these tools to make a good image even better.

Chapter ACA Objectives

DOMAIN 4.0
CREATING DIGITAL IMAGES USING ADOBE PHOTOSHOP

4.2 Import assets into a project.

4.4 Transform images.

4.6 Use basic retouching techniques—including color correction, blending, cloning, and filters—to manipulate a digital image.

4.9 Add filters.

DOMAIN 5.0
PUBLISHING DIGITAL IMAGES USING ADOBE PHOTOSHOP

5.1 Prepare images for export to web, print, and video.

5.2 Export or save digital images to various file formats.

CHAPTER 2

Fast Photo Fixes

Let's get started with some quick photo fixes that you can use straight away on images destined for social media and the web. Everything you'll do in this fast-paced chapter is a simple way to create a decent-looking image in record time. The projects you'll start also ease you into the Photoshop way of downloading and saving files that we touched on at the end of the previous chapter.

These quick and easy solutions may not always be the best solutions. For social media or the web, however, image quality is honestly not that important. Most online platforms recompress your images and alter their quality anyway to enable fast online access.

It's all about applying the right technique to the right job. For example, the methods you would use to create images for larger-format printers would be quite different from the techniques discussed in this chapter.

Just know that the **destructive editing** used in this chapter isn't right for every job. Destructive editing cannot be undone once the file is saved and closed. When you open that document again, you cannot go back to the original, untouched document. These are great for quick, simple fixes. In the next chapter, you'll learn ways to work **nondestructively** so that you can always tweak or undo your changes later.

Video 2.1 *Fast Photo Fixes*

Cleaning Up Your First Image

This section is a quick discussion of how to remove redeye and optimize an image for the web. Most new cameras have flash technology to reduce redeye, so it's a less common problem than it used to be, but it remains a common problem in older images. In the following projects, you'll learn some basic photo editing methods for making images that are quickly prepped for social media to look their best. Let's get started by opening an image in Photoshop.

★ *ACA Objective 4.2*

Opening Images

Video 2.2 *Opening Images in Photoshop*

Opening an image in Photoshop is similar to opening a document in any application. The most common way is to choose File > Open, and then locate the image. This works perfectly when you're opening documents stored on your computer. However, in today's web-connected world, you'll often be grabbing images from the Internet or another source location. Let's look at the three ways you can open an image in Photoshop.

- **Choose File > Open:** Choosing this command will open an image file already saved on your hard drive.
- **Drag the image into the interface:** You can open an image by dragging the image file into the Photoshop interface. If images are already open, you'll need to drag the image file into the title bar of the document window to open it as a separate document; otherwise the image will open as a new layer in the current document.
- **Copy and paste:** This method is becoming more popular as people grab images from the web. First, make sure to copy the largest size image available to you, and be sure to do so before you create a new document. Now that the image is in the clipboard memory, Photoshop will automatically set the image dimensions of a new document to that size. Create the document, and paste your image into Photoshop.

TIP

When copying from the web, be sure to get the full size image, not a thumbnail (reduced size) copy.

To follow along with the video, open both the 201-redeye.jpg and 202-BBR&John.jpg images in Photoshop using the method you prefer from this list (**Figure 2.1**). You'll find instructions for accessing the lesson files in the "Getting Started" section (page xi).

Figure 2.1 You can have multiple images open in the tabbed interface of Photoshop.

TIP

The Redeye tool doesn't work on images of pets, which tend to feature "green eye." You need to fix that manually. See the "Level Up Challenge: Fix Redeye Manually" later in this chapter.

Fixing Redeye

★ *ACA Objective 4.6*

▶ ***Video 2.3*** *Remove Redeye from Your Photos*

In older color photographs taken with a flash, you often need to remove redeye, especially from people with light or blue eyes. In most of today's cameras and even camera phones, the flash uses technology to reduce redeye, but it still appears occasionally. The fix is a really simple tool, and a good way to get started editing your first image.

To remove redeye from a photo:

1. Click the Redeye tool icon, found under the Spot Healing brush. The pointer changes to a crosshair and eye cursor.
2. Place the crosshair over the center of the pupil with redeye and click.
3. Repeat this process for any other eyes with redeye (**Figure 2.2**).

Your first Photoshop fix is complete!

WARNING

Don't try to use the Redeye tool to circle or fill in an area on the image, or anything like that. This can cause problems. Just click once when you have the crosshair over the pupil's center.

Figure 2.2 The Redeye tool in action

Shrink, Sharpen, and Save for the Web

You'll perform the next three steps whenever you want to prepare an image for social media or the web. Most camera images are much too big (in both dimensions and file size) for web use. It benefits you and your viewers to shrink the images to smaller sizes to speed display time. I always remember this as the "Three S's" for prepping images online: Shrink, Sharpen, and Save it for the web.

Resize Images

★ *ACA Objective 4.4*

***Video 2.4** Resize Images*

The first step is to shrink the image. For the web, you'll typically want to reduce your images to around 1200 pixels in the largest dimension. This size works well for phones and most social media sites, and is great for the web because the smaller size images display much quicker.

> **NOTE** *Image size is mainly measured in two basic ways: the image dimensions (measuring the height and width of an image in pixels) and the image file size (measuring the total number of bytes in an image). Shrinking the image dimensions will always reduce the file's byte size, so the method you're currently learning helps reduce both.*

1. Choose Image > Image Size (**Figure 2.3**).
2. Enter the desired dimensions in pixels (1200) in either the Width or Height field.
3. At the bottom of the Image Size dialog box, select Resample.
4. Select the proper resampling method from the menu. In this case, select Bicubic Sharper (reduction) because you are shrinking an image (**Figure 2.4**).
5. Click OK.

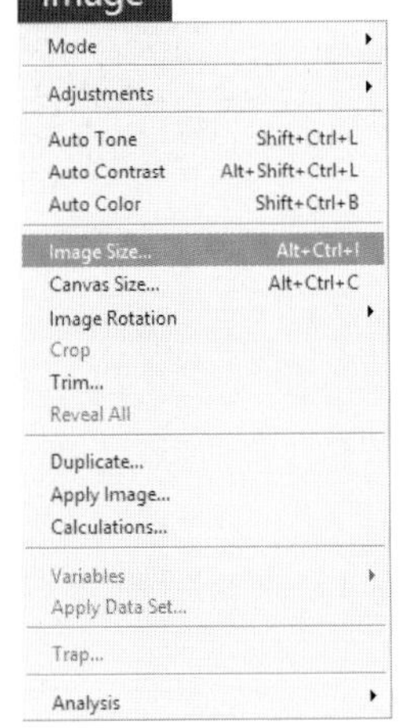

Figure 2.3 Select Image Size from the Image menu.

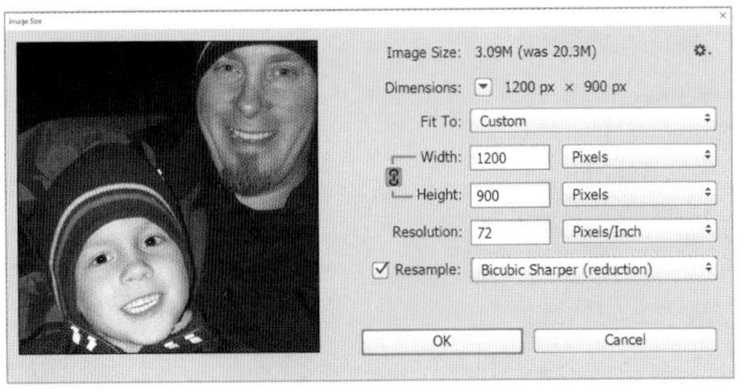

Figure 2.4 The Image Size dialog box with Bicubic Sharper (reduction) selected

For best results, it's important to specify the proper resampling mode. The notes in parentheses next to the resampling options should help you select the method that best suits your image and its use.

Sharpen Using Unsharp Mask

★ ACA Objective 4.9

Video 2.5 Sharpen Using Unsharp Mask

When creating images for the web, it's a good idea to **sharpen** it after reducing its size. Adding contrast to the fuzzy details makes an image look crisper. However, many sharpening methods—even within Photoshop—can cause skin and other smooth textures to get really gritty. To solve this, Photoshop has a **filter** called **Unsharp Mask** that sharpens only the edges within the subject of the photo while retaining the overall smooth textures of skin, clothing, and sky.

1 Choose Filter > Sharpen > Unsharp Mask (**Figure 2.5**).

2 Adjust the following settings in the Unsharp Mask dialog box (**Figure 2.6**).

- **Amount** specifies the level of contrast added to the edges. *Higher numbers sharpen more.*
- **Radius** sets how wide the sharpening should extend past the edges. *Higher numbers sharpen more* by increasing the width of edges.
- **Threshold** adjusts how much sharpening is applied to the spaces between detected edges. *Higher numbers sharpen less* between these edges.

TIP

Use Unsharp Mask rather than Sharpen Edges for detailed control over your image sharpening. Unsharp Mask is the best option for sharpening only the edges within your image.

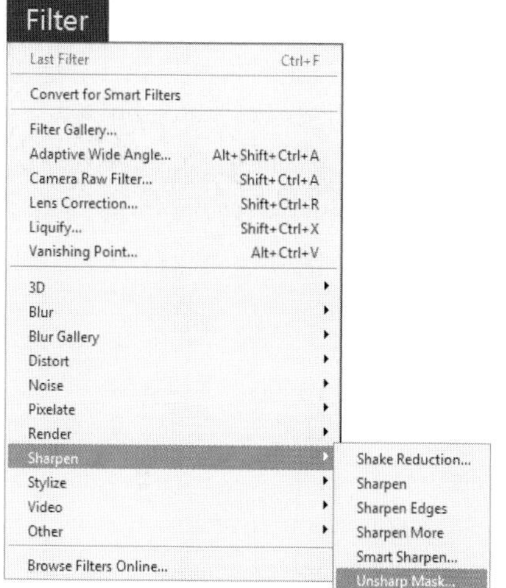

Figure 2.5 Choosing Unsharp Mask

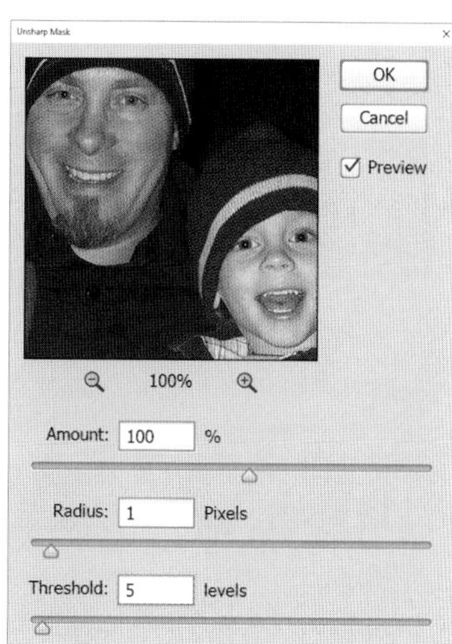

Figure 2.6 Adjusting settings for Unsharp Mask

TIP

Good starting values when sharpening pictures of people are: Amount 100%, Radius 1 pixel, and Threshold 5 levels.

3 Select Preview to compare the sharpened image to the original. (The dialog box always shows the sharpened image, so selecting Preview also shows the change on the image itself.)

4 Adjust the settings until the image edges look crisp but the smooth areas (skin, clothing, sky) are still smooth and pleasant looking.

5 Click OK to accept the sharpening.

That's all there is to it! Sharpening images with Unsharp Mask can help your images "pop" a little more by tightening up edges without distorting the smooth areas or gradients. The next step in our Three S's is to save your image for the web to share on social media or via email.

★ *ACA Objective 5.1*

Save Images for the Web

Using the Save For Web feature is the best way to save images in a format that is web friendly and will work with any Internet-related task: social media, websites, email, texting. What's more, the feature is designed to make the smallest file possible, so it will remove any unnecessary data from the image files, including **metadata** (you can select how much metadata to retain).

▶ ***Video 2.6*** *Save Images for the Web*

Saving for the web can be a little confusing initially because you have to choose from multiple online-friendly formats. Let's talk about the three image formats that are most popular online and when to use each.

- **JPEG** (pronounced "jay-peg") is the most popular format for photographic images. You can set image quality when saving in Photoshop to find the best balance between file size and image quality. JPEG files can end in a .jpg or .jpeg extension.
- **GIF** (pronounced "jiff" or "ghif") is a popular image format for images without a lot of colors. The format is also popular when making very small moving images or animations and can include transparent pixels based on a specific color. GIF images are best used for logos, graphs, and clip art images that have few colors. For higher quality images, the GIF format is falling out of favor and being replaced with PNG files. GIF files end in a .gif extension.
- **PNG** (pronounced "ping" or "pee en gee") is a relatively new format that was originally designed to replace GIF. It's an open source format that includes indexed as well as true color images, supports true alpha transparency, and is widely supported by applications and browsers. In many ways, PNG offers the best of the JPEG and GIF formats and is becoming more popular. (However, JPEG is still used for photographs because it tends to create smaller files.) PNG files end in a .png extension.

To save an image for the web, do the following:

1. Choose File > Export > Save For Web (Legacy) (**Figure 2.7**).
2. Select the desired format for your image.
3. Adjust the settings at the top of the Save For Web dialog box to determine the image quality.

   Choose your quality setting visually—depending on the image, the quality you will need will change. Medium often works for creating very small files where quality isn't a major concern.

   Select the JPEG medium preset (**Figure 2.8**).

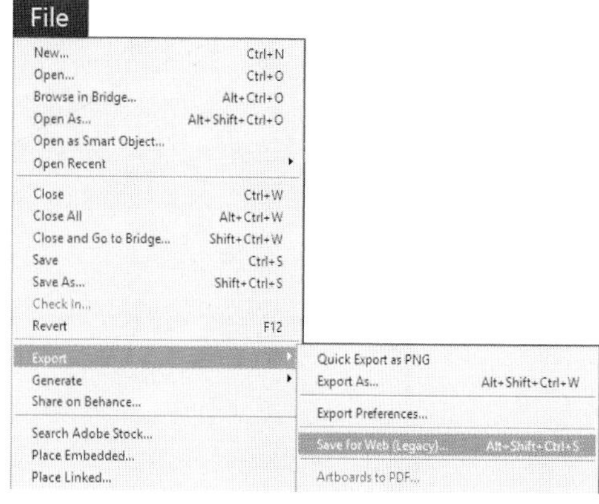

Figure 2.7 The Save For Web option

4. To specify the image size:
   - In the lower-right corner, enter values in the W or H field, or enter a value in the Percent field.
   - When Constrain Proportions (the chain link icon) is selected, adjusting the value in the W field automatically adjusts the value in the H field to maintain the proportions (aspect ratio) of the image.
   - Deselect Constrain Proportions if you're distorting an image for an effect.
5. Click Save and choose a location to save your document.

   Name the document `redeyefix.jpg`.

In the Save For Web dialog box, you can change your view to 2-up or 4-up to compare the quality between different file formats or settings with the same image.

Figure 2.8 The Quality is set to 30 for this example.

Close Your Image

You've corrected your first photo! You won't be needing this image any more so you can close this image. Since you have made changes, Photoshop will ask if you would like to save changes. You don't need to save the little you've done to this image, so you can click No in the dialog box that appears (**Figure 2.9**).

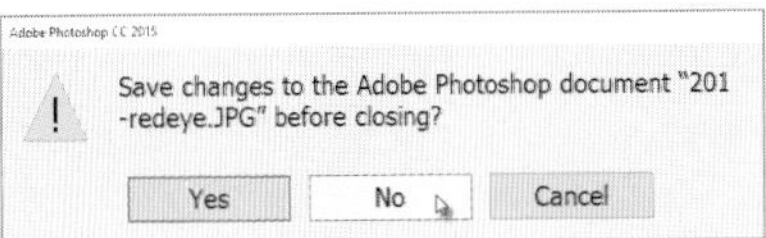

Figure 2.9 You can close the images without saving changes by selecting No in the dialog box.

★ *ACA Objective 4.6*

Fix Color Balance

***Video 2.7** Correct Color Balance*

The next image was also taken with a digital camera, but the settings were improperly set on the camera, creating a problematic **white balance**. This means the color of the lighting is visible in the photo. Our eyes do a lot of adjusting to the colors we see, and this is difficult for a camera to do. If a camera is set wrong or taking pictures in mixed lighting, then you can get a **color cast** where the color of the light is tinting the image (**Figure 2.10**). You will correct the color cast for this image and fix the redeye, and then save for web as you just learned with the last image.

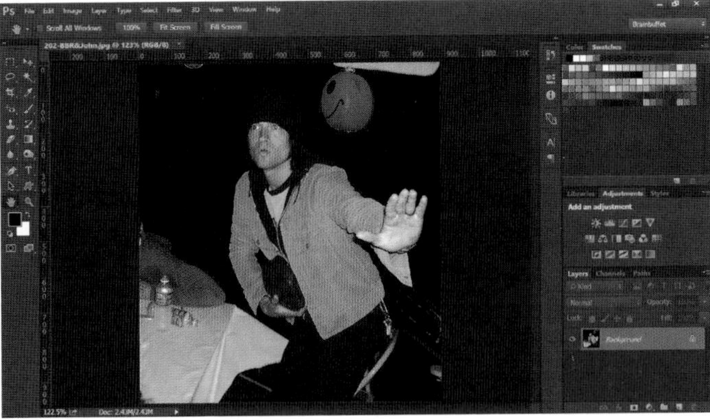

Figure 2.10 The blue tint in this image is caused by improper color balance (also called white balance) in the camera's settings.

Automatically Adjust White Balance

To automatically adjust the white balance of the image, you will use an automatic feature of Photoshop created to solve this common photo problem in older photos and in mixed lighting.

To automatically correct the color balance of an image, choose Image > Auto Color from the menu. This will remove the image color cast and balance the image colors properly. Note that when you select this setting, it is automatically applied to the entire image.

To automatically correct the white balance of an image:

1 Choose Image > Auto Color, or press Shift+Ctrl+B (Windows) or Shift+Command+B (Mac OS) (**Figure 2.11**).

2 Use Ctrl+Z to undo so you can compare the two images quickly (Command+Z in Mac OS).

   Smile because your image looks great!

You should see that the color balance in your image was easily fixed using the Auto Color command. However, sometimes you will need to tweak colors by hand. We will look at that later in the book, but most of the time, the automatic fix works just fine.

Image
Mode
Adjustments
Auto Tone Shift+Ctrl+L
Auto Contrast Alt+Shift+Ctrl+L
Auto Color Shift+Ctrl+B
Image Size... Alt+Ctrl+I
Canvas Size... Alt+Ctrl+C
Image Rotation

Figure 2.11 Choose Auto Color to automatically set the white balance of an image.

Fix Redeye

You can also see that this image has some redeye in John's eyes; let's correct that as you did in the last project. You'll have some problems with his left eye; the same problem often occurs with animals where the redeye tool will not be able to fix the image. You don't need to worry about it now, but feel free to take the challenge to learn how to solve this problem.

LEVEL UP CHALLENGE: FIX REDEYE MANUALLY

The Redeye tool doesn't always work. Pets often get "green eye" (in photographs, not real life) and sometimes a person's redeye is so bright that Photoshop doesn't recognize that the glowing dot is an eye. In these cases, you'll need to fix the redeye manually using the Sponge and Burn tools. The Sponge tool absorbs color, and the Burn tool lightens or darkens.

Video 2.8 When the Redeye Tool Won't Work

1 Select the Sponge tool to remove the color of (or **desaturate**) the eye and remove the red or green cast.

2 Press the Left and Right Bracket keys ([and]) to resize the Sponge tool pointer until it is exactly the size of the pupil or a bit smaller.

3 Click the pupil until the color is removed while being careful not to remove the color from the iris.

4 Select the Burn tool .

5 Adjust the pointer to the size of the pupil or a bit smaller using the bracket keys.

6 Click until the pupil is as dark as you want it.

Basic Photo Restoration

Video 2.9 Basic Photo Restoration

The next couple of images will help you learn to repair and restore old scanned photos. These images have unique problems that won't occur in digital images, such as dust, scratches, tears, and other physical damage to the photo. The tools you will use in this section of the chapter will help you restore photos when they have been damaged with age (**Figure 2.12**).

Figure 2.12 This photo has been damaged by age and needs significant work.

Flip or Rotate the Image

ACA Objective 4.4

You often receive images that are sideways or upside-down because of the way they were shot with a digital camera, or because of the way they were placed on the scanner. This is an easy fix with a method that you can also use to creatively work with images and play with perspective. This same method also includes tools that you can use to create a vertical or horizontal mirror image.

To flip or rotate an image:

1. Choose Image > Image Rotation (**Figure 2.13**).
2. From the Image Rotation submenu, choose the proper rotation or flip for your needs (**Figure 2.14**).

   When you flip an image, you will get a mirror image that reverses any text and numbers. Keep this in mind when you flip an image.

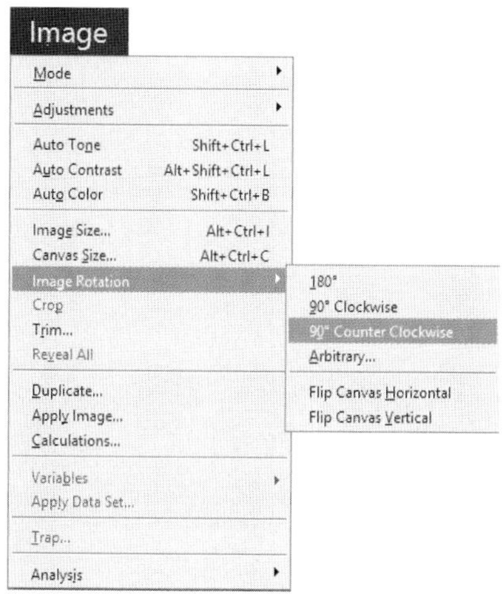

Figure 2.13 The Image Rotation submenu of the Image menu

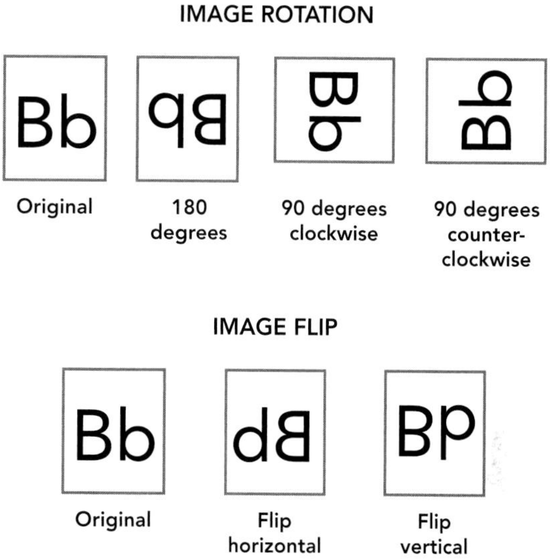

IMAGE ROTATION

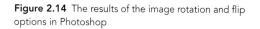

Original | 180 degrees | 90 degrees clockwise | 90 degrees counter-clockwise

IMAGE FLIP

Original | Flip horizontal | Flip vertical

Figure 2.14 The results of the image rotation and flip options in Photoshop

Crop the Image

Cropping images is a common task in the design industry when you need to resize or reframe an image. Simply changing the crop of an image can drastically affect its feeling. When you crop the image, you are also adjusting its focal point and compositional balance.

To crop an image:

1. On the Tools panel, select the Crop tool.
2. Drag the tool from the upper-left corner to the lower-left corner to define your crop area, or drag the crop handles from the corners or sides of the image (**Figure 2.15**).
3. Click Commit in the Options bar to crop the image.

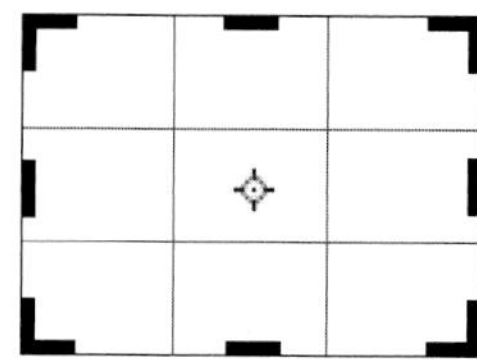

Figure 2.15 Drag the crop handles or corners on the crop overlay to adjust an image's cropping.

Now the edges of the image have been removed, so the color adjustments can be completed. The white borders of scanned images can make Photoshop's image correction tools behave unpredictably.

★ ACA Objective 4.6

Video 2.10
Restoring Color in Aged Photos

Fix Color in Aged Photos

It is not uncommon for aged photos to begin to shift colors. This can be from the yellowing of the paper or from damage from light. There are some tools within Photoshop to help solve some of these common problems quickly. Later in the book you will learn to manually adjust many of these settings to perfect them, but you'll see in the next few steps that Photoshop can do an excellent job with these one-click tools.

Using Auto Color and Auto Tone

You've seen how Auto Color in Photoshop can automatically fix improper white balance settings in photos, but the **Auto Tone** tool is much more helpful with old, damaged photos. This tool will automatically set the black and white points in the image to make the blacks become truly black and the whites become truly white. This often corrects the tonal shifts as well as the color problems in an image (**Figure 2.16**).

To correct the tone and color of the image:

1. Choose Image > Auto Tone to automatically set the black and white points of the image.

   The image will change significantly, but results will vary depending on the source image.

2. Choose Image > Auto Color to see if an additional correction helps.

   The correction does enhance this image, but you'll find it does not for all images. If it seems to make the image appear worse, you can undo the step by pressing Ctrl+Z (Windows) or Control+Z (Mac OS).

These changes really helped fix this image, but there is some discoloration that would take a lot of time and effort to repair. Depending on the use, this may not matter much, but when there are irregular colors in an image, you can convert it to black and white to hide the color problems.

Now get this image ready for the web as you've done before. Shrink, sharpen, and save your web-ready image as `nostalgia.jpg`.

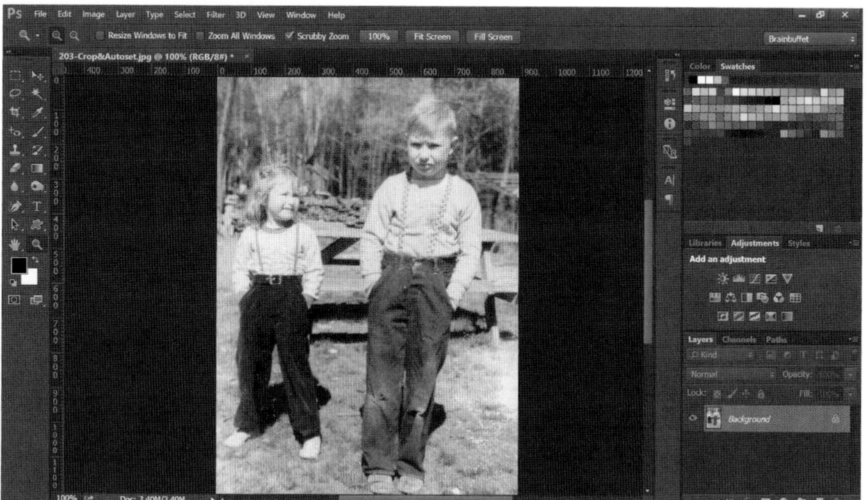

Figure 2.16 The auto correction tools in Photoshop can really change the quality of an image.

Converting Images to Black and White

You can often improve a weak color image by converting it to black and white. Doing so will not only discard any color casts but also allow viewers to focus on the image contents. Black-and-white photographs also have a much different feel; they can create a great mood with the beauty of the levels of light and dark in the image. Photoshop offers many ways to convert to black and white, but the preferred method gives you complete control over how the image is rendered in its final black and white form.

Video 2.11
Convert Images to Black and White

NOTE *Choosing Desaturate will also remove the color from the image, but will not give you any control over the final image. It's best practice to always use the Black & White adjustment for the ideal result.*

To convert an image to black and white:

1. Choose Image > Adjustments > Black & White (**Figure 2.17**).
2. Click Auto or browse the options from the Preset menu.

TIP *The Preview option will show your changes in real time on the image in the background.*

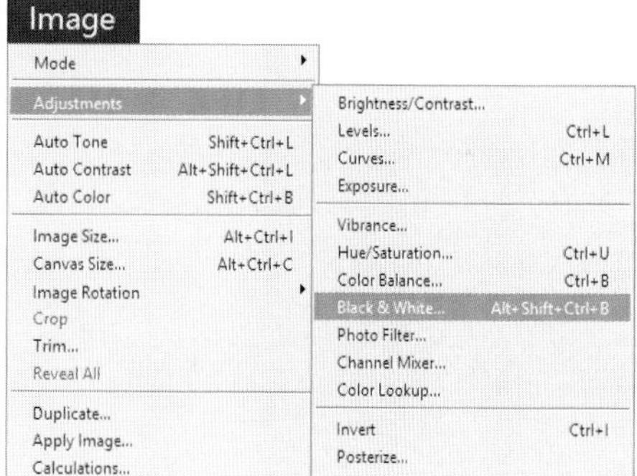

Figure 2.17 Use Black & White adjustments to convert images.

3 Manually adjust each color of your image to achieve the results you desire (**Figure 2.18**).

   Some images will look great after just choosing Auto or selecting a preset, but often you can get it looking even better with a little experimenting.

4 Click OK to accept the changes.

The image looks great (**Figure 2.19**). The conversion to black and white helps give it a nostalgic feeling which works for this photo. Now you will shrink, sharpen, and save this image for the web as you have the other images.

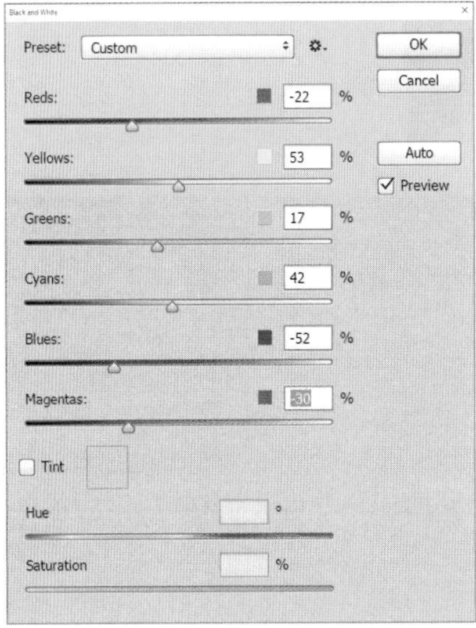

Figure 2.18 Experiment with each color adjustment to perfect your image.

Figure 2.19 The feeling in this image was enhanced by converting to black and white.

Shrink, Sharpen, and Save

As you've done before, you need to get this image ready for the web. Save your processed image as `nostalgiaBW.jpg`. After you've saved your images, close your document in Photoshop without saving changes.

Removing Dust and Scratches

The last damaged photo is one that has faded with time, and also has dust and scratches on the image. You will use many of the same tools you've used in the past to complete this task, so we'll only go into detail here with the new step of removing scratches. The videos will walk you through the whole process, though, so be sure to watch those.

Video 2.12
Removing Dust and Scratches

Open and Rotate the Image

First open the image as you have the others, but this time you'll see that the image is upside down. Rotate the image 180 degrees using the Image > Image Rotation command (**Figure 2.20**). Then crop the image as you have before to crop off the border and torn corner.

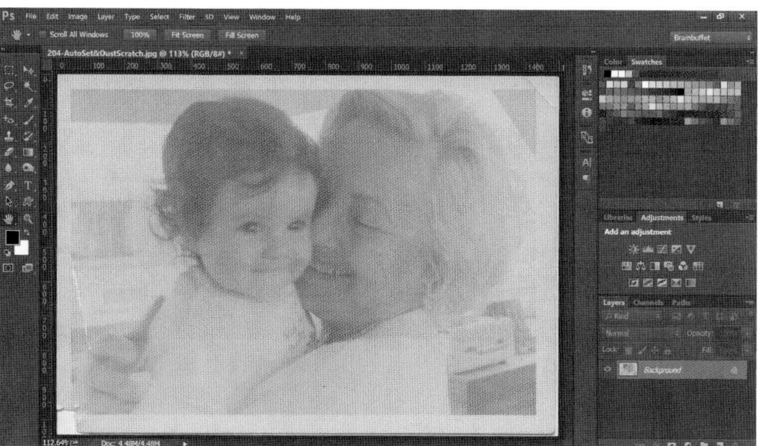

Figure 2.20 The image after rotating 180 degrees

The next step you want to take is to remove the dust and scratches from this image. There are a lot of minor problems in the image that can be corrected in one step using this tool.

To remove dust and scratches:

1. Choose Filter > Noise > Dust & Scratches from the menu (**Figure 2.21**).

   The Dust and Scratches dialog box appears.

2. Set the Radius and Threshold values according to your image.

   I used a Radius of 4 and a Threshold of 21 (**Figure 2.22**).

3. Click OK to accept the changes.

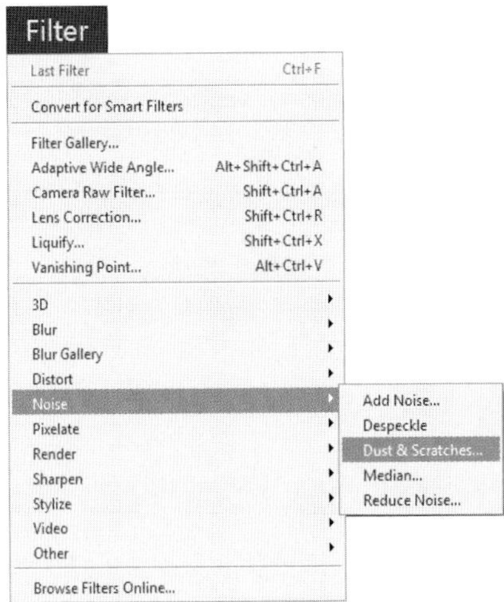

Figure 2.21 Dust & Scratches is a filter that reduces noise in the image.

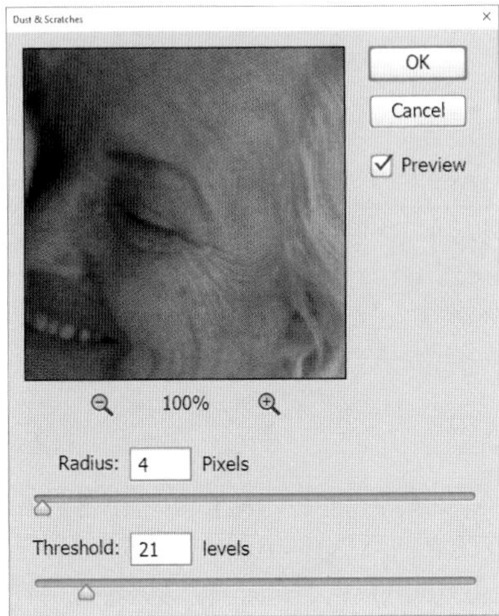

Figure 2.22 The Dust & Scratches filter dialog box

You can see that this does an impressive job removing dust and scratches on the image (**Figure 2.23**). This tool is a bit of a blunt instrument since it performs the same changes to the entire image. This chapter intentionally focused on how to fix damage to photos that are one-click or one dialog box type fixes. To dig a little deeper we need to move into the types of tools that allow us to choose exactly what gets fixed. The next chapter will discuss most of these tools in depth and teach you all you need to know to become skilled at repairing old photos.

Figure 2.23 The image after being repaired with the image-wide adjustment tools in Photoshop

Shrink, Sharpen, and Save

Once again, it's time to get this image ready for the web. Shrink to 1000 pixels in the largest dimension, sharpen with Unsharp Mask, and save for the web as a JPEG named `dustscratch.jpg`. After you've saved your image, close your original document in Photoshop without saving changes.

Perfecting Great Images

In this chapter, you used Photoshop features to repair damaged photos, but you can also use them to perfect excellent photos. Let's explore how the features you're already familiar with can transform images that don't need much help into visual masterpieces (**Figure 2.24**).

Video 2.13
Perfecting a Great Image

Figure 2.24 The original image is nice already, but you can improve it slightly for a more dramatic effect.

Use Auto Tone to Improve Images

Once again use Auto Tone to set the black and white point levels in the image automatically. This will give the image a more complete range of color and tone. You will see a slight change to the image, but it is an improvement. Most changes to images *should be subtle*. Beware the beginner's error of taking your changes too far.

Boost Color in an Image

Most images seen in magazines and advertising are color enhanced. An image rarely comes perfectly balanced "out of camera" (OOC in the design world). Especially in advertising, images are boosted with a little extra color. When clients ask for "pop" in their images, they're referring to boosting levels for enhanced contrast, as well as boosting **saturation** and **vibrance**. Increasing saturation boosts all color evenly, whereas increasing vibrance boosts the muted colors more than the already well-saturated areas of the image.

To adjust saturation and vibrance:

1. Choose Image > Adjustments > Vibrance (**Figure 2.25**).
2. Adjust the Vibrance and/or Saturation of your image by dragging the sliders or entering specific values (**Figure 2.26**).
3. Select Preview to compare the original and adjusted images.
4. Click OK to accept the edited version and admire the result (**Figure 2.27**).

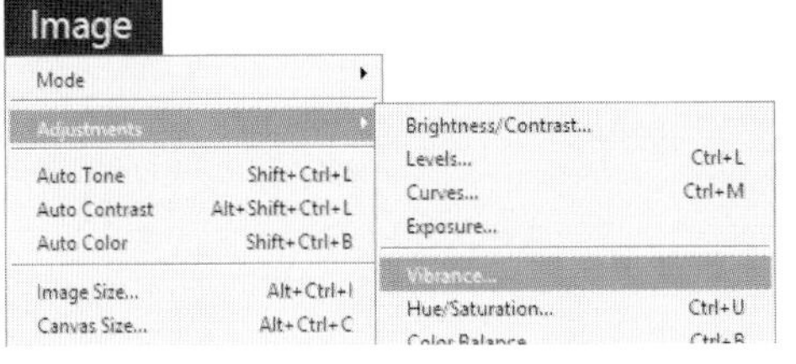

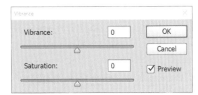

Figure 2.25 Selecting the vibrance adjustment from the menu

Vibrance: 0
Saturation: 0
OK
Cancel
Preview

Figure 2.26 The Vibrance settings are normally set visually using the preview.

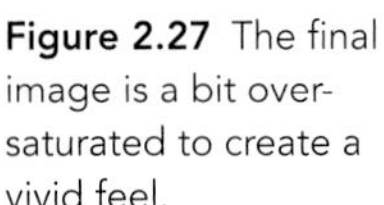

Figure 2.27 The final image is a bit over-saturated to create a vivid feel.

Shrink, Sharpen, and Save

For the last time this chapter, get this image ready for the web. Shrink to 1000 pixels in the largest dimension, sharpen with Unsharp Mask, and save for the web as a JPEG named `grapes.jpg`. After you've saved your image, close your original document in Photoshop without saving changes.

Wrapping Up

You've learned some amazing quick tricks to help images get to a decent level for sharing on the web or social media sites. This is great for Throwback Thursday images on Facebook! You learned not only how to fix common problems, but how to enhance an already good image and make it great.

Most of what you did introduced some tools and features that are relatively automatic in function. You also performed most of these image edits **destructively**. That is, you actually changed the image information without reserving the ability to undo or modify the changes later. Destructive edits are often "quick and dirty" photo fixes that can be completed so fast that it doesn't matter much if you have to redo your work.

Starting with the next chapter, you'll be applying a nondestructive workflow, which is a more desirable way to work because you can later remove or redo all of the changes you make to an image. A destructive workflow isn't bad; it's just less flexible and very resistant to change.

LEVEL UP CHALLENGE: FIX ON YOUR OWN

We've provided some extra images in the downloads folder that are either scanned old photographs or SOOC (straight out of camera) to challenge you. If you have them, I encourage you to experiment with your own challenge images. Fix these images using the tools and techniques you've learned about in this chapter.

- **Level I:** Fix the images using methods you learned in this chapter and save the images for the web.
- **Level II:** Take your own images with your camera phone or digital camera, and enhance them.
- **Level III:** Scan or photograph an older, faded photograph and restore it.

Video 2.14 Fix On Your Own

CHAPTER OBJECTIVES

Chapter Learning Objectives

- Open, repair, and restore damaged photos.
- Colorize black-and-white photos.
- Create, manage, and organize layers.
- Enter, edit, and format type.
- Combine and export layers.

Chapter ACA Objectives

For full descriptions of objectives, see the table on pages 256–261.

DOMAIN 3.0
UNDERSTANDING ADOBE PHOTOSHOP
3.2, 3.3, 3.6

DOMAIN 4.0
CREATING DIGITAL IMAGES USING ADOBE PHOTOSHOP
4.2, 4.4, 4.5, 4.6, 4.8

DOMAIN 5.0
PUBLISHING DIGITAL IMAGES USING ADOBE PHOTOSHOP
5.1, 5.2

CHAPTER 3

Restoring and Colorizing Damaged Photos

In the previous chapter, you learned how to perform many image-wide tweaks and fixes. Now you're going to dig a little deeper to learn about the most powerful feature of Photoshop: layers. Layers are an absolutely critical concept for mastering Photoshop. Adobe introduced layers in Photoshop 3 way back in 1995. Today, nearly every graphics program of note features this important innovation in digital imaging.

Layers are exactly what they sound like: a way to put some elements in front of, or behind, others. When items are on separate layers you can manipulate one area without affecting another, even if the two are in exactly the same area of the image.

In this chapter, you'll go beyond automatically fixing an image and enter the realm of enhancing and creating new elements in your image. You'll learn more about concepts that you've already explored, and then check out some really amazing new features and tools.

During the exercises, remember that it's more important to understand what each tool does than what it does for the particular image you're working on. It's helpful to experiment with the tools on your own images. Experimenting might be a bit harder than following along with the edits for this particular image, but you'll be more likely to retain the information in the long run.

★ ACA Objective 4.2

Restore Damaged Photos

Video 3.1 Restore Damaged Photos

I've been using this exercise for years to teach photo enhancement. You're going to restore an old, faded, torn image (**Figure 3.1**), and then convert the image to color. As with all of the projects in this book, the concepts you learn here can be adapted and used in a thousand different ways.

To get started, open the image named `EnaTheBallerina.jpg` from your Chapter 3 downloads folder. You'll notice that it needs a bit of work! (Many images that are nearly a century old will need work.) Take a little time to first examine the image and think about the fixes it will need.

Although we're going to modify it beyond what you're probably imagining, I want to make a point. As digital artists, our eyes are the most valuable tools we have. An experienced artist will spend a minute just looking and thinking about the image before jumping in with the edits. Sharpen that visual and analytical skill! Don't become so focused on what you're about to do that you lose sight of the step that comes before the action: determining what needs to be done. Most Photoshop books have you jump right into fixing the image, but being a Photoshop artist means thinking before you start working.

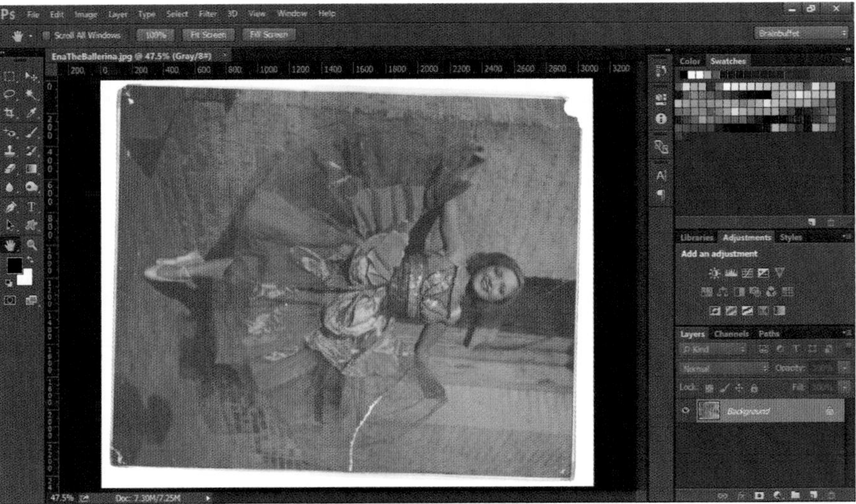

Figure 3.1 You will be restoring a damaged image and converting it from black-and-white to color in this chapter.

LEVEL UP CHALLENGE: SEE LIKE AN ARTIST

▶ *Video 3.2 See Like an Artist*

You will obviously acquire a lot of important technical and digital skills using these videos and this book, but it's also important that you know *when* to apply those skills. Taking 60 seconds to reflect, think, analyze, and identify your starting point is an effective practice.

This practice is called mindfulness or awareness. It's taking the time to really look and see before you jump to conclusions about how to solve a problem.

- **Level I:** Look at the image and think about what needs to be done to it.
- **Level II:** Discuss the image with a partner. Did she see something you missed? How can you avoid that blind spot with future projects?
- **Level III:** Find a different damaged image and try to fix it using the tools and tricks you learn in this chapter. You'll have a little less guidance because your image will require different fixes.

Rotate and Straighten the Image

ACA Objective 4.4

▶ *Video 3.3 Rotate, Crop and Straighten an Image*

Many images need to be rotated, but you'll also sometimes need to straighten images. Doing so requires a little more work than just rotating the image because you need to find a proper edge to use as a guide for straightening it. In this exercise, you will use a feature of the Crop tool that will automatically straighten the image.

To get started, first rotate the image so it's vertical:

1 Choose Image > Image Rotation.

2 Note the options in the Image Rotation submenu.

3 Choose 90° Counter Clockwise (**Figure 3.2**) to properly rotate the image of the ballerina.

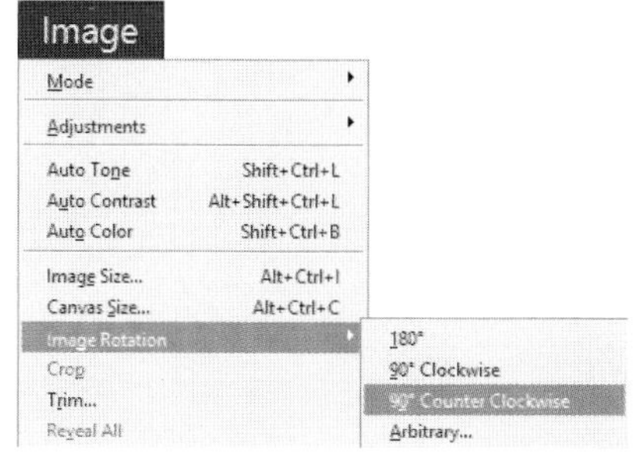

Figure 3.2 Choose Image > Image Rotation > 90° Counter Clockwise.

Crop and Straighten the Image

When working with scanned images, a common problem you will encounter is crooked images. This happens when images are not placed on the scanner precisely. Often, the white of the scanner bed is visible around the image, which throws off the auto color processing in Photoshop. In the following exercise, you will automatically straighten and crop an image in a few simple steps using the Straighten function of the Crop tool.

The Options bar provides a variety of options for the Crop tool (**Figure 3.3**):

- **Select Crop Presets** by aspect ratio or dimensions and resolution.
- **Enter and swap width and height** by entering dimensions or clicking the arrows to switch the width and height.
- **Clear the manual settings** for the crop width and height.
- **Straighten the image** using the straight edges of horizontal and vertical elements in the image.
- **Select Crop Overlays** to use compositional aids such as the Rule of Thirds, the Golden Ratio, or the Golden Spiral.
- **Adjust Crop tool options** to adjust the way the Crop tool operates.
- **Select Delete Cropped Pixels** to *destructively* delete cropped pixels or deselect it to *nondestructively* crop by retaining pixel data beyond the canvas.

To crop and straighten the image:

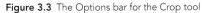

1. Select the Crop tool.
2. Identify a vertical or horizontal edge in your image such as the side of a building or the top of a sign.

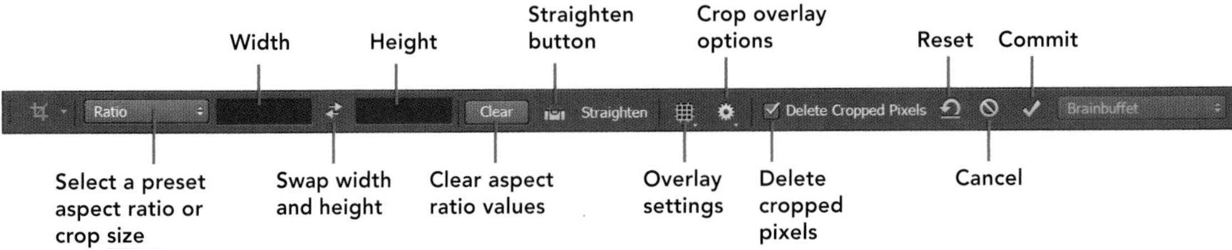

Figure 3.3 The Options bar for the Crop tool

3 To straighten your image, click Straighten on the Options bar.

- Drag a line across the vertical or horizontal reference point you have chosen.
- Release the mouse button to straighten the image and crop the edges.

4 If your image needs to be cropped more, drag the corners or edges of the Crop Preview box (**Figure 3.4**) to adjust the edges of the crop. (Don't crop out the torn corner, you'll be working on that next.)

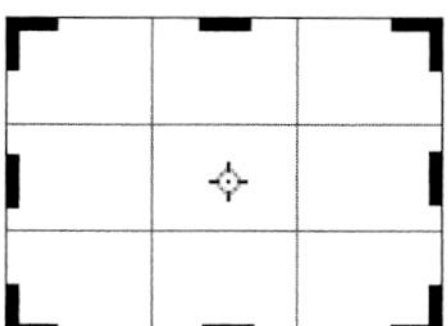

Figure 3.4 Drag the crop handles or corners on the crop overlay to adjust an image's cropping.

5 In the Options bar, click the Commit button to crop the image.

Using the Crop tool to automatically straighten and crop the image is an excellent way to fix photos with a crooked horizon or buildings that are leaning. This lesser-known use of the Crop tool saves time and you'll find it comes in handy on many photos, not just crooked scans.

Adjust Levels Manually

ACA Objective 4.6

Video 3.4 *Manual Levels Adjustments*

This image looks "muddy," as they say in the industry. The problem is that, over time, many old photographs fade and no longer have a good range of luminance contrast and balance. To modify the luminance balance, you can automatically or manually adjust the levels of the image. Manual adjustments work best when you want to add a little extra range to your image.

1 Choose Image > Adjustments > Levels (**Figure 3.5**), or press Ctrl+L (Windows) or Command+L (Mac OS).

TIP

You can click the Auto button in the Levels dialog box to automatically set the black and white levels of the image.

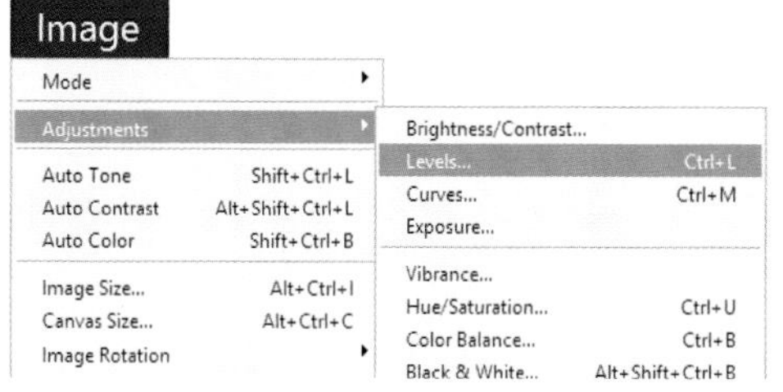

Figure 3.5 The Levels command in the Adjustments menu

NOTE

A histogram is a graph that represents how many pixels of each tonal value exist within the image.

2 In the Levels dialog box (**Figure 3.6**), first select Preview so you can see the changes on the image.

3 Start by dragging the black Shadow Input slider until you start to see data appearing in the left side of the histogram as shown in Figure 3.6.

4 Drag the Highlight Input slider toward the data appearing on the right side of the histogram.

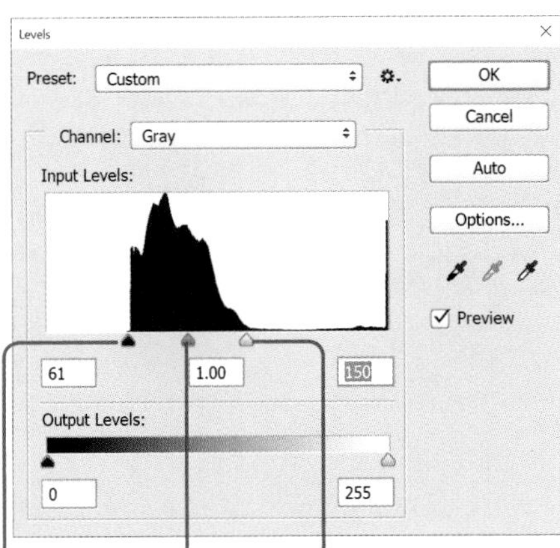

Figure 3.6 The Levels dialog box for adjusting luminance

TIP

Think about the histogram as a mountain and the sliders as cars. To adjust the levels, simply drive the cars to the base of the mountain on each side.

5 Drag the Midtone Input slider to the left or right to adjust the midtones depending on your image.

6 Click OK to accept the level adjustments.

As you can see in **Figure 3.7**, you can drastically change an image by adjusting its levels. Doing so will also reveal whether the image is evenly exposed. Remember that some images *should* have an uneven histogram to emphasize a mood, so you always need to consider the use and intention of the image when adjusting levels. Images that have little information in the brighter areas are called **low key**, and images that lack darker areas are referred to as **high key** (**Figure 3.8**).

Figure 3.7 The image is radically different after rotating, cropping (straightening), and changing levels.

Low key means little to no data in the light areas.

High key means little or no data in the dark areas.

Figure 3.8 Here, the unbalanced histogram of each image adds to the effect the image creates. Low key images (left) are dark and moody, while high key images (right) are bright and fresh.

Use Content-Aware Fill

▶ *Video 3.5*
Content-Aware Fill

The **Content-Aware fill** enables you to remove a selected object from an image and have Photoshop automatically fill in the blank area. The feature analyzes the area surrounding the pixels to be deleted, and then fills the area with similar pixels. You will use this feature to fill in the top-left torn corner with the surrounding texture, rebuilding the wall (**Figure 3.9**).

Figure 3.9 Content-Aware fill is an excellent tool for filling in larger areas of the image with surrounding image data.

To use the Content-Aware fill:

1 Using the Lasso tool, drag to select the area of the image you want to remove.

Select the top-left corner of the image with the torn corner.

2 Choose Edit > Fill (**Figure 3.10**).

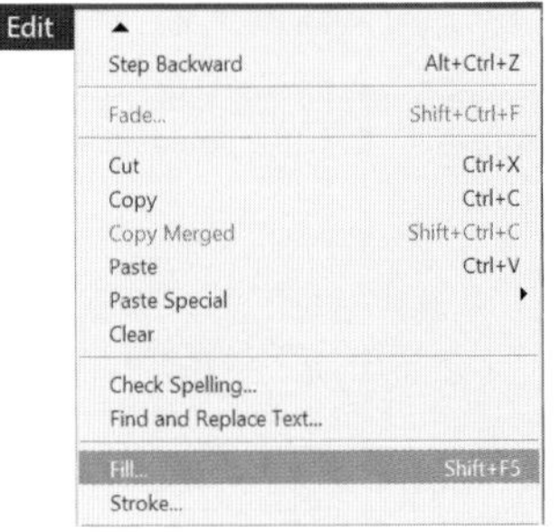

Figure 3.10 The Fill command in the Edit menu

3 In the Fill dialog box, select Content-Aware from the Contents menu (**Figure 3.11**).

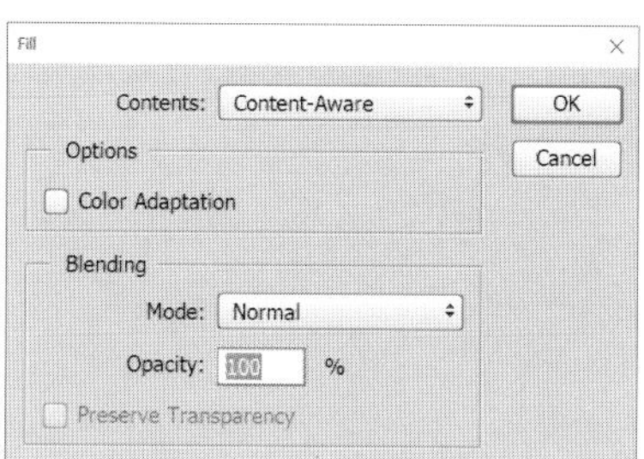

Figure 3.11 The Fill dialog box for applying a Content-Aware fill

4 Select Color Adaptation to help blend gradients (such as sunsets) or color variations in the blended area.

5 Leave the settings in the Blending area alone.

6 Click OK.

After removing the missing top-left corner, try using Content-Aware fill on the shadow in the bottom right of the image and other large areas that need attention (**Figure 3.12**).

Figure 3.12 The image after using Content-Aware fill to remove the tear and the photographer's shadow in the image

Using the Content-Aware fill is a fairly straightforward process, but realize that Photoshop can't always tell which pixels belong, which should be removed, and how to properly blend those pixels into the image.

If the Content-Aware fill does not work well for a particular task, press Ctrl+Z (Windows) or Command+Z (Mac OS) to undo the action. Then try making a new selection that varies slightly from the selection you used earlier. Doing so will cause Photoshop to recalculate the Content-Aware fill, which can often fix any undesired results. If it still doesn't work, you may need to try our next method, using the Spot Healing Brush.

Paint Perfection with the Spot Healing Brush

Video 3.6 The Spot Healing Brush

The Content-Aware fill is the best solution for removing large objects or elements from an image, but it's a bit tedious for smaller marks and scratches. For small fixes, the best tool is the **Spot Healing brush** (**Figure 3.13**). This tool enables you to paint away image imperfections quickly and easily.

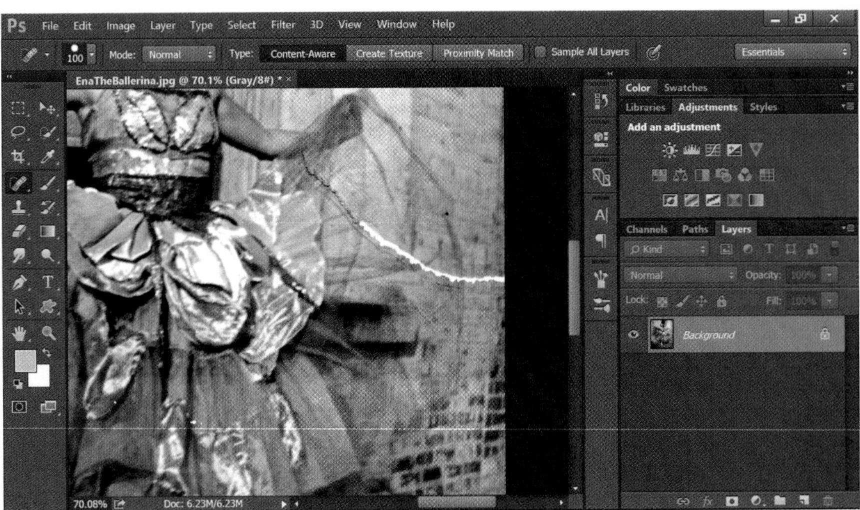

Figure 3.13 You can use the Spot Healing brush to quickly remove tears and scratches in the image.

TIP

To easily move around within an image, hold down the spacebar to activate the Hand tool and drag as if you were sliding the image on a tabletop.

To heal images with the Spot Healing brush:

1. Select the Spot Healing brush.
2. Press the Left and Right Bracket keys ([and]) to adjust the cursor. In this situation, you want to make it just large enough to cover the damage in a single stroke.

   The brush size displays on the cursor as you adjust the size of the brush. Pressing the Caps Lock key toggles the precision cursor that displays as a crosshair. It's not a bug, it's a feature, but it can catch you off guard if you press it accidentally!

3 Drag the brush cursor over the element you want to remove from the image.

When you release the mouse it will attempt to correct the problem (**Figure 3.14**).

Figure 3.14 The Spot Healing brush indicates the area it is covering while you paint with the tool.

TIP

The Spot Healing brush is intelligent, but not perfect. Just like the Content-Aware fill, if the results you get from the tool aren't what you want, undo the last action and try again. Sometimes just painting in a different direction will do the trick.

The Spot Healing brush will show you a preview of the area it will heal while you are dragging the brush on the image. As soon as you release, it will attempt to correct the problem in the image.

Use the Spot Healing brush to correct the other problems in the image (**Figure 3.15**). Remember to watch the video for tips and tricks that are best communicated visually.

Figure 3.15 The image after the defects are removed is quite impressive, considering how it started.

Sharpen and Save

▶ *Video 3.7 Sharpen and Save*

Although you haven't completed all of the improvements to this image, it's a good time to save it. Over the years I've learned that the best time to save a file is when you reach a point where you've done enough work that you don't want to lose it.

My first computer teacher back in middle school taught me an acronym that's popular in the computer industry: SOS. It stands for "**S**ave **O**ften, **S**tupid." Today it's hard to get away with that in some schools with our current "politically correct" culture, so I changed it to SOBS: **S**ave **O**ften or **B**e **S**orry. And if you don't save often, eventually you'll cry over losing hours of work...so just develop the habit and remember whichever acronym works for you.

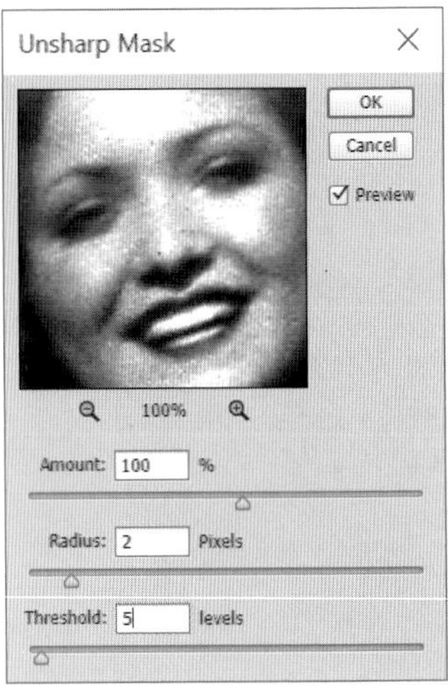

Figure 3.16 The Unsharp Mask dialog box

Sharpen the Image Edges with Unsharp Mask

Before saving your image, you should quickly sharpen the edges with an unsharp mask. Remember, this mask retains the smoothness of the image in large areas, but finds image edges and sharpens them. You will want to do this on the layers that contain the ballerina.

To apply the Unsharp Mask filter:

1 Choose Filter > Sharpen > Unsharp Mask.

2 In the Unsharp Mask dialog box, try the following settings (**Figure 3.16**):

- Amount: **100%**
- Radius: **2 pixels**
- Threshold: **5 levels**

3 Select and deselect Preview to compare the sharpened image to the original.

4 Click OK to accept the sharpening.

Save as PSD

★ *ACA Objective 5.2*

We will be saving this image as a Photoshop document. At the end of this chapter, I'll explain a little more of the advantages of this format. For now, just know that when you are continuing to work in Photoshop, Photoshop Document (PSD) is the best format to save in.

To save your image as a Photoshop Document:

1 Choose File > Save As.
2 In the File Name field (Windows) or Save As field (Mac OS), enter the filename `BallerinaBW.psd`.
3 From the Save As Type menu (Windows) or the Format menu (Mac OS), select Photoshop.
4 Browse to the location where you would like to save this document.
5 Click Save.

You've learned a lot of amazing Photoshop features already, but everything you've done so far was enhancing or repairing images to a previous state. In the next exercise, you're going to actually transform an image into something new. In this case, you will add color to this black-and-white image.

Colorize Black-and-White Images

In this section, you'll add color to the image. You may not be aware, however, that you couldn't do that right now if you tried. If you select a color from the Tools panel, you'll see that the color is converted to the closest shade of gray. (Go ahead and give it a try, I'll wait.) This is because the image is not in the appropriate **color mode**.

Choose a Color Mode

The color mode (also called the **image mode**) determines the color model that Photoshop uses to create the image. The most popular mode for working with images in Photoshop is RGB. That's the default color space for Photoshop and the most common mode for all digital devices and images. The CMYK color mode, on the other hand, is popular for printing because commercial presses use these four colors for reproduction.

▶ ***Video 3.8*** *Color Modes and Color*

You'll explore color and color modes later in Chapter 4, but for now just be aware of the existence of color modes, and know how to switch from one mode to another. The image you've been working with is in grayscale mode, which is why you can't apply colors to it yet. Let's convert this image to RGB color mode to allow Photoshop to work in its native mode and give us the largest array of tools to use.

To convert this image to RGB:

1. Choose Image > Mode > RGB Color.
2. Look at the title bar at the top of the document window. It now says RGB/8 after the name so you know the image has been converted (**Figures 3.17** and **3.18**).

EnaTheBallerina.jpg @ 42.4% (Gray/8#) *

Figure 3.17 The title bar in the document window for the grayscale image

EnaTheBallerina.jpg @ 42.4% (RGB/8) *

Figure 3.18 The title bar in the document window for the RGB image

There's very little fanfare, but you've just opened a world of possibilities!

The most important thing to take away from this is to *always* work in RGB unless you have a specific reason not to. Even when designing for print, it's best to do most of your work in RGB to have access to the widest variety of tools while editing your images. If the document will be commercially printed, you can then convert the image to CMYK at the end. We'll get to the details of working on documents intended for print in Chapter 4, where I'll discuss more about that process.

★ *ACA Objective 3.6*

Work with Layers

Video 3.9 Work with Layers

You will use **layers** to work on different areas of the image separately; this enables you to adjust each color without affecting the rest of the image. With layers, you can isolate separate elements of an image and adjust the way it is positioned, displayed, and mixed with elements on other layers in the image.

Photoshop was the first graphics application to introduce layers, and they have evolved a great deal since their introduction. To understand layers, imagine a stack of magic panes of glass. Each layer of glass can be moved above or below other layers, and the images on them can be made to blend, cover, or mix with the other panes' images in various ways. Now imagine this in a digital world, where the Layers panel in Photoshop is enabling you to create and modify these layers (**Figure 3.19**).

When you're looking at a Photoshop image, you're looking at this stack of panes from the top down. In the Layers panel, the stack is listed from top to bottom. The lower the layer is in the stack list, the farther toward the bottom it is when viewing the image. This is important to remember because the stacking order of the layers determines what's visible and what's hidden behind the content in other layers.

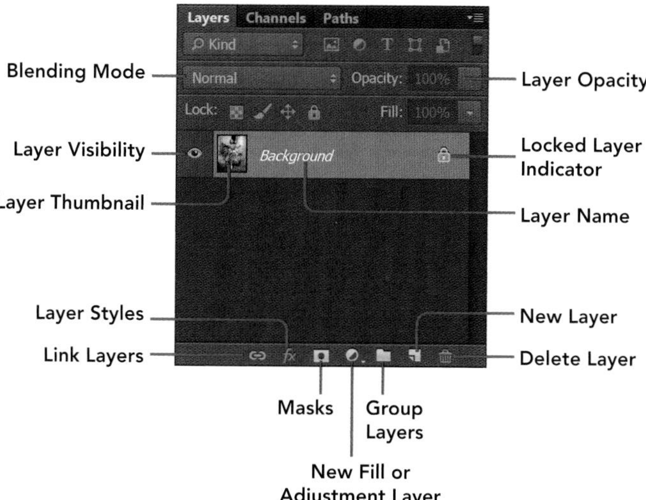

Figure 3.19 The Layers panel serves as a dashboard for your Photoshop documents.

Adding a new layer to an image is a simple process. Much like changing the color mode, the simplicity of adding a layer belies its power. To add a new layer to an image:

1. In the Layers panel, click the New Layer icon . You can also choose Layer > New > Layer, or press Ctrl+Shift+N (Windows) or Command+Shift+N (Mac OS).
2. Enter a name for the layer (often related to its use, such as "text") in the Name field. Don't worry about the other settings for now.
3. Click OK to create the layer (**Figure 3.20**).

   The layer appears in the Layers panel above the currently selected layer (**Figure 3.21**).

TIP

New layers will always be placed above the currently selected layer. In an image with multiple layers, select the layer that you want to be directly below the new layer, and then create the new layer.

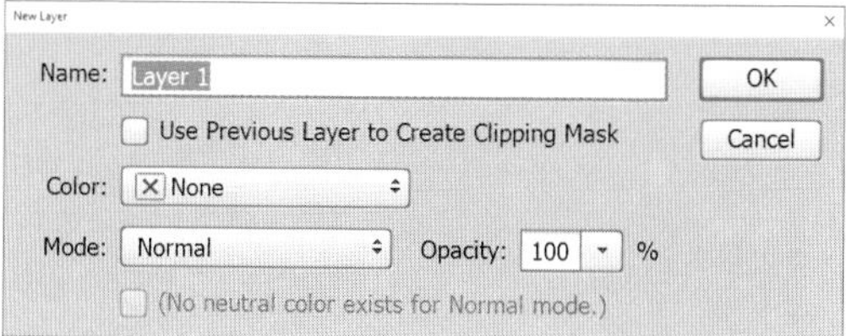

Figure 3.20 ▲ The New Layer dialog box

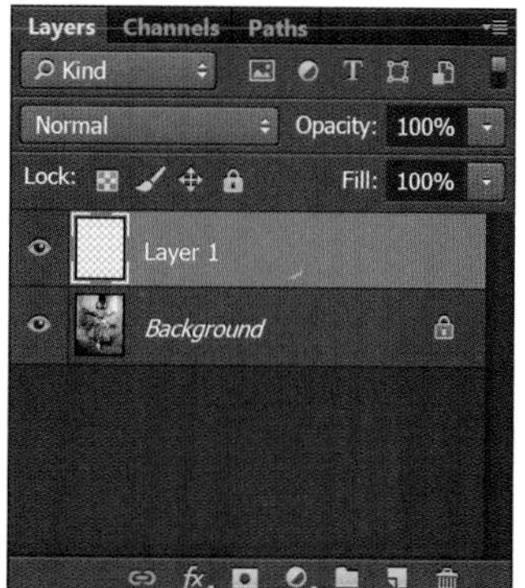

Figure 3.21 ◄ The Layers panel with a new layer above the Background layer

When the new layer is created, you're ready to start adding color. In the following exercise, you will use the power of blending modes to colorize the image. We will cover all of these steps in detail.

> **NOTE** *Make sure that you create a separate layer for each color you intend to experiment with. Doing so will allow you to perfect each color in your image individually without changing the other colors.*

★ *ACA Objective 3.3*

Brush Color on an Image

Video 3.10 *Brushing Color on an Image*

To add color to an image, it's best to isolate every color on a different layer. This enables you to modify the color without affecting any of the other colors, and it prevents a lot of headaches down the road. To begin, we're going to paint in the ballerina's skin tone. The main focus here is to get control of the Brush tool and learn how to use it with a fair degree of accuracy. This project will help you learn most of the tricks that designers use on a daily basis with the Brush tool.

To paint with the Brush tool:

1 From the Tool panel, select the Brush tool (**Figure 3.22**).

2 In the Tools panel, click the foreground color (Figure 3.22).

3 In the Color Picker (Foreground Color) dialog box, select a color that looks close to skin color (**Figure 3.23**).

To do this, first, click the color in the gradient slider (it looks like a vertical rainbow to the right of the color field) to select it, and then click the shade of that color in the large color field to the left of the gradient. You will be shifting this color, so its specific shade and hue aren't critical. Try to select a color that is somewhat similar to skin color.

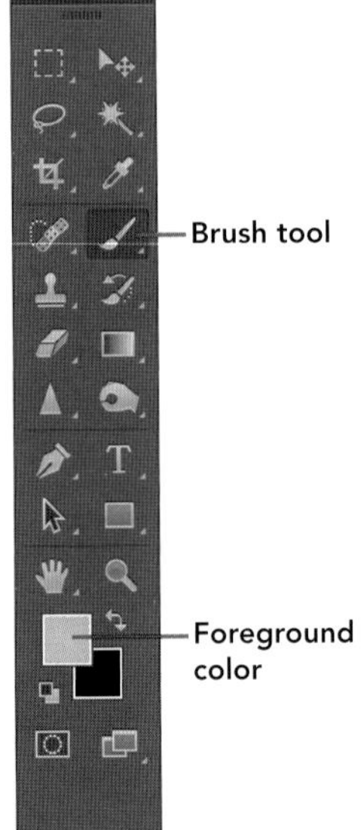

Figure 3.22 Selecting the Brush tool and checking the foreground color

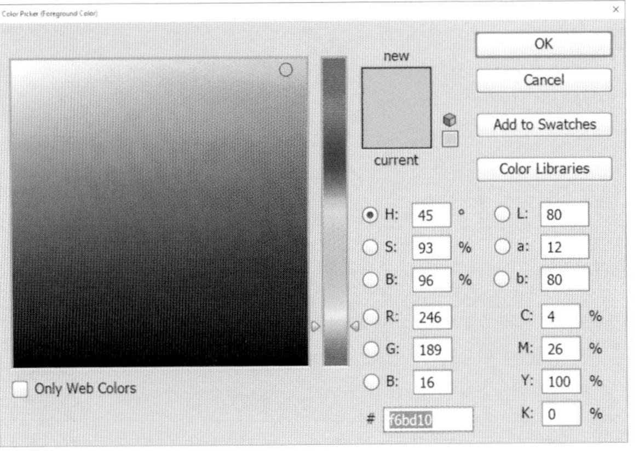

Figure 3.23 The Color Picker (Foreground Color) dialog box

4 Click OK to use the color.

5 In the Layers panel, select the layer you want to paint on. In this case, it should be Layer 1.

Layers are highlighted in light gray when they are active (selected). Any edits you make will affect only the active layers (**Figure 3.24**).

6 In the Options bar, adjust the size and **hardness** of the brush, or press the Left and Right Bracket keys ([and]) to adjust the size of the brush. The cursor should indicate the size of the brush.

The hardness of the brush determines how much the brush fades from its center point. A brush with a hardness of 100 has no fade, and a hardness of 0 has the maximum fade (**Figure 3.25**).

7 On the image, brush over the ballerina's skin to paint in a flesh tone.

NOTE *The Brush tool cursor will indicate the brush size and tip unless the precision cursor (which looks like a crosshair) is enabled. If your brush is not reflecting the size change, try pressing the Caps Lock key to return to the brush preview cursor.*

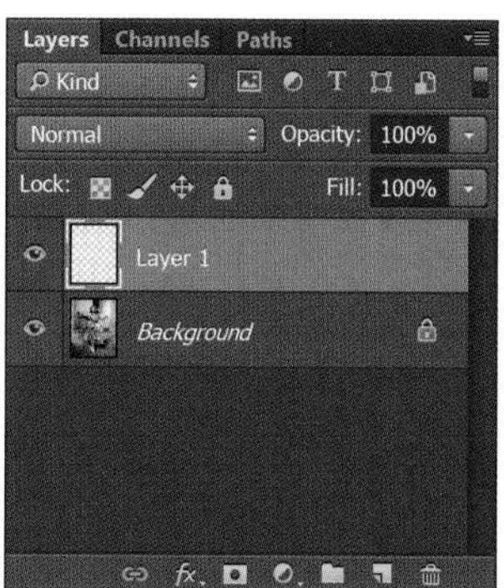

Figure 3.24 The Layers panel with Layer 1 active

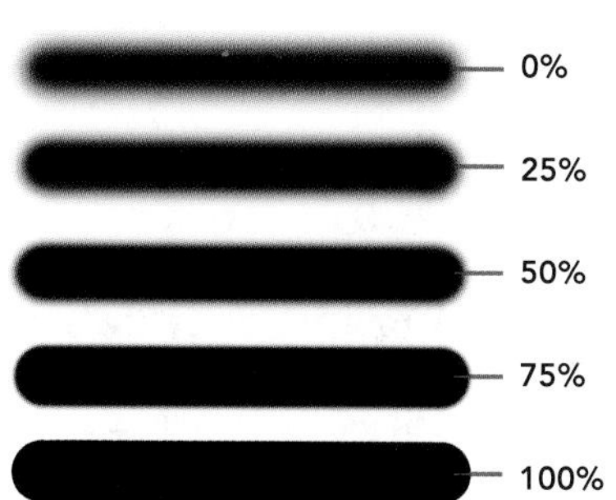

Figure 3.25 This image shows the relative difference in brush hardness settings in 25% increments.

You'll notice that when you initially paint, the results are opaque and look terrible. That's not how they should look—people aren't meant to be painted! To get the color and settings right, you will first need to paint the ballerina with the opaque color. But it's difficult to see where you're painting with the image getting covered up. Let's look at how to make the new color blend in to the image rather than cover it up.

WARNING *You might be tempted to try to fix the color right now, but don't! It's important that the color be uniform across the entire layer so that you can adjust the color and the blending mode uniformly.*

★ ACA Objective 3.6

Tweak Layer Settings and Color for a Natural Look

▶ **Video 3.11** Tweaking Layer Settings for a Natural Look

The reason the ballerina is being covered by the foreground color is because of the **blending mode** settings and the **opacity** of the layer. The blending mode of a layer determines *how* the layer blends with the layers beneath it. The opacity value of the layer determines how opaque or transparent that layer is. A layer with an opacity of 100% is completely opaque and solid, while an opacity of 0 makes all of the elements on that layer transparent.

To make this layer blend as desired and adjust the color to a natural appearance, you will need to adjust the blending mode and the color you selected.

The first step is to change the layer's blending mode to mix the painted color with the image in a way that enables you to see the image. The color will be addressed in the next step; this change will help you paint the skin areas accurately.

1. In the Layers panel, select the layer you want to edit.
2. Select a blending mode from the menu at the top of the panel. For this exercise, select the Color blending mode (**Figure 3.26**).
3. Drag the Opacity slider or enter a value in the field until the desired transparency is reached (**Figure 3.27**).

NOTE

Many artists cycle through the various blending modes to see what they prefer. To do this, select the Move tool and press Shift+plus sign (+) and Shift+minus sign (–) to cycle through the blending modes. On Windows, you can also press the Up and Down Arrow keys to cycle through the menu options.

As you can see, this change enables you to get fairly close to the desired effect. However, using the color I selected, the ballerina is still too orange. This often

Figure 3.26 ◀ The blending mode selected in the Layers panel changes the way layers blend with the layers beneath them.

Figure 3.27 ▲ Adjusting the opacity of the layer

happens. No single setting works in all cases. You will fix this color when you are finished painting, but at the moment it's important to finish painting the skin tones to be sure the color will be consistent across the subject's skin.

Erase Mistakes

★ *ACA Objective 3.3*

Video 3.12 *Erase Mistakes*

At this point, you need to finish painting the ballerina's skin layer. Don't worry about going beyond the skin—painting outside the lines as it were—as you can erase errors easily. It's more important to watch your layers at this point. If you are painting directly on the ballerina's layer or erasing on that layer, you will ruin the original image. All of your work should be confined to Layer 1.

TIP

You may find it easier to do this part while you're zoomed in on the image. While zoomed in, you may need to navigate within the image. Press the spacebar to temporarily switch the cursor to the Hand tool to pan around the image.

The Eraser tool works exactly like the Brush tool, except that it removes rather than adds information from the layer. The settings for the two tools are all identical and the steps are the same.

1. In the Tools panel, select the Eraser tool.
2. In the Options bar, set the brush Size and Hardness.
3. In the Layers panel, select the layer you want to work on.
4. Drag the Eraser tool cursor over the pixels you want to erase.

   Once again, note that layers are highlighted when they are active. Any changes you make will affect only the active layers.

Work on perfecting your image by verifying that all of the exposed skin areas are painted (**Figure 3.28**). It's important to get this right so that when you adjust the color in the next exercise, all the color is changed at once.

Figure 3.28 The skin color is unnatural, but focus on making the painted areas evenly covered.

★ ACA Objective 4.6

▶ *Video 3.13* *Shifting Colors*

Shift Colors

Almost every time you do this kind of project, you will want to adjust the colors in the layers you are painting. This is why it is so critical to put each color that you use on its own layer. As you adjust the colors, it will adjust everything else on the active layer. If you place a bad color on the same layer as a good color, fixing the bad one will ruin the good one!

1. In the Layers panel, select the layer you want to adjust.
2. Choose Image > Adjustments > Hue/Saturation, or press Ctrl+U (Windows) or Command+U (Mac OS).
3. In the Hue/Saturation dialog box, ensure that Preview is selected so you can see the image changing in the background (**Figure 3.29**).
4. Adjust the **Hue**, **Saturation**, and **Lightness** to suit your image (**Figure 3.30**).
   - Hue adjusts the color of the selected area or layer.
   - Saturation adjusts how saturated or vivid the color is in the selected area or layer.
   - Lightness adjusts the tone of the selected area or layer.
5. Click OK to accept the changes.

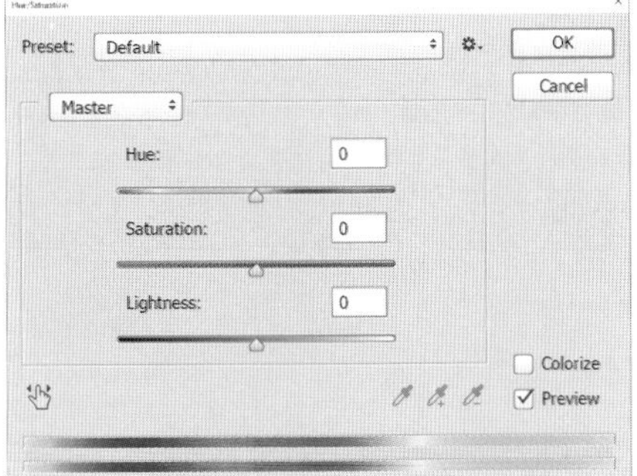

Figure 3.29 The Hue/Saturation dialog box

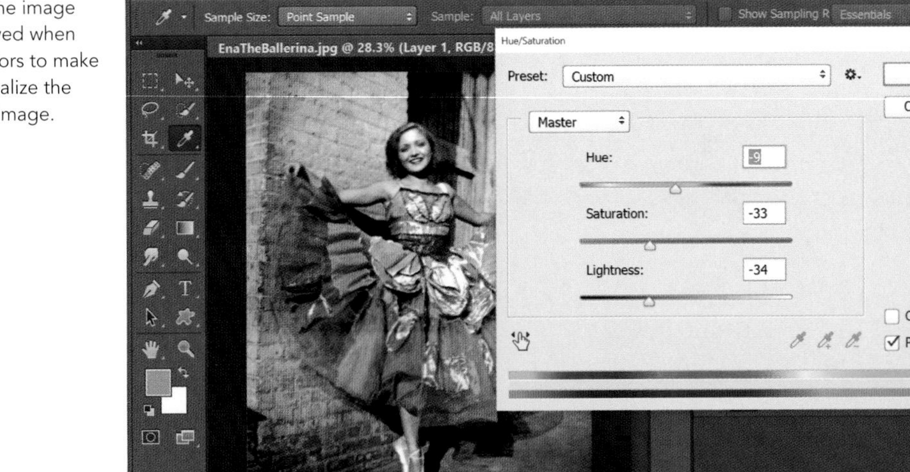

Figure 3.30 The image can be previewed when shifting the colors to make it easier to visualize the effect on your image.

Name Layers

★ ACA Objective 3.2

★ ACA Objective 3.6

Video 3.14 Naming Layers

In addition to creating a new layer for each color you add to the image, it's a smart practice to give the layers descriptive names to make them easier to identify later. It won't be long before you have multiple layers, and it will be difficult to remember if Layer 1, 2, 3, or 4 had the hair color.

You can name a layer when you create it or anytime thereafter. To name a layer when creating it, enter a name into the New Layer dialog box (**Figure 3.31**). To rename a layer, double-click its name in the Layers panel, enter a new name, and press Enter (Windows) or Return (Mac OS) (**Figure 3.32**). Once the layers have descriptive names, you can quickly select the right one to work on (**Figure 3.33**).

NOTE

You must double-click the layer name itself to change it. Double-clicking other areas of the layer will perform different functions.

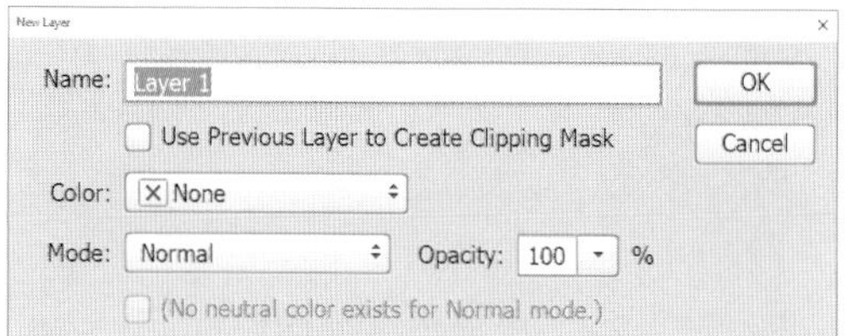

Figure 3.31 Naming a layer in the New Layer dialog box

Layer 1

Figure 3.32 Renaming a layer in the Layers panel

Figure 3.33 When layers are named descriptively, it's easier to determine what layer each element is on.

★ ACA Objective 3.6

Add More Layers and Colors

Video 3.15 *Adding Layers for New Colors*

Now that you know how to add color to the image, let's attempt to color the rest of the picture. My grandmother told me that the dress was supposed to look like a red rose with silver in the background, but feel free to create whatever color scheme you prefer. Photoshop is about artistic expression, not color-by-numbers replication.

Video 3.16 *Ballerina Mission*

LEVEL UP CHALLENGE: BALLERINA MISSION

This project enables you a lot of creative freedom, so you have plenty of ways to challenge yourself.

- **Level I:** Apply color to the ballerina (don't forget her lips and hair!) and make her dress one color.
- **Level II:** Apply color to the ballerina and make her dress three colors or more.
- **Level III:** Apply color to the entire image, leaving no black-and-white areas.

★ ACA Objective 4.5

Organize Layers

Video 3.17 *Organize Layers*

Some Photoshop projects can become unwieldy with literally dozens—and sometimes *hundreds*!—of layers. Managing layers well is like managing documents well on your computer. Photoshop allows you to group layers to help you organize your work on the image.

You can group and organize your layers many ways in Photoshop. I'm going to show you a few methods, but remember that you can mix and match them as necessary.

To group layers into a folder:

1. In the Layers panel, Ctrl-click (Windows) or Command-click (Mac OS) the layers for the group.

   The layers highlight in light gray when selected.

   TIP *To quickly select a contiguous range of layers, Shift-click the first and last layer in the range.*

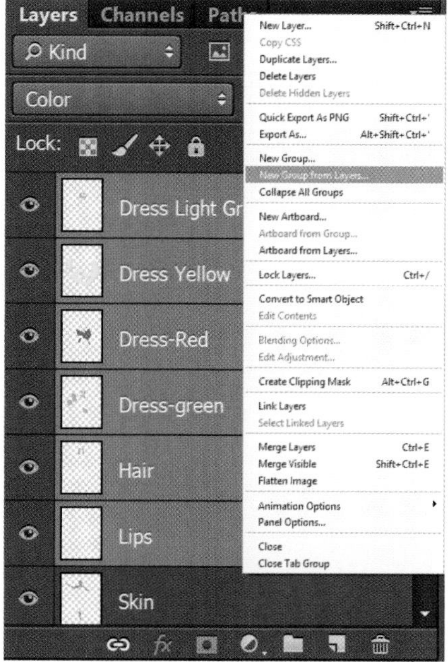

Figure 3.34 ◀ The New Group From Layers command in the Layers panel menu enables you to group selected layers into a folder.

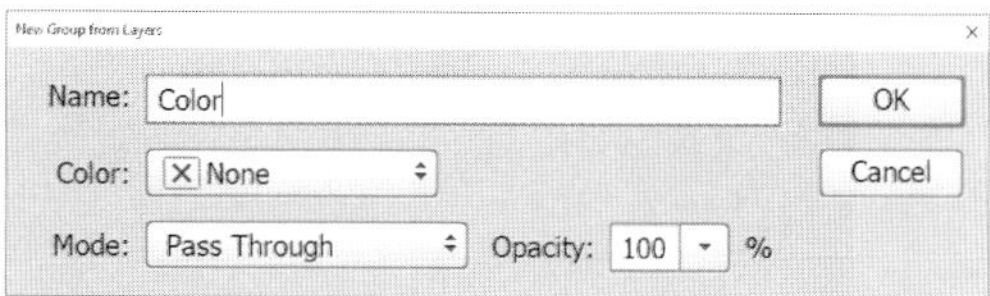

Figure 3.35 ▲ Naming a new group in the New Group From Layers dialog box

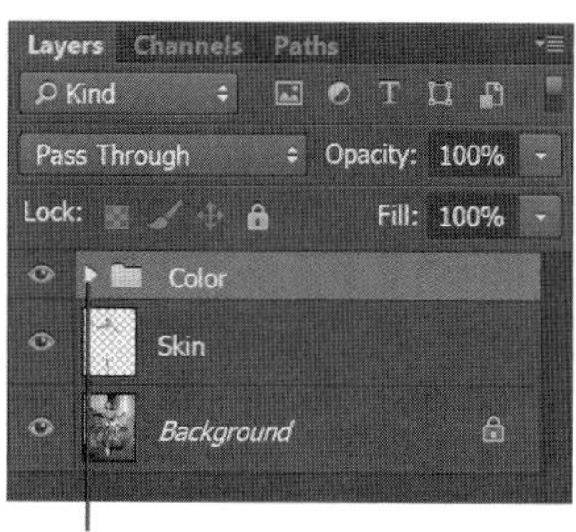

New layer group

Figure 3.36 ◀ The new Color layer group in the Layers panel

2 Select New Group From Layers from the Layers panel menu . You can also right-click (Windows) or Control-click (Mac OS) the selected layers and select Group From Layers from the Layers panel menu (**Figure 3.34**).

3 In the New Group From Layers dialog box, enter a descriptive name for the layer group in the Name field (**Figure 3.35**).

4 If you want to identify the layers in the group by color, you can select an option from the Color menu.

5 You can specify the Opacity and Mode for each layer in the group here, but it's best to leave these at their default values unless you have a specific reason to change them.

6 Click OK.

The grouped layers display in a folder with a disclosure triangle so you can expand the folder as necessary (**Figure 3.36**).

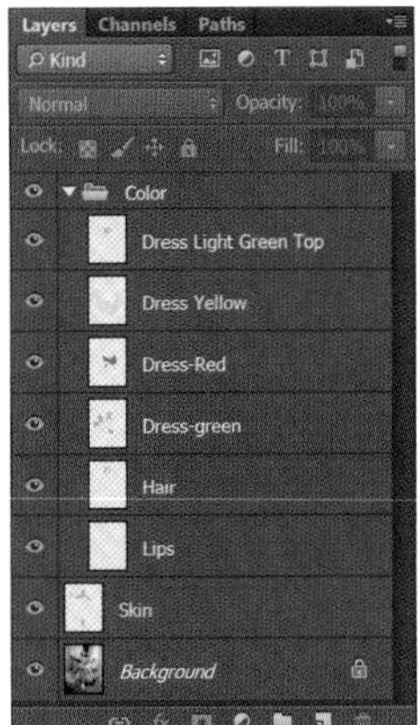

Figure 3.37 An expanded layer group

Work with Layer Groups

Grouping layers is a great way to organize your document with little downside. To view the individual layers within a group, click the disclosure triangle next to the folder icon to expand and collapse the layer group (**Figure 3.37**). When it's expanded, you can rearrange, rename, and modify the layers within the group the same way you would if they were not in a group.

You can modify a selected group in many of the same ways you can modify a single layer: by changing the order, opacity, and blending mode.

> **NOTE** *A new Pass Through blending mode is available for groups. This default mode for groups allows each layer in the group to maintain its own layer settings.*

Unlock the Background Layer

***Video 3.18** Unlock and Reorder Layers*

By default, when you open a new image file in Photoshop, the image is placed on the Background layer. Notice that the Background layer displays a lock icon at right. The Background layer is different from other layers because it cannot be moved, it cannot have transparent pixels, and it cannot be repositioned in the layer stack. To remove these limitations of the Background layer, let's unlock it.

To be able to edit the content on the Background layer:

1. Double-click the Background layer name.

   > **TIP** *You can also select the Background layer and choose Layer > New > Layer From Background. Or, you can right-click (Windows) or Control-click (Mac OS) the Background layer and select Layer From Background from the context menu.*

2. In the New Layer dialog box, enter `Ballerina` in the Name field.
3. Click OK.

   Now the Ballerina layer is properly named, and you've turned it into a regular layer that is free from the limitations of the Background layer.

Reorder Layers

A critical Photoshop concept to understand is the importance of layer order. The Layers panel lists all the layers in the document from top to bottom, while the image area shows a top-down view.

To illustrate this, move the Ballerina layer to the top and see how changing the layer stacking order affects the image (**Figure 3.38**).

1 In the Layers panel, select the layer that you want to move.

  Select the Ballerina layer.

2 Drag the layer to a new position in the stack.

  Drag the ballerina to the top of the layer stack. You will see a blue line when moving the layer just like when you arrange panels.

3 Release the mouse button to relocate the layer.

  The ballerina covers all of the layer contents.

Figure 3.38 The Ballerina layer hides all the layers below because it is on top of the stack, covering up all the other layers.

Now to undo this action, you can drag the Ballerina layer back to the bottom of the layer stack to see the colors again.

Remember that the higher a layer appears in the list, the closer it is to the top view of the image. Learning the ways to manage and creatively reorder layer positions and blending modes will help you become a more creative and efficient designer. It seems really simple at this point, but as your documents become more complex and you become more experienced using Photoshop, the order of layers combined with all the variations of layer settings can drastically change the way a document looks and the number of effects you can apply.

★ *ACA Objective 5.2*

Save Your Work

▶ ***Video 3.19** Save Color Version*

You've come a long way, and it's a good time to save your document again (**Figure 3.39**). This time, save it as `BallerinaColor.psd`. I'm not going to explain how to do it, but try to remember how you saved a Photoshop document previously. You don't need to worry about saving in JPEG format just yet. You'll do that later, when we invite you to show off your creation on social media.

Figure 3.39 Your final image after repairing all the damage and adding color to the image

From Photo Editing to Designing

▶ ***Video 3.20** Designing in Photoshop*

Your image looks good! You've turned a faded, torn, and damaged photo into a colorized image. Colorizing takes a lot of practice to make the results look accurate, and this image is particularly difficult to colorize because of the bricks and concrete. They are notoriously difficult to get right.

Let's now move beyond the basic photo retouching skills and change the document into a designed piece. You're about to cross a threshold that may seem insignificant, but we're moving now from restoring to actually designing.

Limiting yourself to editing images in order to restore the original look is a *technical* skill. Moving forward into design and editing is a *creative* skill. You'll have technical steps, of course, but the decisions you'll make won't have a direct, real-world reference. The work becomes all about how *you* think the image should look.

If you aren't comfortable with the design decisions at first, that's okay. (There's a whole chapter at the end of this book dedicated to design and creativity.) It just takes time and experience of actually looking at—*and looking for*—creative uses of design elements for it to start to become natural. You may think you are not creative, but you just haven't yet *practiced* creativity.

To move forward with this image, add a few touches to learn some design and creative tools in Photoshop that will make it look a little better when you show it off by posting it online. Let's give it a border and add some text to identify the image.

Expand the Canvas

★ *ACA Objective 4.4*

▶ ***Video 3.21*** *Expand the Canvas*

Your next tweak for this image is to place a border around it. To do so, you must first expand the dimensions and change the shape of the canvas, the working area of the image. The end result will be a border around the image that is thicker at its bottom to accommodate the addition of some text.

1 Choose Image > Canvas Size to open the Canvas Size dialog box (**Figure 3.40**).

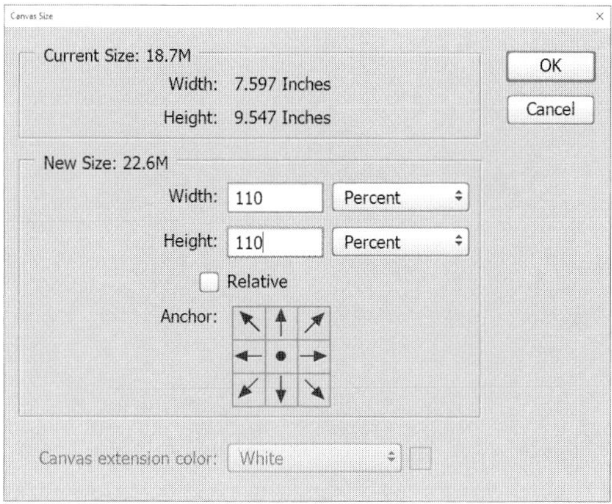

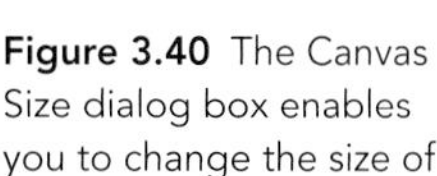

Figure 3.40 The Canvas Size dialog box enables you to change the size of the image area.

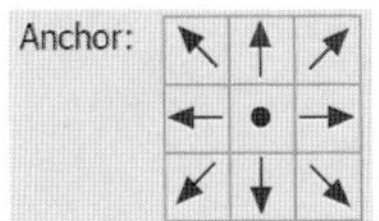

Figure 3.41 The Anchor indicates the directions in which you want to expand or decrease the canvas size.

NOTE

The Relative option lets you toggle between entering total and added percentage. If you want to add 10%, you enter 110% with Relative deselected and 10% with Relative selected.

2 In the New Size area, select Percent from the Unit menus next to the Width and Height fields.

   The menu can be changed to use various units of measure. During this exercise, you will work with Percent, Pixels, and Inches.

3 Enter **110** in the Width and Height fields to increase the canvas size by 10%. This will produce a 5% increase on each side of the canvas.

4 Make sure Relative is deselected.

5 In the Anchor grid, make sure the center is selected and shows arrows extending in all directions (**Figure 3.41**).

   This indicates that you want to expand the canvas in all directions.

6 Click OK.

The canvas expands equally in all directions because you increased the Horizontal and Vertical axes and anchored the image in the center of the canvas, thereby allowing the canvas to expand in every direction. The next step for changing the canvas shape is very similar, but you will increase the canvas size in only one direction using a different unit of measure.

1 Choose Image > Canvas Size to open the Canvas Size dialog box again.

2 Select Relative.

3 Select Inches from the Units menus next to the Width and Height fields.

4 In the Height field, type **1** to add an extra inch of height to the canvas.

   Leave the Width field at 0, because you want to expand the canvas only downward. Entering a value in the Width field would also expand its left-to-right dimension.

5 In the Anchor grid, select the top center point, so that arrows extend in all directions *except* upward (**Figure 3.42**).

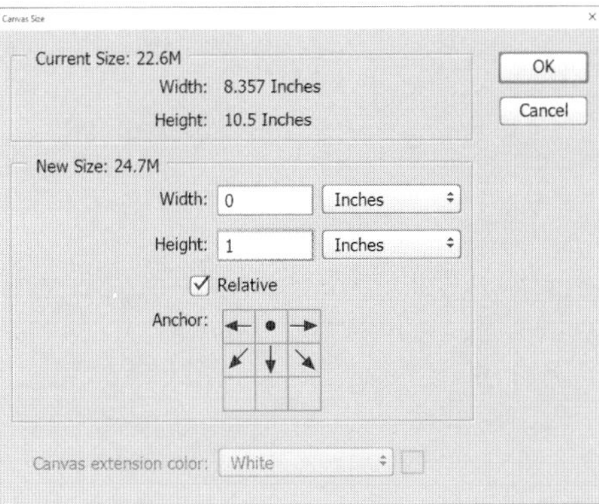

Figure 3.42 With Relative selected, Photoshop adds any new values in the Width and Height fields to the current dimensions. The top of the image is anchored, so the canvas will not expand upward.

Think of the Anchor grid selection as pinning down a section of the image. With the upper center point locked, the canvas can expand down and to the sides only. The arrows indicate the directions in which the image can expand (**Figure 3.43**).

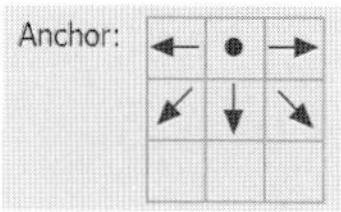

Anchor:

Figure 3.43 The Anchor grid shows the direction in which the image can expand.

6 Click OK.

You can see that the canvas expanded downward only, because you "pinned" the top of the canvas so that it couldn't be changed (**Figure 3.44**). The image didn't grow to the right or left because you didn't change the Width setting.

NOTE *The Anchor grid in the Canvas Size dialog box enables you to pin the center, any of the four sides, or any of the four corners of the canvas when you want to force the expansion of the canvas in one or more specific direction. Feel free to experiment with this grid. Even if you make an error, you can just undo the last action and try again (Edit > Undo).*

Figure 3.44 The image after the canvas is expanded. Note that transparency is indicated in Photoshop by displaying a checkerboard pattern.

Add a Solid Color Fill Layer

★ *ACA Objective 4.5*

Video 3.22 Add Solid Fill Layer

Solid Color fill layers are layers that automatically extend to the full dimensions of the canvas even when the canvas is resized. A solid color fill layer is essentially an infinite plane of color. You cannot paint on these layers, but you can still edit layer settings—such as opacity, blending mode, and masks—on a solid color fill layer.

NOTE

The current foreground color is selected by default when you create a solid color fill layer.

TIP

If you want to change the color of the Color Fill layer, double-click the color thumbnail in the Layers panel. From the Color Picker, select a new color.

Let's add a Solid Color fill layer to the document.

1. Choose Layer > New Fill Layer > Solid Color to open the New Layer dialog box (**Figure 3.45**).
2. Name the layer, if desired, and click OK.
3. In the Color Picker (Solid Color) dialog box, select a color for the layer, and click OK (**Figure 3.46**).

   The Color Fill 1 layer appears in the Layers panel (**Figure 3.47**).
4. Drag the Color Fill 1 layer below (behind) the Ballerina layer in the list (**Figure 3.48**). This creates a black background for the image (**Figure 3.49**).

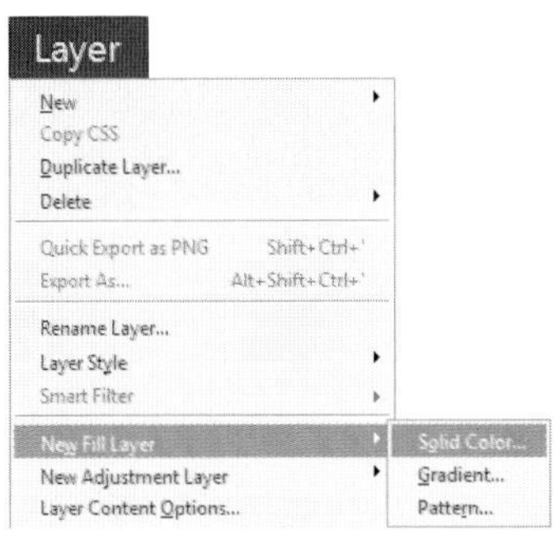

Figure 3.45 Creating a solid color fill layer

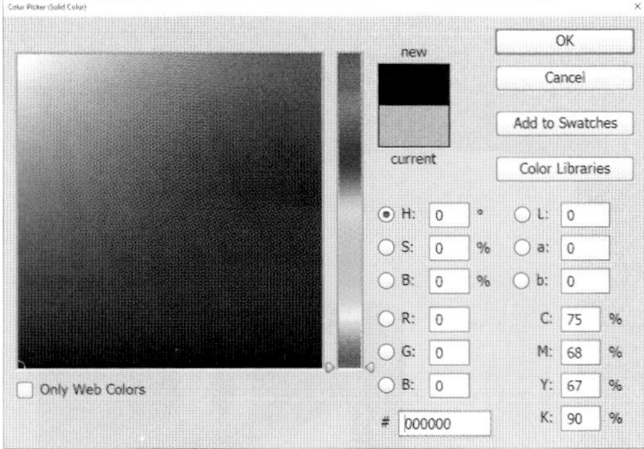

Figure 3.46 The Color Picker (Solid Color) enables you to select a color for the new Solid Color fill layer.

Figure 3.47 The Color Fill 1 layer is added to the Color layer group.

Figure 3.48 The Color Fill 1 layer is moved below (behind) the Ballerina layer.

Figure 3.49 The image after adding the solid fill layer as a background

Add Text

★ *ACA Objective 4.8*

▶ ***Video 3.23*** *Add Text*

Your next step is to add a type layer to the document. **Type layers** are like Solid Color fill layers, but as the name suggests, they are specifically designed to contain text. Type layers are **vector layers**, meaning that they are not created by an arrangement of pixels, but by data that can be manipulated without the quality loss that occurs when editing **raster** (pixel-based) images.

You're going to add a small bit of text to the bottom of the image to identify the time and location of the photo.

1. Select the layer that you want the new type layer to appear directly above.
2. Select the Type tool T.
3. Click on the image where you want to enter the text. In this case, click in the center of the black border added to the bottom of the image.

   A cursor appears where you click. Keep your text alignment in mind when clicking to enter the text.
4. In the Options bar, set the text color to be white. Format the text any way you prefer or use these settings (**Figure 3.50**):
   - Font: **Mostra Nuova**
   - Style: **Bold**
   - Size: **30 points**
   - Alignment: **Center**

   You're now ready to enter the text.

NOTE

The font Mostra Nuova Bold is available with your Adobe Creative Cloud subscription as part of Typekit. If the font is not available, select a different sans serif font such as Helvetica or Arial.

Figure 3.50 In the Options bar, you can specify font, alignment, color, and detailed character settings.

NOTE *A font baseline appears under the text as you enter it, but the underline will not appear in the final results unless you specifically select Underline as a formatting option.*

5 Enter **Ena The Ballerina**.

6 In the Options panel, click the Commit button to commit the text to the layer.

After you commit the changes, the new type layer will appear on your document. You can use the Move tool to adjust the placement of the text on your document.

Edit Type Layers

At times, you may need to edit an existing type layer to correct spelling or to change the formatting choices such as font, color, or other character or paragraph settings.

Figure 3.51 The Type icon displays for a text layer's thumbnail regardless of the text on the layer.

1 In the Layers panel, double-click the type layer's thumbnail (**Figure 3.51**).

The text on that layer is highlighted on the image.

NOTE *When you double-click the thumbnail for the layer, it preselects your previously entered text. Click where you need to edit before typing or your text will be replaced.*

2 Add the text **-Radio City Music Hall** to the end of the text on this layer.

3 In the Options bar, edit the type settings to suit your design.

4 Click the Commit button in the Options bar to save your changes.

Work with Advanced Character Settings

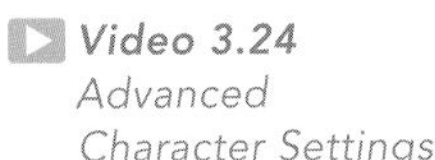

Video 3.24 *Advanced Character Settings*

Now that you've entered and edited text, you're going to add another text layer and save a few different versions. With this next text layer, you'll learn a little more about the advanced settings you can apply.

1 In the Layers panel, select the layer want to be below the new text layer.

2 In the Tools panel, click the Type tool.

3 Place the cursor where you want to enter the text.

TIP *If you want to place text on top of previous text, press and hold the Shift key with the Text tool selected. This will also prevent you from editing previously entered text.*

4 Click where you want to enter the text.

The cursor appears where you click. Keep in mind your alignment when clicking to enter the text.

5 Enter the text **New York City, 1938**.

6 In the Options bar, click the Character and Paragraph toggle button to open the Character panel (**Figure 3.52**) and Paragraph panel.

7 Select all of the text on the layer.

8 In the Character panel, enter **100** in the Tracking field.

The amount of space between characters increases.

9 Click the Commit button in the Options bar to save your text.

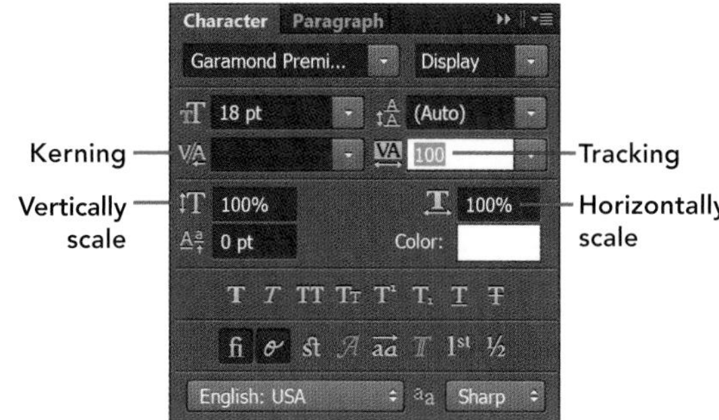

Figure 3.52 In the Character panel, you can specify the typeface, kerning, tracking, vertical scaling, horizontal scaling, and more.

You're done! You have come a long way with this image (**Figure 3.53**). The last thing you need to do is save this image in multiple formats and versions for different uses.

NOTE

The Character and Paragraph panel button toggles the panels open and closed.

Figure 3.53 A comparison of the beginning point and our ending point after editing

Save for Multiple Purposes

Video 3.25
Save for Multiple Purposes

You've created an image with multiple layers, and now want to prepare it for multiple uses. Let's explore some of the most common ways to save this project in a Photoshop workflow, and the advantages and disadvantages of each. You've already learned many of these steps, so much of this is review. Be sure to watch the videos for more details. We will also explore a way to save the image with two versions: black and white, as well as color.

ACA Objective 5.1

Save as a PSD Document

You have saved this image a few times with different names throughout this project. Let's save it one more time as `BallerinaFinal.psd`. You should already know how to do so, but just to review, here is how to save the image as a Photoshop document with a new name.

Layered Photoshop Document

ADVANTAGES	DISADVANTAGES
Retains the full power of Photoshop	Large file sizes
Most versatile and editable image	Can be opened only with Photoshop

1. Choose File > Save As.
2. In the Name field (Windows) or the Save As field (Mac OS), enter `BallerinaFinal.psd`.
3. If necessary, select Photoshop (*.PSD) from the Type menu (Windows) or the Format menu (Mac OS).
4. Browse to the location where you would like to save this document.
5. Click Save.

It is a good practice to save your document frequently throughout the design process. Doing so allows you to return to earlier states of the image, and also backs up multiple copies of the project should something go wrong with a file. Saving to cloud-based backup folders is also recommended, especially for critical documents. If you have a Creative Cloud account, the Creative Cloud folder is perfect for this purpose and is available as part of your free account. This will automatically back up your folder in case your local files or drive get corrupted.

Merge and Flatten Layers

★ *ACA Objective 4.5*

Video 3.26 Merge and Flatten Layers

The Photoshop document you created has multiple layers, and each layer adds to the size of the document. This image has three distinct areas: the black background and text, the ballerina picture, and the color layers. In this exercise, you will merge some of the layers into a single Photoshop layer to reduce file size and avoid accidental moving of these layers. This process is similar to **flattening** the image, which converts all the layers into a single **raster** image layer. **Merging** combines and rasterizes *selected* layers, while flattening combines and rasterizes *all* of the layers in the document.

Merged or Flattened Photoshop Document

ADVANTAGES	DISADVANTAGES
Smaller file sizes Retains full saved image quality	Rasterizes layers and thereby removes the ability to edit text, shapes, layer positioning, layer styles, and layer settings Can be opened only with Photoshop Larger file size than other common file formats

Raster images are created by pixels, each with its own color and transparency information. The process of converting non-pixel-based images to pixel-based images is called **rasterizing**.

1 Ctrl-click (Windows) or Command-click (Mac OS) the layers or groups you want to merge. In this case, select the text layers and the solid color layer. The layers are highlighted.

2 Select Merge Layers from the Layers panel menu (**Figure 3.54**).

The text and solid color layers are merged into a single raster layer. The new layer inherits the name of the topmost selected layer, in this case, New York City, 1938 (**Figure 3.55**).

3 Double-click the layer name and enter a new name, such as **Background**.

It might seem as if you could easily flatten the Colors group, but because you have different blending modes in the layers within that group, flattening will not work properly because a layer can have only a single blending mode. There is, however, a workaround. (There almost always is in Photoshop!) The key is to duplicate the layers first.

Figure 3.54 ▼ Merging selected layers using the Merge Layers command in the Layers panel menu

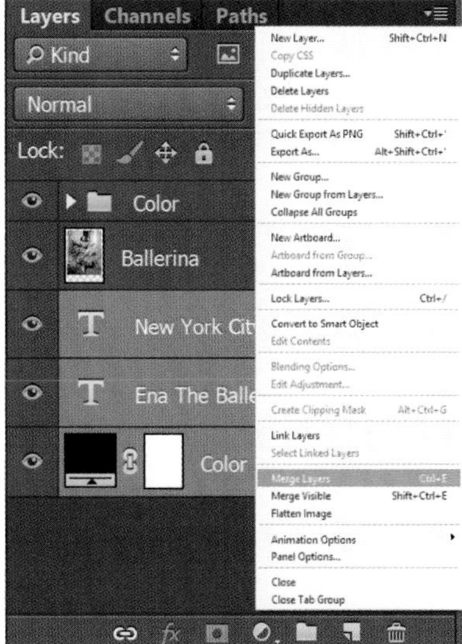

Figure 3.55 A new layer created by merging layers

Duplicate and Merge Layers

Video 3.27 *Duplicating Layers*

You want to end up with two complete images, each containing text. One is a color image, and other is black and white. To do this, you will need two copies of the ballerina and the text background to merge together.

To duplicate layers:

1. In the Layers panel, select one or more layers you want to duplicate. For this exercise, select the Ballerina and Background layers.
2. Drag the layers to the New Layer icon at the bottom of the Layers panel.

   The duplicate layers appear with the word "copy" added to the layer names.

Now that you have the copied layers, you want to select and merge the layers to end up with just two layers. Make one layer by merging both copy layers and the color group, and another layer by merging the Background and Ballerina layers (**Figure 3.56**).

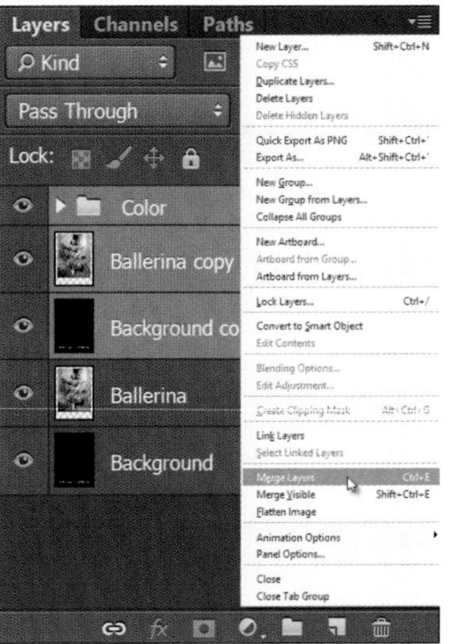

Figure 3.56 The Color group and duplicated layers are selected and about to be merged.

At this point, you have two copies of complete images in a single Photoshop document: one in color, and one in black and white. This is one way to keep multiple versions of the same document together in one file, but it only works when the images and changes are small. We will look at other ways to accomplish this later in the book that allow more flexibility. For this small image, this is an easy solution.

When you have two layers of complete merged images, save the document as a Photoshop document called `BallerinaMergedVersions.psd`. You can easily toggle the visibility (eye icon) of the Color layer to compare the two versions (**Figure 3.57**).

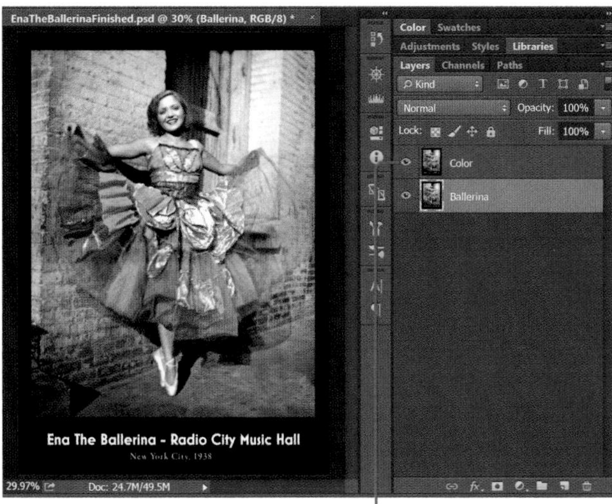

Figure 3.57 Toggle the layer visibility using the icon that looks like an eye.

Export Layers as Separate Files

ACA Objective 5.2

Video 3.28 *Export Single Layers*

Let's say you want a color version of this image and a black-and-white version. One way to do this would be to hide the Color layer and save a black-and-white version of the image, and then show the Color layer and save a color version. You can, however, export multiple versions of an image in a single file. To do this:

1. Choose File > Export > Layers To Files (**Figure 3.58**) to open the Export Layers To Files dialog box.
2. Specify the following settings for the exported files (**Figure 3.59**):
   - Destination: **Photoshop folder**
   - File Name Prefix: **Ballerina**
   - File Type: **JPEG**
   - Quality: **8**

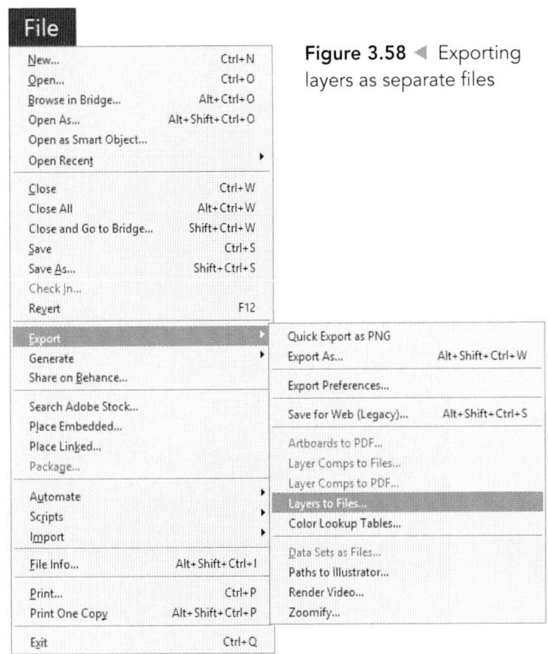

Figure 3.58 ◀ Exporting layers as separate files

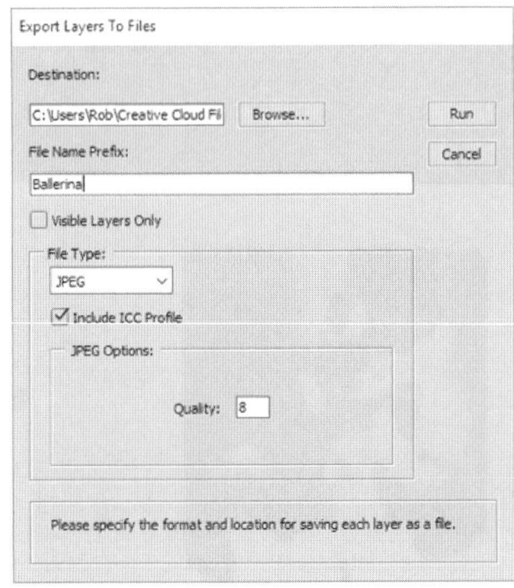

Figure 3.59 The Export Layers To Files dialog box

The File Name Prefix will become the beginning of the filename, followed by a number, and then the layer name (such as Ballerina_0000_Color.jpg).

3 Click Run to export the layers as separate JPEG files.

This process saves the documents as full-size JPEG files with the quality setting you selected. These files are not optimized for the web, which is the last step.

★ *ACA Objective 5.1*

Save for Social Media Use

▶ ***Video 3.29*** *Save for Social Media Use*

Let's show off what you've learned! The last step is to save the image for sharing on your social media account.

1. Choose File > Export > Save For Web (Legacy).
2. Select appropriate image formats for sharing the image on social media. We recommend a Medium quality JPEG format with the largest dimension at 1000.
3. Navigate to a location and click Save to save the file.

LEVEL UP CHALLENGE: BONUS ROUND

You have learned everything you need to know to colorize old photos. Take one or more of these challenges to level up your skills and let the concepts sink in.

- **Level I:** Find a quality black-and-white image and colorize it.
- **Level II:** Find a damaged photo online, fix the damage, and colorize the photo.
- **Level III:** Find an old family photo, scan it, and restore or color the image.
- **Level IV:** Share your image on Social Media! Tag it with **#PPBBlrnPS**, or **#PPBBlrnPS3** for this project specifically. Visit *http://brainbuffet.com/peachpit* to learn how to connect with us socially, join the conversation, and connect with other learners like you!

CHAPTER OBJECTIVES

Chapter Learning Objectives

- Learn to set up documents for commercial printing.
- Use non-printing tools in Photoshop to assist in design.
- Learn to work with RAW images and develop them in Photoshop for future use.
- Learn to work with multiple lines and multiple layers of text.
- Explore how to use Photoshop styles and filters to create effects on text, graphics, or photos.
- Learn how to soft proof and review your images with a client to troubleshoot and refine images.

Chapter ACA Objectives

For full descriptions of objectives, see the table on pages 256–261.

DOMAIN 2.0
UNDERSTANDING DIGITAL IMAGES
2.3

DOMAIN 3.0
UNDERSTANDING ADOBE PHOTOSHOP
3.2, 3.3, 3.5, 3.6, 3.8

DOMAIN 4.0
CREATING DIGITAL IMAGES USING ADOBE PHOTOSHOP
4.1, 4.2, 4.3, 4.5, 4.6, 4.8, 4.9

DOMAIN 5.0
PUBLISHING DIGITAL IMAGES USING ADOBE PHOTOSHOP
5.1, 5.2

CHAPTER 4

Event Flyer

In previous chapters you explored how to work with images to restore them to their original state or enhance them. In this chapter, you'll start designing images rather than restoring them. You will learn some awesome new concepts that most Photoshop designers work with on a weekly basis. Plus, you will start learning some amazing new tricks that you can apply to creative images while experimenting with the Photoshop design tools.

You're about to design a flyer for a concert at a comic convention featuring the band Gasoline Heart. The demographic is older teenagers to twentysomethings at a convention after-party to be held at a local venue. The flyer should let people know the event offers discounted prices at the door and a free drink with admission, but should also promote the concert for people not attending the convention.

NOTE

If the design stuff doesn't come naturally to you, that's okay. We'll talk about design and improving your artistic skills much more in a later chapter.

Video 4.1 *Event Flyer*

So far, you've been designing digital images for the screen. Whether it's a computer screen or a TV screen doesn't matter much as the color space and units of measure are the same. When designing for paper, things are different, as you'll discover in this chapter.

Designing for Print

Video 4.2 Designing for Print

By default, screens are black and paper is white. This fundamental difference is the reason you need to use different ways of blending colors for print.

Paper is also measured in inches rather than pixels. Therefore, you measure the finished project in inches and determine the image quality in pixels (or dots) per inch. This pixel density (how many pixels per inch) of an image is called its **resolution**, and it is critical that you set it properly when working for print.

NOTE

dpi and ppi both mean the number of colored points that make up the image. ppi is normally used when working on screens, and dpi is normally used to describe images on paper. When you're working on screen for a paper project, it can get confusing!

To make things simpler and more consistent, industry standards exist for print output. Unless told otherwise, you can assume that images created for print will need to be in the CMYK color space with a resolution of 240 to 300 dots per inch, or **dpi**. On screen you can think of it as pixels per inch (ppi). Even when a document is measured in centimeters, the resolution is defined in terms of ppi. This is a critical setting when initially setting up your document, because *images don't scale-up well.* If an image starts with a screen resolution of 72ppi, the image will have less than 25% of the resolution necessary for it to print accurately. And just scaling up to the higher ppi will result in a fuzzy, poor-quality image when printed.

For example, in **Figure 4.1** the left image began as 300dpi and looks good. The other began as 72dpi and at actual size it's hard to see detail. When you take the 72dpi image and force it to be larger the results are not good, as shown at the right. The skin is splotchy and all the time and energy to perfect the skin is lost.

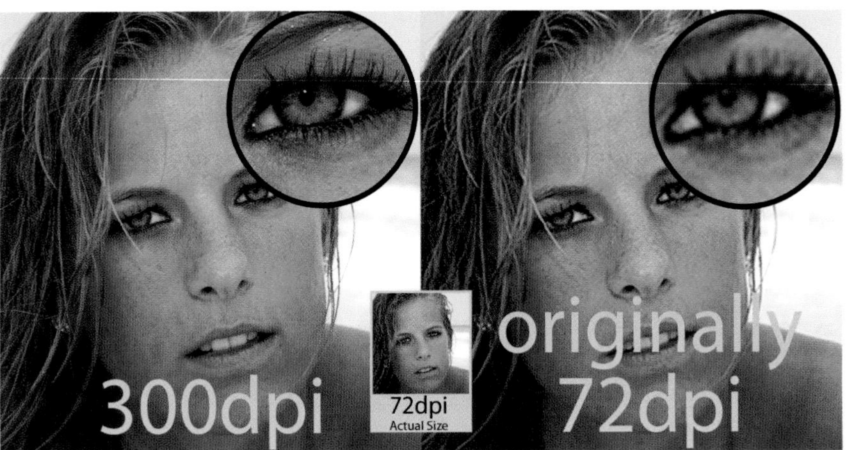

Figure 4.1 These images are shown as they would appear at actual size on your screen.

Create a Print Document

★ *ACA Objective 4.1*

Video 4.3 Create a New Print Document

When working toward a specific print size, you should first set up the document for the final printed size you will need. This document is for a standard one-quarter page club flyer (4.25 x 5.5 inches) printed edge-to-edge with no border around the image. You need to create extra space around your document, called **bleed,** which can be cut away later to get your document to the proper size after printing. So, you'll want to add an extra .25 inch around every side of the document, and an additional .25 inch to both the width and height of the document.

To create a new document for print:

1 Choose File > New.

The New document dialog box appears (**Figure 4.2**).

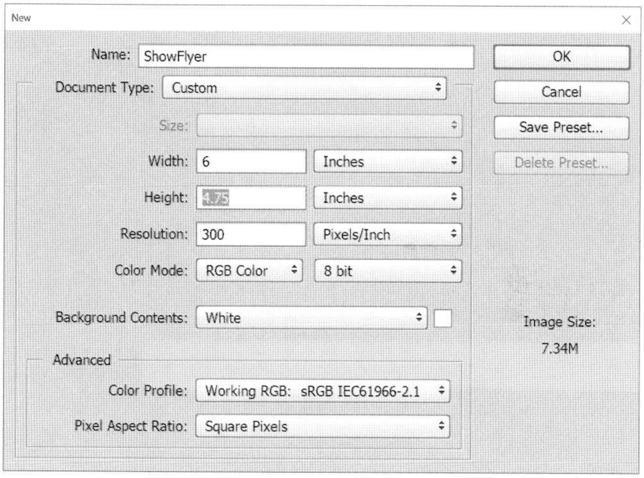

New
Name: ShowFlyer
Document Type: Custom
Size:
Width: 6 Inches
Height: 4.75 Inches
Resolution: 300 Pixels/Inch
Color Mode: RGB Color 8 bit
Background Contents: White
Advanced
Color Profile: Working RGB: sRGB IEC61966-2.1
Pixel Aspect Ratio: Square Pixels
OK
Cancel
Save Preset...
Delete Preset...
Image Size:
7.34M

Figure 4.2 The New document dialog box

2 Name the document `ShowFlyer`.

3 From the Document Type menu, select U.S. Paper.

Doing so sets the resolution to 300ppi and the units of measure to inches.

4 To change the size of the document, enter a Width of **6** inches, and a Height of **4.75** inches.

5 Click OK.

You've set up your document to the size you need with that extra .25 inch bleed. To finish setting up your document, you'll create some guides to help locate the edges when the final printed page is cut to size.

Soft Proof Colors

★ *ACA Objective 4.1*

Video 4.4 *Soft Proof Colors*

With soft proofing, you can work in RGB color, which is the native color space for Photoshop, while approximating how images will look when printed on a commercial offset press. You should work in this view to be sure that when adjusting the colors and look of your design, you will get the visual results you want in the CYMK color space.

1 To soft proof a document in order to simulate the color space of an offset commercial press, choose View > Proof Setup and make sure Working CMYK is selected.

2 Choose View > Proof Colors (**Figure 4.3**), or press Ctrl+Y (Windows) or Command+Y (Mac OS).

You won't see anything happen, but the magic is going on behind the scenes. When you're soft proofing, the document's title bar will indicate a simulated color space after the name (**Figure 4.4**).

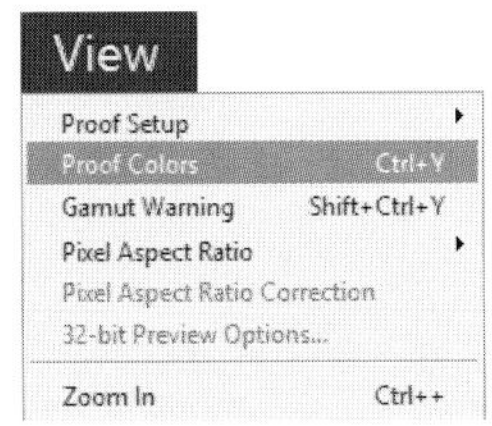

Figure 4.3 Soft proofing simulates onscreen how colors will look when printed on an offset commercial press.

The CYMK color space is largely reserved for commercial printing on an offset press. Most home and office printers actually prefer the RGB color space, so use CMYK soft proofing only when you know it's necessary. High-end color inkjet printers used by design houses and photographers for proofs are calibrated to work best in the RGB color space.

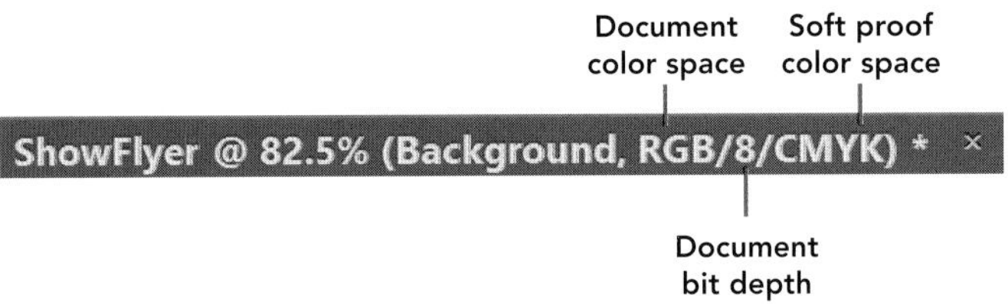

Figure 4.4 The title bar of a Photoshop document shows the color space of the document, the bit depth, and any soft-proofing color space in effect.

Work with Rulers and Guides

★ *ACA Objective 3.5*

Video 4.5 *Guides and Rulers*

Rulers and guides are features that help you align the elements of your design. Rulers help you determine where the elements of the design will appear in your document when printed. Guides allow you to line up elements and define the printable area of your document. Neither rulers nor guides appear in your final printed product.

DISPLAY RULERS

1 To show rulers on your document, choose View > Rulers (**Figure 4.5**), or press Ctrl+R (Windows) or Command+R (Mac OS).

The rulers will be visible on the **canvas**—the image area—to help determine the placement of elements on your printed document.

2 To change the units of measure for each ruler, right-click (Windows) or Control-click (Mac OS) the ruler to display the menu. Choose which unit of measure you prefer.

Set your image to inches; this is the standard for US printing companies.

Note that the current unit of measure is indicated by a check mark (**Figure 4.6**).

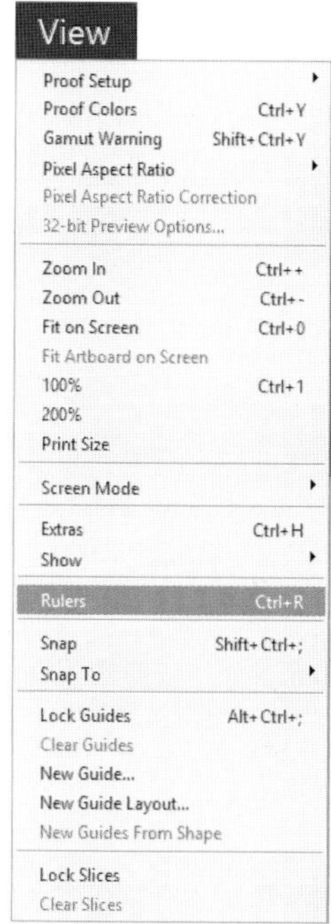

Figure 4.5 ◀ The View > Rulers command for displaying horizontal and vertical rulers on the document window

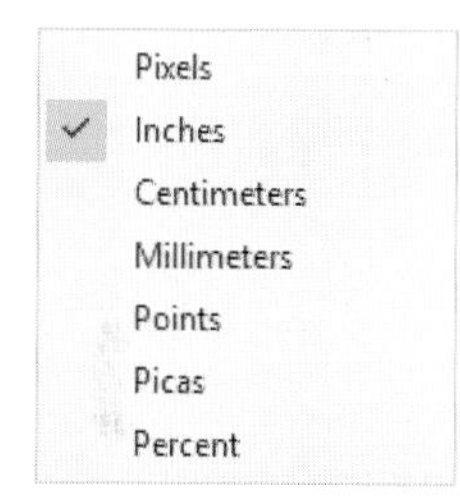

Figure 4.6 ▲ The context menu enables you to select the units of measure for your ruler. Right-click or Control-click the ruler to display this menu.

CREATE GUIDES

Guides are almost as easy to set up as rulers. You can do so by entering their location manually, or by dragging them into the document from the rulers.

To create a guide in your document, drag one out from the ruler and release the mouse button when the guide is in position. This is a visual way to create guides and is best when you want to use them to visually assist with layout.

To place a guide at a specific location:

1 Choose View > New Guide to open the New Guide dialog box (**Figure 4.7**).

2 Click Horizontal or Vertical for the Orientation.

3 Enter a value in the Position field to specify the location of the new guide. In this case, enter **.25 in**.

4 Click OK.

You have placed a horizontal guide .25 inches from the top of your document.

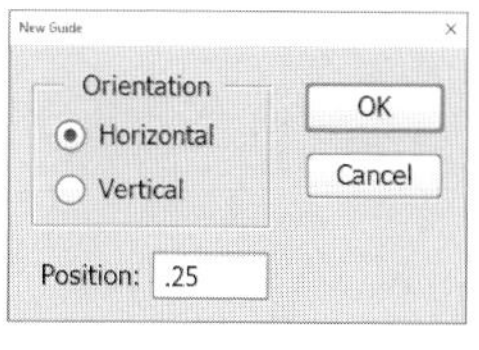

Figure 4.7 The New Guide dialog box

Repeat the steps again to place a guide .25 inches from the left edge of your document by following the same steps but selecting Vertical for the orientation.

After placing the top and left guides, use the mouse to click inside the ruler and drag guides .25 inches from the right edge and bottom edge of your document (at 5.75 and 4.5 inches respectively). When completed, your document should look like **Figure 4.8.**

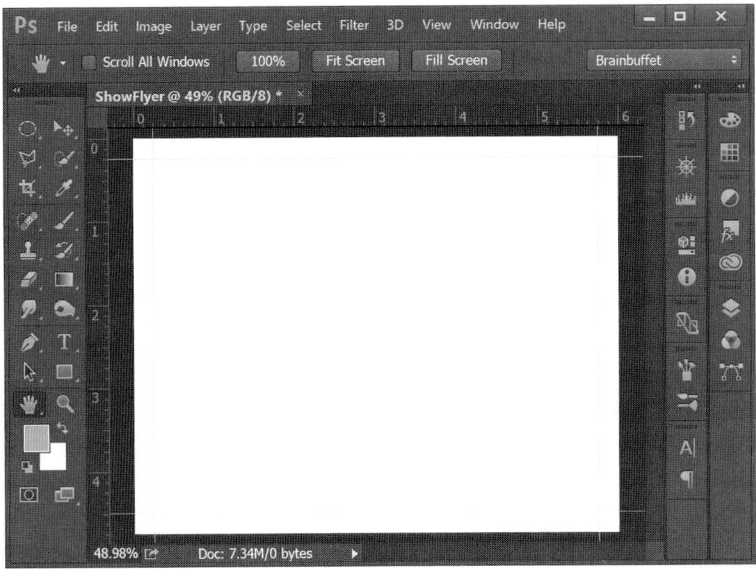

Figure 4.8 The document with vertical and horizontal guides delineating the printed page area

MOVE, DELETE, AND LOCK GUIDES

As you work more with guides, you'll find that you need to move and delete them. In addition, you might want to lock guides so they can't be repositioned accidentally. To work with guides:

- **Move:** To reposition a guide, select the Move tool, click the guide, and drag it to a new location.
- **Delete:** To delete a guide, drag it back onto the ruler. Choose View > Clear Guides to remove all guides.
- **Lock:** Lock the guides you created by choosing View > Lock Guides. For this project, the guides should stay in place.

TIP

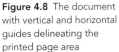

You can move guides by pressing Ctrl (Command on Mac OS) to temporarily switch to the Move tool and dragging the guides, except when the Hand tool is active. In that case, you must select the Move tool manually.

Import Images

ACA Objective 4.2

Video 4.6 About Opening and Placing Images

Previously, you opened files directly in Photoshop, which places the image as the background layer of the document. (You've already learned about the special challenges of the Background layer.) But now you're going to import images into an open document. You can open images into Photoshop in many ways:

- **File > Open:** Opens the file as a new document with the image as the background layer.
- **File > Open As Smart Object:** Opens the file as a new document with the image as a smart object.
- **Dragging onto an open document:** Opens the file on a new layer of the open document.
- **Dragging into an empty area of the interface:** Opens the file in a new document window.
- **File > Place Embedded:** Places the image on a new smart layer in its current saved state.
- **File > Place Linked:** Places the image as a smart object and updates it as the original image is updated.

NOTE

You'll learn about smart objects later in this chapter.

Depending on your needs, you might want to open a document in one of these specific ways.

Browse with Bridge

★ ACA Objective 5.2

Video 4.7 Browsing with Bridge

Bridge is an important application for designers because it enables you to browse, manage, and view Adobe documents without the need to open the application that created it. When you're browsing a folder full of Photoshop, Illustrator, and/or InDesign files on your desktop, you see only the icons for those files. When using Bridge, you can preview the files, so you can choose the right shot from a photo shoot or the correct layout for a flyer (**Figure 4.9**).

Aside from the ease of navigating and viewing your documents, Bridge also makes it easy to view each document's **metadata**. Metadata is a collection of information about a file that is invisibly attached to the file. It can include copyright information, color swatches used in the file, camera and lens information, and even GPS coordinates that identify where a photo was shot.

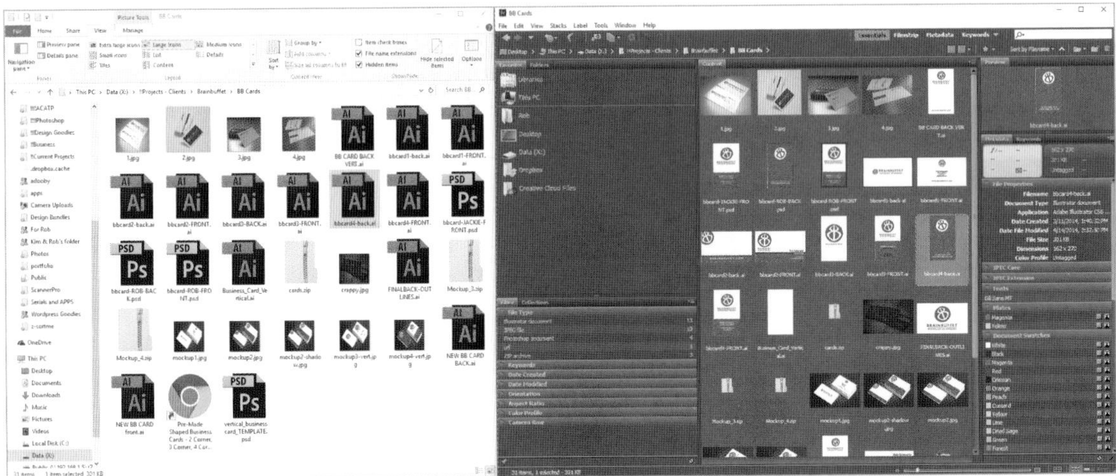

Figure 4.9 Unlike system file browsers (left), Bridge makes it easy to locate your design documents by displaying previews of all supported file types.

Modern operating systems are getting better at connecting with and previewing files when browsing, but Bridge provides a reliable way to locate and preview any of the images you might want to bring into your Photoshop project. The browsing options in Bridge are also more full featured and easier to use.

NOTE

To increase the size of the file thumbnails to find the perfect image for your project, drag the slider at the bottom of the Bridge Browser.

To browse for a document in Bridge:

1. Choose File > Browse In Bridge to open Bridge.
2. Browse for the file you want to open into Photoshop. For this project, you locate the file `GH-JohnBass.CR2` in the `Downloads` folder.
3. Right-click the image thumbnail and choose Place > In Photoshop (Control-click in Mac OS).
4. Your image is placed in the current Photoshop document on a new layer as a smart object.

   Because this file is in the RAW format, it opens into Photoshop as a Camera RAW file that is ready for processing in the RAW window. Let's explore what's special about files in RAW format and learn how to process them.

Work with RAW images

RAW files are images that can be created only in a camera, and they contain the unprocessed image data directly from the camera's image sensor. When your clients are providing images, always get the RAW files when you can. Although RAW files are much larger in size than a JPEG file, they're also much more useful and versatile. Because they contain all of the original image sensor data, nothing is thrown away—even the unseen information in the shadows is retained! You can often recover image details from a RAW file that you would not be able to recover from a JPEG file.

▶ ***Video 4.8*** *Raw Images*

You can open a RAW file in Photoshop as you would open any other file. Choose File > Open or File > Place to open a RAW file directly into Photoshop. You already told Photoshop to place this image, so let's look at the Camera Raw Interface.

NOTE

Choosing Open creates a new file while choosing Place opens the image as a smart object on a new layer in the active document.

To develop RAW images in Camera Raw:

1 Using the Camera Raw interface (**Figure 4.10**), fine-tune the image settings.

  You can automatically set the white balance, and then manually set each development setting to meet your image needs.

2 Click OK to place the image in your document as a smart object.

Once the image is in your document, notice that the layer has a small icon in the corner of the thumbnail. The icon indicates that this is a smart object. Let's talk about the advantages of using this special type of image layer in Photoshop.

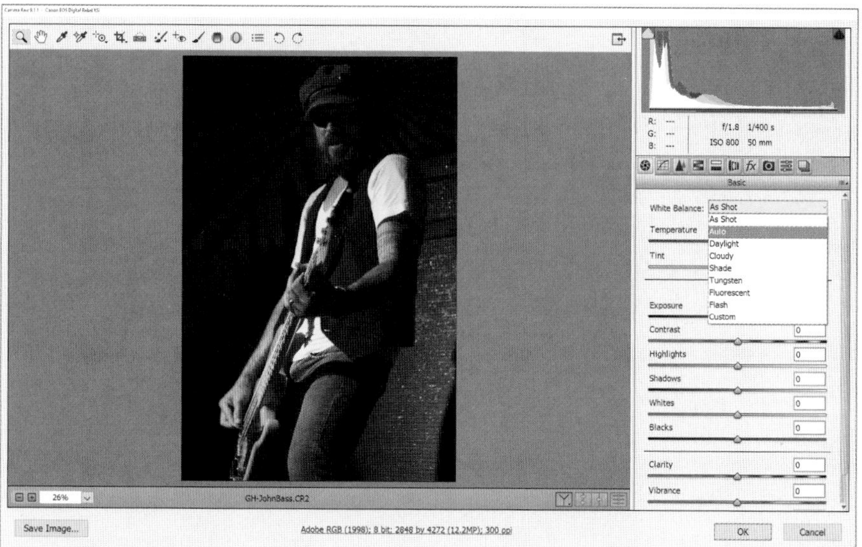

Figure 4.10 The Camera Raw interface in Photoshop

Understand Smart Objects

▶ *Video 4.9 Smart Objects*

Opening a file as a smart object is often the smartest way to work because the image opens as a **smart object**. You can identify them by the Smart Object icon (**Figure 4.11**). Smart objects are nondestructive layers in Photoshop—no matter what you do to them, you can always return to the original image, even after the document is saved. This is a huge advantage that has very few drawbacks. If you need to change a smart object into a regular layer, you can simply rasterize the image and change it into pixel data. Smart objects offer a few distinct advantages over regular layers:

TIP

Make text a smart object so you can apply filters to it while retaining the ability to edit the words.

- They are nondestructive, so they can always be returned to their original state.
- Filters applied to smart objects become smart filters that can be edited after they are applied.
- Smart objects can be linked, so that if the original file is updated, the update will automatically be reflected in the document.
- Smart objects can be used across Adobe applications.

Figure 4.11 Identify smart objects by the Smart Object icon in the lower-right corner of the layer thumbnail.

Create a Solid Fill Layer

▶ *Video 4.10 Solid Fill Review*

Since our image is fairly dark, you're going to create a dark background you can fade your image in to. To create a plane of solid black that will always fill your image, you will again create a solid fill layer as you did previously.

To create a solid fill layer:

1. Choose Layer > New Fill Layer > Solid Color.
2. Select black as the solid color.
3. Click OK to create the layer.
4. Move the solid fill layer below your smart object layer.

Blend the Image

The next step in creating the poster is to blend our bass player smoothly from the photo to the black area. You have a few ways to do this, but let's use a nondestructive method. When erasing parts of an image, the nondestructive method is to use a **mask**. You create a mask on a layer, and then paint black on the mask to hide the layer contents or paint white to reveal the contents.

Create a Layer Mask

★ *ACA Objective 3.6*

▶ ***Video 4.11** Layer Masks*

Let's create a mask on the layer containing your image so that you can fade the image into the black area. Then you'll add some text to the document.

1. Click the layer on which you want to add a mask. In this case, click the layer with the bass player.
2. In the Layers panel, click the Mask button.

   The Mask is added to the layer (**Figure 4.12**).

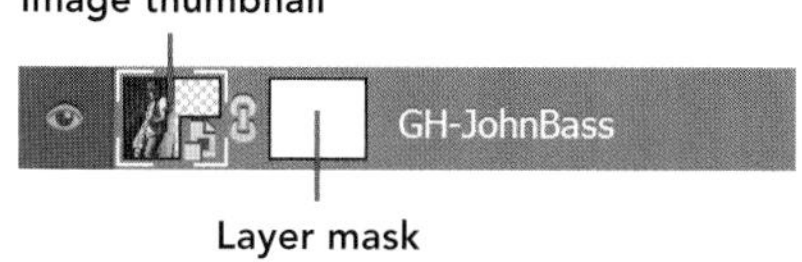

Figure 4.12 Creating a layer mask

A mask displays as a thumbnail to the right of the image thumbnail in the Layers panel.

Because there was no active selection, the mask is initially all white, thereby revealing the entire layer. If a selection is active when you create a mask, the new mask will reveal only the active selection.

Fade the Image Using a Mask

★ *ACA Objective 3.6*

★ *ACA Objective 4.5*

▶ ***Video 4.12** Gradients to Blend with Masks*

Now you will fade out the image using the mask. For this task, you will create a gradient on the mask that goes from black to white. As the gradient moves from black to white, the image will move from hidden to visible.

Gradients in Photoshop can be fairly complex, but let's start with a simple preset gradient.

1. Select the Gradient tool.
2. Click the layer mask thumbnail to activate the mask.

   When the layer mask is active, white corners display around the thumbnail of the mask, but not the layer (**Figure 4.13**).

Figure 4.13 An active layer mask

3 In the Options bar, select the gradient that is white to black (**Figure 4.14**). If the first option in the gradient selector is not white to black, press the D key to return to the default colors.

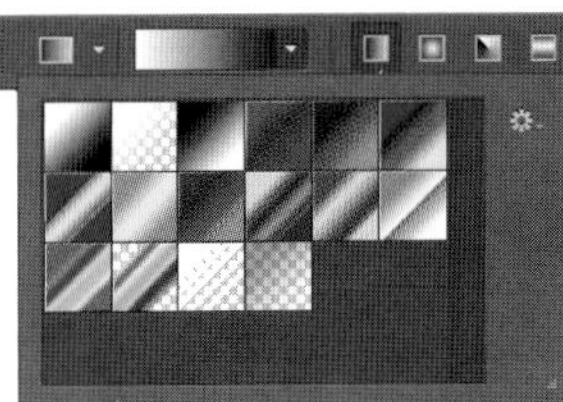

Figure 4.14 The preset white to black gradient selected in the Options bar

4 Drag a gradient on your image to fade the image from visible to hidden. You can Shift-drag to constrain the gradient's angle, dragging from the arm to the image edge.

The image should fade from visible to transparent, fading away into the black background layer.

5 Save your work by pressing Ctrl+S (Windows) or Command+S (Mac OS).

This effect gives a nice transition to your image rather than a hard edge, thereby making the image feel less separated from the rest of the document and providing a little more freedom for the text.

Master Text

★ *ACA Objective 3.2*

★ *ACA Objective 3.3*

★ *ACA Objective 4.8*

You'll now focus on text. Most beginning designers overlook this detail, but it's absolutely critical for excellence in design. Even people who don't know about design have a subconscious awareness of the unity and elegance of well-placed type in a composition. Though they might not be able to say *why* one design looks better than another, they will be able to identify which design *is better*. A good designer knows this and takes the extra 15 minutes that might be needed to properly tweak the text.

Design with Type

Video 4.13 *Designing with Type*

You learned the basics of adding text in an earlier chapter, so let's dig a little deeper and really start to design the text. You will be moving past basic, one-line text entries to explore the spacing and alignment options available within multiline text. Doing so opens a few other typographical options that will help express the feeling of your design.

To create multiline text:

1. When you add text, it is placed on a layer. To indicate where you want this layer to go, select the layer that will be immediately below the text layer. For this exercise, select the top layer.
2. Select the Type tool.
3. Click on the document where you want to enter the text. A text insert point appears where you click.
4. In the Options bar, select Myriad Pro Regular, 30 pt, and centered, white text (**Figure 4.15**).
5. On the document, enter **Gasoline**. Press Enter (Windows) or Return (Mac OS), then enter **Heart**. Note that Photoshop shows the baseline of the text as you enter it.
6. Click Commit in the Options bar to place the text on the document.

   The text layer is created and the baseline is hidden (**Figure 4.16**).

Figure 4.15 Setting type formatting in the Options bar

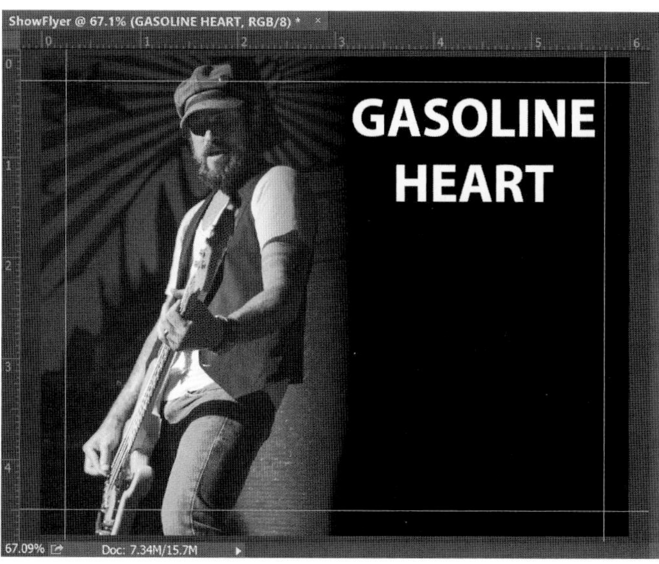

Figure 4.16 The default settings for text are not suitable for every design. A good designer learns when to adjust the settings for a better composition.

ACA Objective 2.3

Tweak Character Settings

Video 4.14
Tweaking Type

TIP

You can scrub the settings of many options in the panels by placing the pointer over the icon for the setting and waiting for the scrub icon to appear. Then adjust the setting visually by dragging left or right.

TIP

Hold down the Ctrl (Windows) key or Command key (Mac OS) while editing text to reshape or move the text frame.

Beginning designers will enter the text and be done with it, but good designers pay attention to typography. Three terms that every designer needs to know about text are **tracking**, **kerning**, and **leading**.

- Tracking adjusts the space between all characters in the selected text.
- Kerning adjusts the space between two characters.
- Leading (rhymes with "*heading*") adjusts the space between lines.

Settings are also available for **horizontal scaling** and **vertical scaling**, which stretch the type in the direction indicated.

To work with the character settings:

1. Start by selecting the text with the Type tool to fine-tune it. On the text layer, select the word "Heart."
2. To improve the look of the text, make the following changes in the Character panel:

   Enter **30** pt for Leading to reduce the space between lines.

   Enter **150** for Horizontal Scale to increase the width of the text (**Figure 4.17**).
3. Click Commit in the Options bar to save the modifications to the text (**Figure 4.18**).

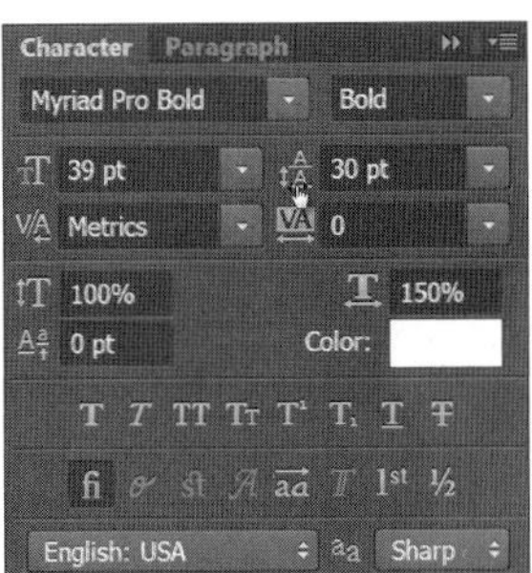

Figure 4.17 Fine-tuning character formatting in the Character panel

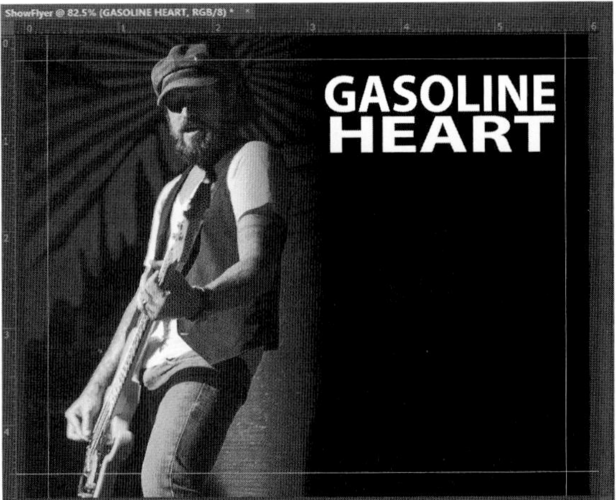

Figure 4.18 The text appears much more unified and stronger with the tweaked settings. Typography matters!

As you can see, making these few minor changes really improved the title section of this flyer. Taking the time to design your text will always pay off. Poor typography and weak design screams "newbie!" and you don't want to convey that feeling to your client. Not only does it diminish the client's confidence in your work, but it weakens your portfolio.

Add Event Information

Your next steps are to add the remaining event information to the flyer. Try entering all the text in one text block, and then use the character settings to design it to resemble the figure. You will next add the venue name to the flyer in a vertical text layer.

Video 4.15 Adding Event Info

1 Use the Type tool to add the following event information to the flyer, each on it's own line:

   04.01.16

   $5 Doors

   726 Peachpit Street

   Roof Access with Event Pass

2 Use the Options bar and other techniques you've learned to format the text as shown (**Figure 4.19**).

3 If your character settings get out of control, you can easily reset them to their default values by choosing Reset Character from the Character panel menu (**Figure 4.20**).

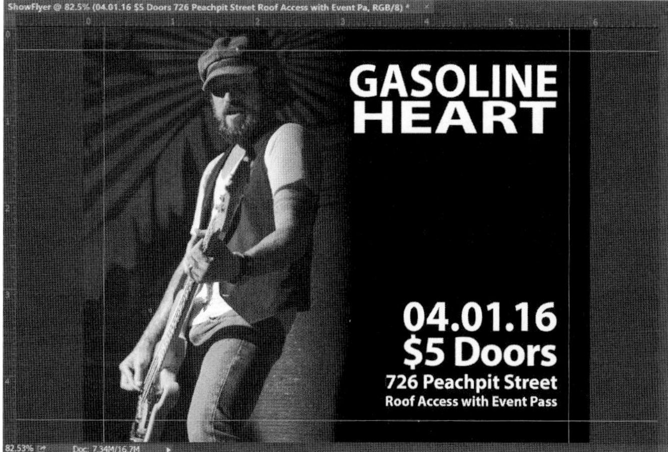

Figure 4.19 The formatted event information added to the poster

Figure 4.20 Selecting Reset Character from the Character panel menu to revert character settings to the defaults

Align Layers

Because all the text you just added is on different layers, you cannot use text alignment tools to line them all up. However, you can easily align multiple layers in a document using the Move tool.

1. From the Tools panel, choose the Move tool, or press V.
2. Select any layer that you want to align, and then Ctrl-click any other layers that you want to add to the layer selection (Command-click in Mac OS).
3. In the Move Options bar, select the alignment you want to use (**Figure 4.21**).

   Align the right edges.

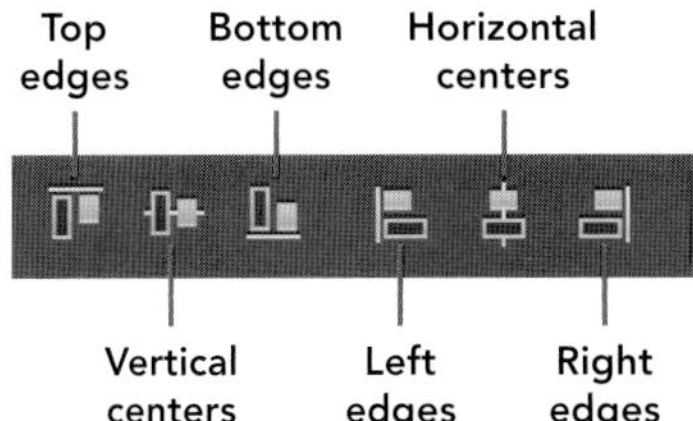

Figure 4.21 The alignment options of the Move Options bar

You can apply these alignment options to any combination of layers, including layers of different types. These tools can speed up design work and help you more easily line up elements in a composition.

Add Vertical Text

Video 4.16 *Adding Vertical Text*

You can create a vertical text effect in two ways: rotate the text 90 degrees or use the Vertical Type tool, which stacks the characters on the text layer.

The after-party venue's sign is from the 1950s, and it's easily visible from the street. To help people find the venue, the client wants to use a similar slightly wide slab serif typeface with vertical stacking.

To do this, you will add a vertical text layer:

1. In the Tools panel, click and hold the Type tool to display a menu of hidden tools. Select the Vertical Type tool (**Figure 4.22**).

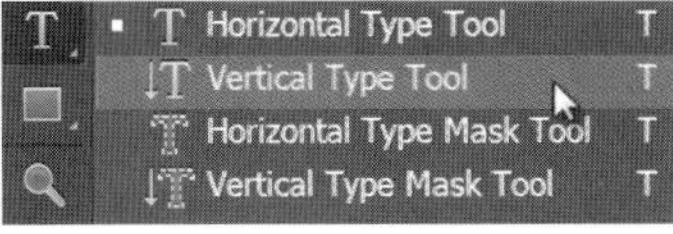

Figure 4.22 Selecting the Vertical Type tool, which is hidden under the Type tool

2 Click where you want to add the text and enter **THE VENUE**. The text appears vertically on your document.

3 Select the text and use the Character panel to format it as follows (**Figure 4.23**):

- Font: **Rockwell Bold** (or a similar slab serif typeface)
- Size: **36 pt**
- Fill: **White**
- Horizontal Scale: **150%**

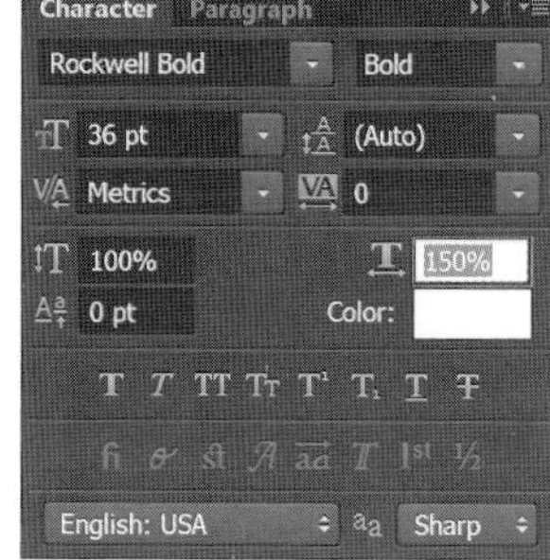

Figure 4.23 Using the Character panel to format the vertical text

4 Click Commit in the Options bar ✓ to create the vertical text layer and place the text on the page (**Figure 4.24**).

Now that all of the text is entered for the poster, you need to take a very important artistic step that is often ignored by beginning designers, but stands as an essential part of good design. You need to *look* at your image.

Looking at the image as an artist is different from looking at it as a technician or computer user. Yes, you can see that all of the information is in there, but what could be fixed, tweaked, or perfected? What's wrong with the image that gets in the way of its message?

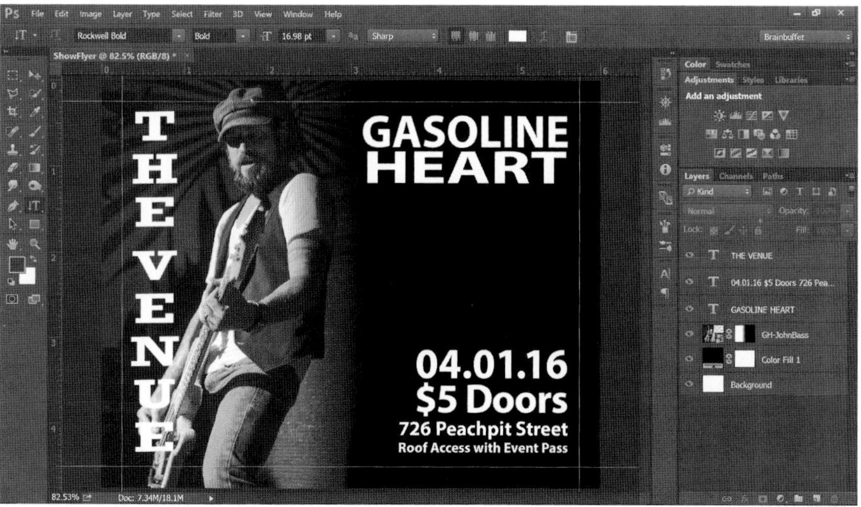

Figure 4.24 The poster with the venue name on a vertical text layer

Video 4.17 *Seeing Like an Artist*

LEVEL UP CHALLENGE: LOOK LIKE AN ARTIST

I'm not talking about growing a pencil moustache and wearing a beret (though that might be kinda cool). I mean look at and see your design as an artist would. In this book I don't want you to just use Photoshop to complete these projects. I want you to learn to use Photoshop to create expressive, communicative designs that exhibit beauty and are visually appealing. Take the time to stop, look, and think. Analyze and question. These are the real skills of an artist.

Using Photoshop is relatively easy. Using it well is much harder. Take the time to critically evaluate your work, and you will develop artistic skills faster and you'll be more fluent.

- **Level I:** Look at your image with a fresh set of eyes. It's typical to be blinded by staring at your own work. It helps to get up and look at something else for a few minutes. Visit a design website. (We have a great list posted at BrainBuffet.com.) Then come back and take a new look at your design. Evaluate it critically. Our technical editor Rocky looks at the image upside down—this is a great trick to force yourself to see it in a new way.
- **Level II:** Get another person's opinion of the design. What does she see? What does she like or dislike about the design?
- **Level III:** Find examples of how other artists have solved the problems you see in your design, and then steal those ideas. It's not plagiarism—it's research! Every artist learns from great masters. Follow that example.

Enhance Designs Using Creative Tools

This is where we move into the things that really make Photoshop designs so spectacular. We're going to learn a few great tricks that I've either learned or developed over the last 20 years working with digital design. These tricks are really simple but uncommon ways to use a couple of the tools I'm about to share with you, and it all came from experimenting, exploring the application, and trying to solve problems. I've failed more than any other designer I know—but I count that as a victory! I fail because I try and experiment—and because I fail so often, I succeed often as well.

As we explore, remember that these are not answers to design problems, but a possible solution to *this* specific design problem. As we explore these tools, think about how the settings we use might be changed and how that might create a different look in your design. It really is all about trying and experimenting.

Solve Design Problems with Styles

★ ACA Objective 3.8

★ ACA Objective 4.5

★ ACA Objective 4.9

Video 4.18 *Using Styles*

One of the most obvious problems in your current project is that the name of the venue—which happens to be "The Venue"—is difficult to read. Because this project is in support of an event, the location is critical, and the client's desire to format the text like the sign at the location is essential.

Unfortunately, while most of the image is fairly dark, the lower-right corner that includes the text happens to be one of the brightest areas in the photo. You could try to mask the left edge of the document but that would create a strange light-streak look on the photo. Fortunately, you can add a style to the layer so that any effects apply to everything on the layer.

NOTE

Layer styles are very similar to layer effects. Technically, a layer effect is a setting that you apply to the layer, and the style is a group of effects and settings that may be applied to a layer. In the industry, many people use the terms interchangeably.

To create a layer style:

1. Select the layer to which you want to add the effect. Select the vertical text layer that reads "The Venue."
2. At the bottom of the Layers panel, click the Add A Layer Style icon fx (**Figure 4.25**).

   An effects menu displays (**Figure 4.26**).
3. From the menu, choose Outer Glow.

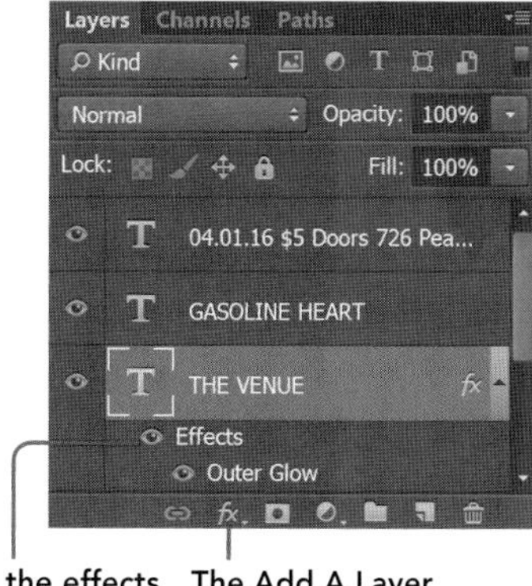

Figure 4.25 Creating a layer style

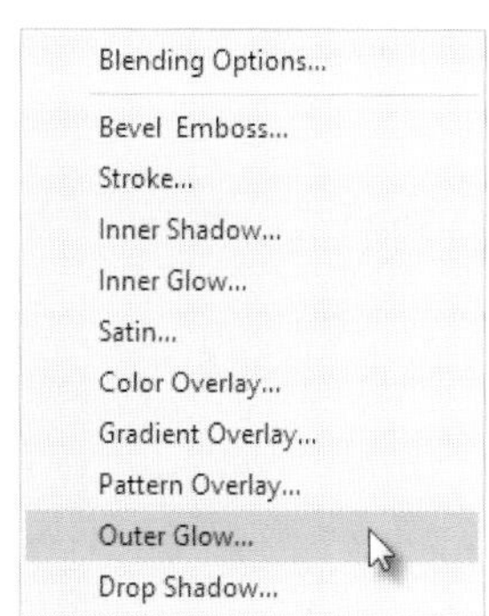

Figure 4.26 The effects menu on the Layers panel

4 In the Outer Glow panel of the Layer Styles dialog box, specify the following (**Figure 4.27**):

- Blend Mode: **Normal**
- Opacity: **81%**
- Color: **Black**
- Spread: **28%**
- Size: **76 px**

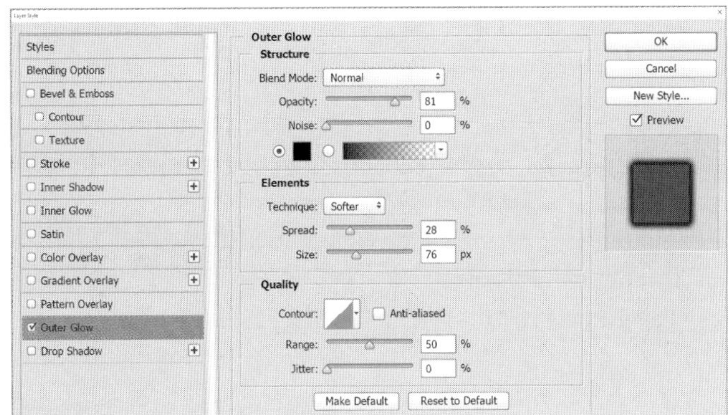

Figure 4.27 The Outer Glow panel of the Layer Style dialog box

You will almost always evaluate and tweak these settings visually, so select Preview to see how the settings affect your layer. Because each project is different, you'll find that these settings will need to be fine-tuned for every new project.

5 Click OK to apply the layer style to the layer (**Figure 4.28**).

Figure 4.28 The black outer glow effect helps distinguish the text from a highly contrasting background image without being too clumsy or obvious.

You can see that placing the dark area just around the letters made the text much easier to read by creating a strong contrast with the background. The softer edge doesn't look as cheap as a solid stroked outline might. By styling the text as somewhat transparent and fading, you minimize the visual distraction that a sharp border could cause.

SAVE STYLES FOR REPEATED USE

Styles sometimes take a while to set up. Even though this one is relatively simple, we should still save it so that you can use it again on another layer or another project. With a style, the effect is applied consistently and you can make global changes easily.

1. Select the layer with the style you want to save. In this case, select the vertical text layer that reads "The Venue."
2. In the Styles panel, click the Create New Style button (**Figure 4.29**).
3. In the New Style dialog box, enter **BlackGlow Title** in the Name field.
4. Select Include Layer Effects and Add To My Current Library, and then click OK (**Figure 4.30**).

Figure 4.29 The New Style button at the bottom of the Styles panel

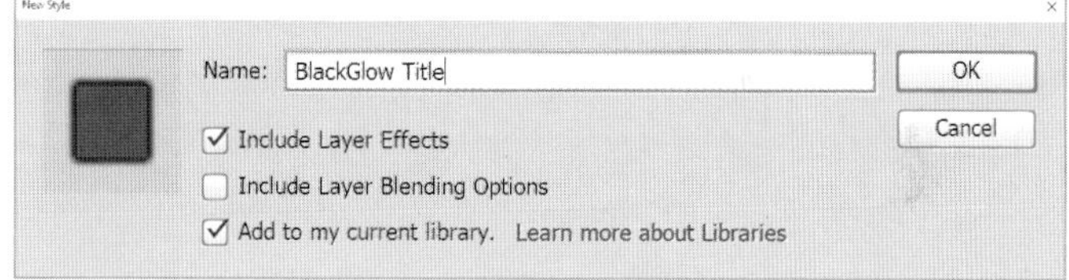

Figure 4.30 Enter the style name in New Style dialog box.

The advantages of saving styles are obvious: you can reuse them at any time! Building a customized set of styles can save you much time on future projects. Furthermore, custom styles will enhance your projects and add a personal design touch to your work.

TIP *To see the name of a style, point at its tile. After a short delay, the name will appear in a tool tip (**Figure 4.31**).*

Figure 4.31 A style name shown in a tool tip

MANAGE STYLES

▶ *Video 4.19 Managing Layer Styles*

Sometimes a style must be changed, hidden, or removed. All are accomplished easily in just a few steps.

- To edit a style on a layer, double-click the style to edit the style settings.
- To hide a style from a layer, click the visibility icon next to the layer style.
- To remove a style from a layer, drag the style to the trash can in the Layers panel. Or, right-click the style and select Clear Layer Style from the context menu (Control-click in Mac OS).
- To copy a style from one layer to another, right-click the layer that has the style you want to copy, and choose Copy Layer Style. Then right-click the destination layer, and choose Paste Layer Style (Control-click in Mac OS).

Format the Flyer Headline

▶ *Video 4.20 The Title Styles*

Your flyer looks okay at this point, but let's bring a little more attention to the headlining band. The client says they're a crowd favorite for locals, and they also think the flyer could use a little more "pop." (Clients *always* say it could use more "pop.") I'm also going to share one of the tricks I've developed over the years that I call the "glowing ghost" effect.

Figure 4.32 Selecting Outer Glow

1. In the Layers panel, select the layer that you want to alter. In this case, select the vertical text layer that reads "Gasoline Heart."
2. Click the Layer Styles icon and choose Outer Glow from the menu (**Figure 4.32**).
3. In the Outer Glow panel of the Layer Styles dialog box, specify what works for your image. We used the following (**Figure 4.33**):
   - Blend Mode: **Normal**
   - Opacity: **100%**
   - Color: **White**
   - Spread: **2%**
   - Size: **54 px**

   Remember to select Preview to see how the changes affect the layer.
4. Click OK to create the layer style for the layer.
5. In the Layers panel, enter **0** in the Fill field (**Figure 4.34**).

If your settings get out of control, click the Reset To Default button to restore them to the default settings.

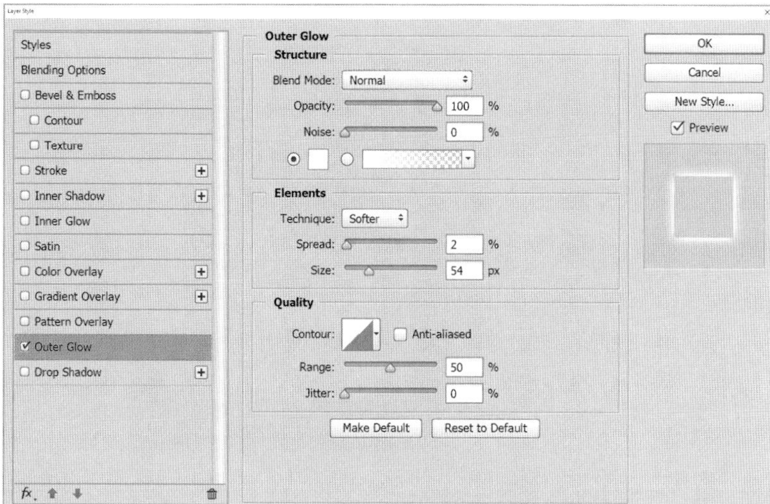

Figure 4.33 The Outer Glow panel of the Layer Style dialog box

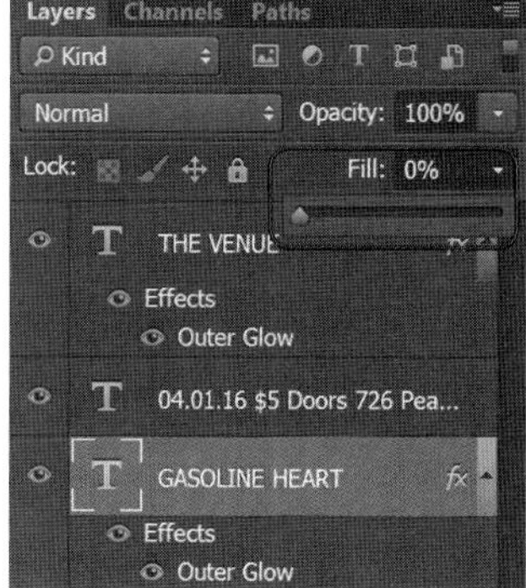

Figure 4.34 The Fill percentage for the layer

The text becomes transparent, but the white, Outer Glow layer style remains (**Figure 4.35**).

This pronounced effect can often be used to help text stand out in your designs without introducing colors or exaggerating the design elements. I also like using these tricks because they represent a slightly unusual use of the Outer Glow effect, and show the flexibility of these tools in Photoshop.

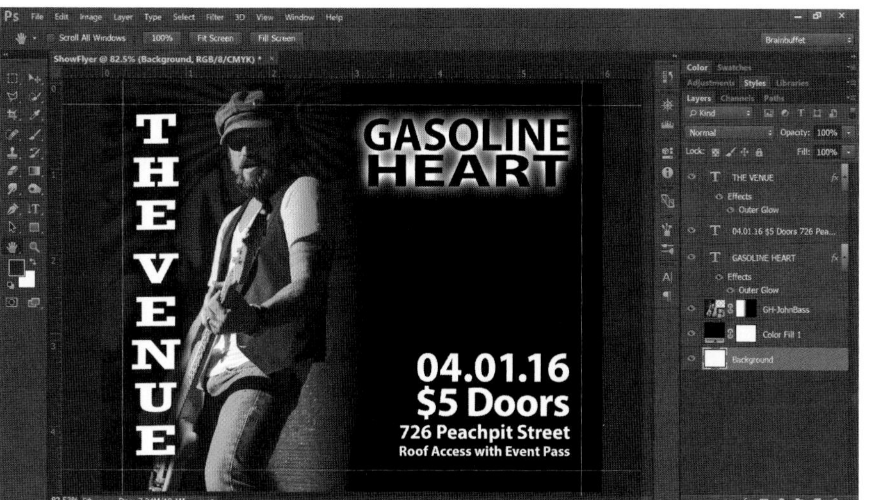

Figure 4.35 Using an effect to distinguish text from the background.

NOTE

Changing the Fill percentage changes the opacity of the layer contents but does not alter the layer effects. However, changing the opacity value alters both the layer and the effects.

Save your work!

Video 4.21 Safer Saving

You've done a lot of work and you're about to shift gears again. Quickly save your work before moving on. I also want to teach you a quick habit that you should acquire. Although some believe this habit is redundant and unnecessary, it's saved me from disaster more than once.

After saving the file, save it again using a different filename. That is, after you've saved the current file as `ShowFlyer.psd`, choose File > Save As and save it as `ShowFlyer-v2.psd` and then continue working.

These steps will create two files: one saved at this point, and another that you will continue working on. This is not a foolproof solution, but can save you in the event that a file gets corrupted. Drive space is cheap; your time is expensive. Develop good habits to help protect your work now to save yourself headaches later.

For now, your flyer looks good. If this were a rush job, I'd even call it acceptable to present to the client. But you can still perform a few more, nonessential refinements to improve the design.

ACA Objective 4.9

Working with Filters

Video 4.22 Working with Filters

Just as you applied effects (through layer styles) to improve the visibility of your text, you can often use **filters** to improve images. Filters, like effects, change the look of the image.

While you can apply both styles and filters to layers, styles are best applied to text and shape layers, whereas filters lend themselves more readily to photos. Filters also generally can perform much more complex adjustments and manipulations to the image. Because your photo layer is a smart object, in this exercise, you will create **smart filters** that are filters applied to a smart object layer. This technique lends the most flexibility and ease of editing to your project.

> **NOTE** *Smart filters used to be very limited, but now nearly every filter is available as a smart filter. It's a best practice to convert a layer to a smart object layer before you edit unless you have a specific reason not to.*

Add Smart Filters

To add a smart filter to a layer:

1. Select the layer containing the smart object. In this case, select the layer with the bass player.

   If the layer is not a smart object, you can convert it into one by choosing Filter > Convert For Smart Filters (**Figure 4.36**).

2. From the Filter menu, choose the filter you want to use on the image. For this exercise, choose Filter > Blur > Surface Blur.

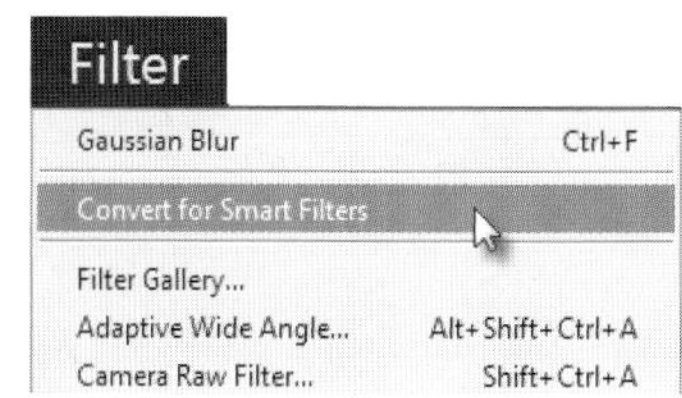

Figure 4.36 Preparing a layer for a smart filter

FILTER GALLERY

In the Filter menu you'll find an option called Filter Gallery that enables you to quickly preview a number of filters (**Figure 4.37**). You're not going to be using them in this project, but take some time to explore them for future use. These include the categories of Artistic, Brush Strokes, Distort, Sketch, Stylize, and Texture.

Figure 4.37 The Filter Gallery is great for experimenting with various filters.

3 In the Surface Blur dialog box, specify the following (**Figure 4.38**):

- Radius: **40 Pixels**
- Threshold: **200 Levels**

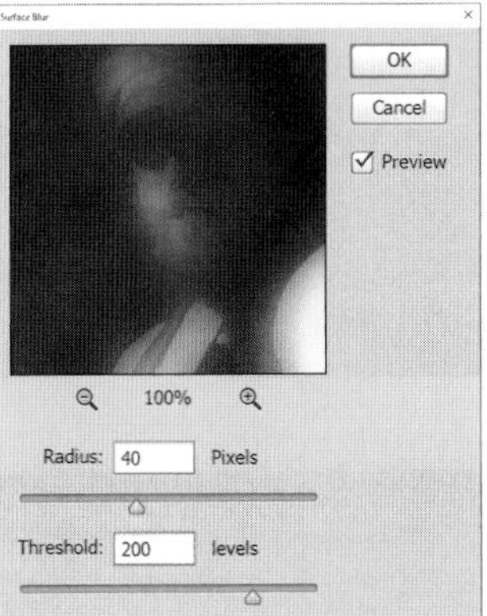

Figure 4.38 The Surface Blur dialog box

4 Select Preview to view your settings on the image, and then click OK.

The smart filter appears in your Layer Stack under the layer that it affects (**Figure 4.39**).

While this doesn't look so great right now, it's okay because you were just prepping for the next step. You're going to cut holes into the filter to hide the filter's effects in certain areas of our image.

Figure 4.39 The smart filters appear in the Layers panel directly under the layer they affect.

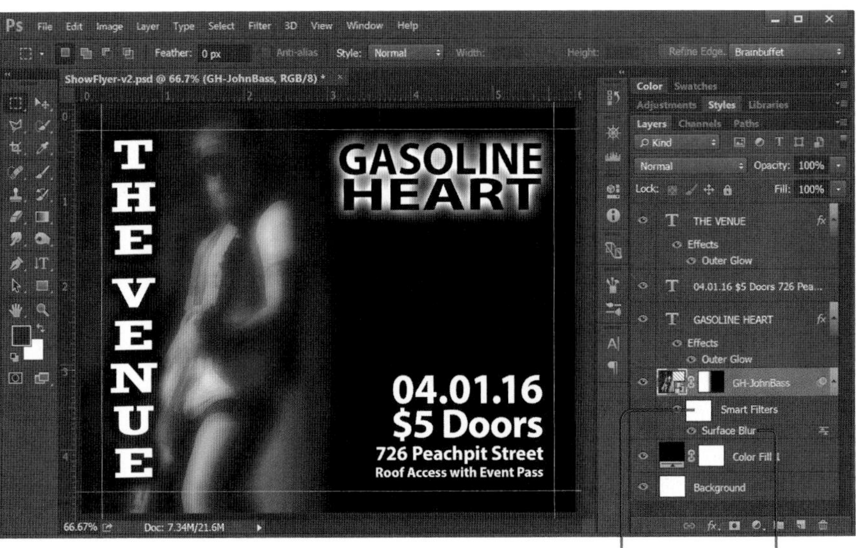

Adjust Smart Filters

★ ACA Objective 4.6

Video 4.22 Adjusting Filters

Although you can preview the results of a smart filter in the Filter dialog box, sometimes you'll later want to adjust the filter settings. When you're not working with a smart filter, you can undo your steps by choosing Edit > Step Backward. You can easily adjust smart filter layer settings in the Layers panel.

1 In the Layers panel, double-click the name of a smart filter layer.
2 In the Smart Filter dialog box, adjust the filter settings as necessary.
3 Click OK to apply the changes to your smart filter layer.
4 To adjust the way a smart filter blends with a smart layer, double-click the Filter Blending Option icon next to the smart filter you want to adjust.

   The Blending Options dialog box appears for that filter (**Figure 4.40**).

5 Select a different blending mode from the Mode menu and enter a different value in the Opacity field to modify the effect.
6 Select Preview to compare the edited and unedited settings, and then click OK to apply the changes to the smart filter layer.

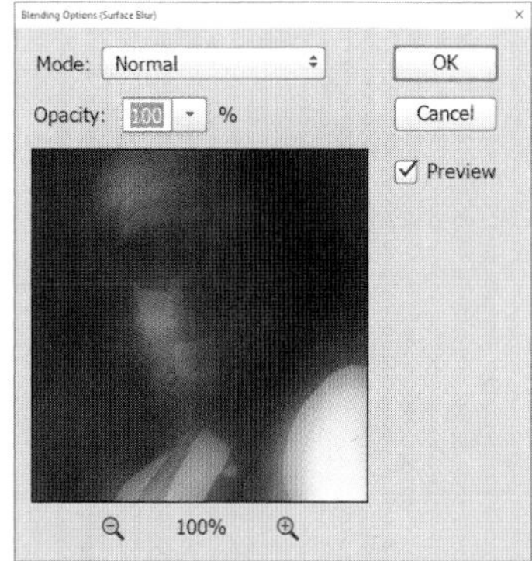

Figure 4.40 The Blending Options dialog box

Smart Filter Masks

★ ACA Objective 3.6

★ ACA Objective 4.3

Similar to masks used on layers, smart filters always include a mask that allows you to control the visibility of the effect on that layer. Previously, you faded a layer using a gradient; now you will just cut holes in a mask to allow the unfiltered image to show through.

You're going to cut through this mask using the Selection tool and then fill in that area on the mask with black. This method introduces a couple of new concepts, but they're pretty simple.

To hide a smart filter in sections of your image:

1 Click the mask for the smart filter.

   White corners appear around the mask to indicate that it is selected (**Figure 4.41**).

Figure 4.41 In the Layers panel, white corners display around the active mask.

TIP

Press X to reverse the foreground and background colors.

2 Press the D key to be sure you are using the default colors of a white foreground and a black background.

3 In the Tools panel, select the Rectangle Selection tool .

The pointer turns into a crosshair.

4 In the Options bar, verify that Feather is set to 0 px and the style is Normal (**Figure 4.42**).

5 Select areas of the image and fill them with black to hide them, or white to reveal the underlying smart filter effect (**Figure 4.43**).

> **TIP** *You can use keyboard shortcuts to fill your selections. Press Alt+Delete (Windows) or Option+Delete (Mac OS) to fill the mask with the foreground color, and press Ctrl+Delete (Windows) or Command+Delete (Mac OS) to fill with the background color.*

With this method, it is easy to modify an effect that you applied to your image. The beauty of using smart filters is that they are nondestructive; you can always alter or remove an effect later by using a mask.

Figure 4.42 The Options bar for the Rectangle Selection tool

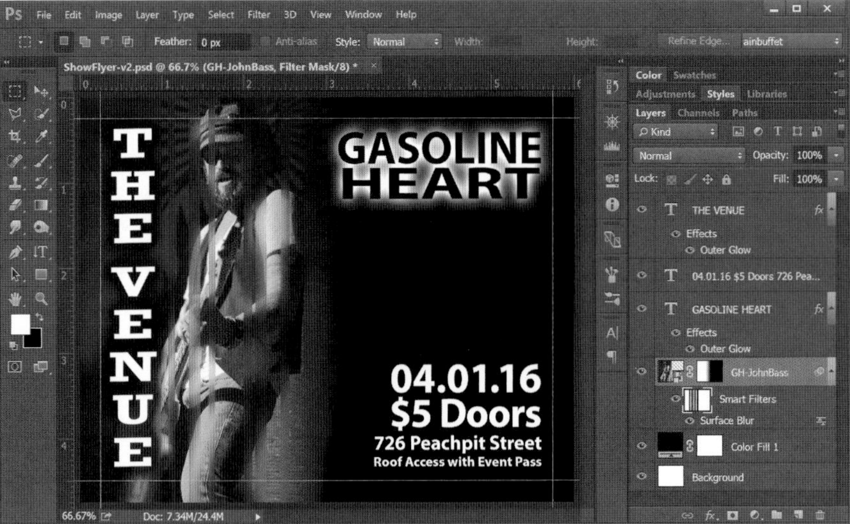

Figure 4.43 Note that the mask corresponds to the affected areas of the image: black hides, white reveals.

Explore Further

Teaching filters, styles, and other effects is a difficult process because if we simply dictate the values to put into the fields you won't be creating your own design. Following instructions by rote is not how you'll get great at Photoshop. In the real world of design, you have to personally experience plenty of experimentation, failure, and guesswork. This is a critical part of the process. You'll need to explore and experiment so that you can stumble onto your own design styles and tricks.

***Video 4.23** Explore Filters Further*

The projects here are pretty simple and easy to follow because they have to be, but I want to make sure that you feel comfortable trying new things. You can always duplicate a layer and do something wild! It doesn't cost anything and it's easy to trash an experimental layer that doesn't work.

Client Review

Finally, you'll get your design ready for client approval, and then save it in a format that you can submit to a commercial printer for offset press reproduction. You want to show the client precisely how the final print results will look in their proper size so that you have no possible misunderstanding when the client gets the final product.

***Video 4.24** Client Review Prep*

Hiding the Bleed

Because your document has a bleed, the Photoshop document is larger than the final print product. I developed a small trick for working with clients that helps eliminate misunderstanding and gives them a better idea of how the final document will look. You'll create a new layer the color of the background, and then cut a hole at the cutlines of the guides to simulate the appearance of the final trimmed document.

1. Click the top layer of your document to select it.
2. In the Layers panel, click the New Layer icon. Name the layer **Bleed Sim**.
3. Select the Eyedropper tool and sample the background color by clicking it.

4 Press Alt+Delete (Windows) or Option+Delete (Mac OS) to fill the layer with the foreground color that you just sampled.

   You may need to adjust the layer to make it match perfectly. Choosing Image > Adjustments > Hue/Saturation often works well with Saturation set to 0 and Lightness set to +9.

5 Select the Rectangular Marquee tool and select the area defined by your guides.

   By default, the cursor will snap to the guides when you get close to the corners. If it doesn't, choose View > Snap.

6 Press the Delete key to delete the selected area.

   Your design now simulates the final trim size and crop of the printed image (**Figure 4.44**).

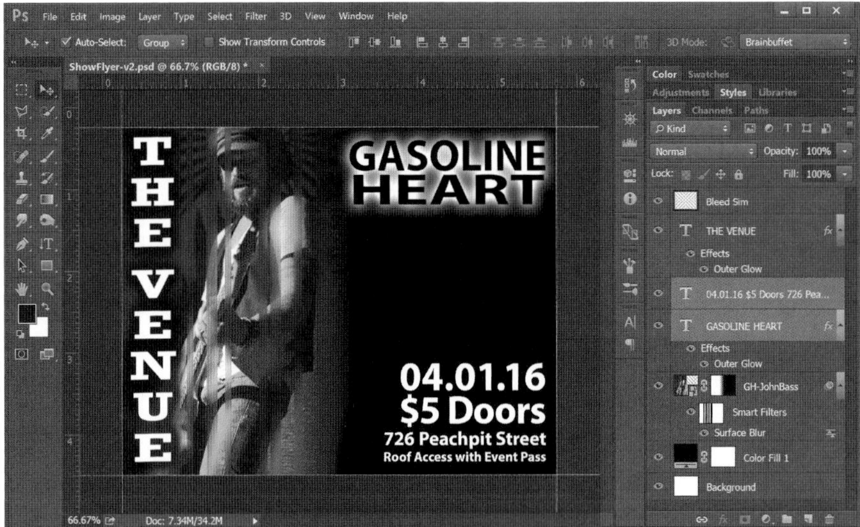

Figure 4.44 After simulating your final print trim, you may wish to adjust the elements on your image.

This method also lets you preview your design as it will look when cut to size. Sometimes it's hard to visualize the cut document from the guides alone. After this layer is created, you may want to nudge elements or resize items. Feel free to make any changes that you think your document needs.

View at Print Size

To view the design at print size, choose View > Print Size (**Figure 4.45**). Doing so will simulate the final print size onscreen using the selected resolution. The results are dependent on the proper calibration of your screen resolution, but they should be close to reality. The main problem you're hoping to avoid with this step is allowing the client to expect a different size because of what she saw onscreen.

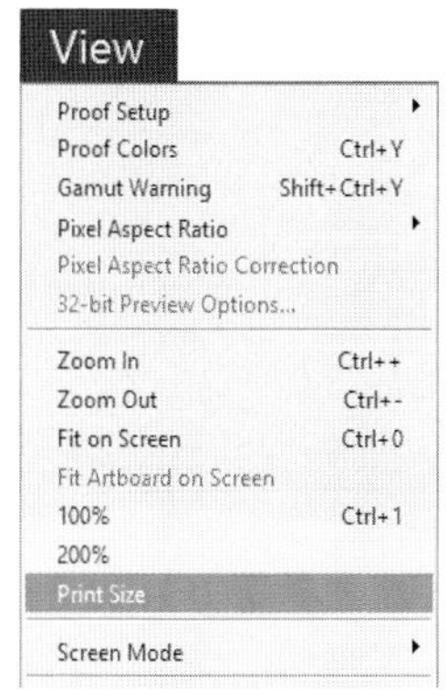

Figure 4.45 Choose View > Print Size to view the design in the approximate size that it will be printed.

Give Proof

We talked about this when you set up the document, but you'll also want to verify once again that your document is in soft proof view. You can tell you're soft proofing because of the CMYK that appears in the title bar of the document panel. You can also toggle the soft proof with Ctrl+Y (Windows) or Command+Y (Mac OS).

At this point, you have a very good simulation onscreen of what the final printed image will look like. Discussing this with the client at this point is critical if you haven't had much communication so far.

Making Adjustments for the Client

Video 4.25 *Making Adjustments*

Sometimes a client asks for changes at the final review. It may be editing text, moving elements, or making other more significant changes.

If the client says that the image is too dark and he wants the bass player to have more "pop," you may have a problem because an adjustment chosen from the Image menu will be limited by the mask you are using for the filters. But you have a simple solution: use an adjustment layer.

Adjustment layers are similar to smart filters in that they affect layers without changing image information. However, by default, an adjustment layer affects *all* of the layers under it, rather than just one layer. This technique can be really helpful at times, and will work for the final image adjustment that the client requested.

To create and use an adjustment layer:

1. In the Layers panel, select the uppermost layer that you want to change.
2. In the Adjustments panel, select the adjustment you want to use. For now, select Curves.

3 In the Properties panel (**Figure 4.46**), click the Auto button to lighten the image. You can also choose a preset or manually adjust the curve.

4 Minimize the Properties panel (**Figure 4.47**).

Depending on the image you have and the style your client wants, you may need to experiment with the adjustments. Adjustment layers are completely nondestructive, so you have no chance of damaging your original image. Plus, you can easily show, hide, and combine adjustment layers to get the look you want.

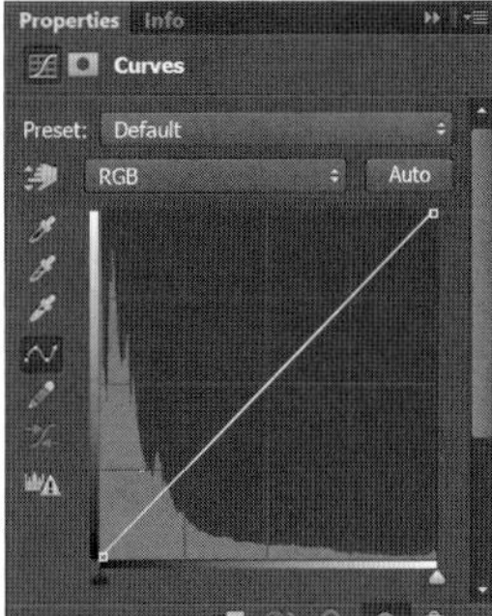

Figure 4.46 The Properties panel for the Curves adjustments

Figure 4.47 The final design after the client's changes were implemented

Save the Document

With all the changes made and the client happy, let's get our final design exported. Before you do, save the document as an unaltered Photoshop file in case the client asks for another change to be made.

> **TIP** *When I'm doing work for clients, I always save a copy for the web at 1000 pixels to add to my portfolio and for the client to use with social media marketing. To do so, save the Photoshop document for the web in JPEG format with a resolution of 1000 px in the largest dimension.*

Making It Final

★ ACA Objective 5.1

★ ACA Objective 5.2

Video 4.26 Making It Final

If the client is happy with the design, it's time to save it in its final forms. Because this is a print job, you are going to save the project in a few formats to support various uses. Often, the final formats you need to deliver will be specified by the client or the print shop you're using. When in doubt, always check with the client to pin down the formats they need for the final design. If the client does not have strong preferences here, you may have to guide the client in making these decisions. A good designer should have a few reputable print houses to refer the clients to where you know the workflow.

Convert to Flat CMYK

You know that this document is going to be commercially printed on an offset press, so you need to convert the Photoshop document to CMYK. You will also flatten the file to reduce its size.

Flattening a document merges all of the visible layers and discards anything that is not visible. Make sure that you have the document in its final visual form, ready to go to press, and then flatten it as follows:

WARNING *If you created a Bleed Sim layer, be sure to hide or delete that layer before flattening the document.*

1. From the Layers panel menu, choose Flatten Image (**Figure 4.48**).
2. When the warning appears asking if you want to discard hidden layers, click OK.

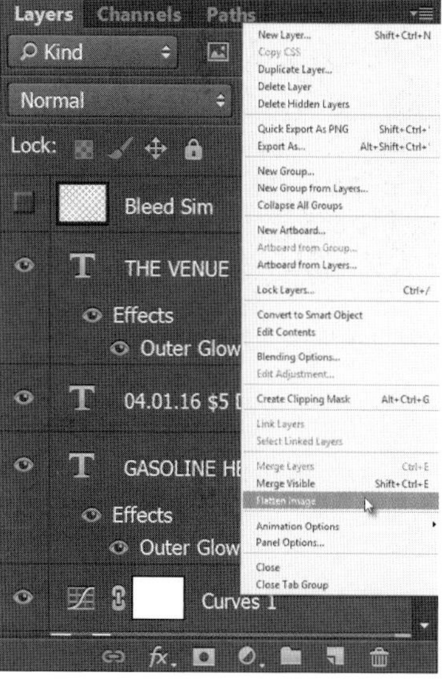

Figure 4.48 You have multiple ways to flatten a document, but using the Layers panel is the most convenient.

The layers are converted into a single background layer.

Now that the Photoshop document is flattened, you will want to convert it to the CMYK color space. To do so, choose Image > Mode > CMYK Color to put the document in the color space that is needed for commercial presses (**Figure 4.49**). Click OK in the confirmation dialog box that appears.

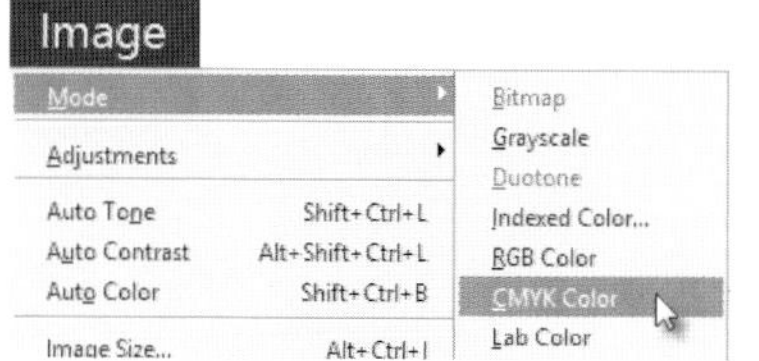

Figure 4.49 CMYK is the color space used by commercial presses. Convert your documents to CMYK before sending them to press to avoid color problems in your final product.

The confirmation dialog box will not appear if you already selected "Don't show again."

Save a Flat Copy

Now that you have flattened this document and converted it to CMYK for the press, you will save the document to send to the printer. Because you do not want to overwrite your layered document, you are going to save the print-ready version as a separate file.

Be sure to choose File > Save As so that you do not overwrite your layered original. Save your document as `ShowFlyerFLATCMYK.psd` in the same location that you saved your original documents.

LEVEL UP CHALLENGE: DREAM EVENT

Video 4.27 Dream Event

In this project you learned about many cool tools for making a document for an event, but every event is different. You'll need different looks, styles, and layouts depending on each client's goals and target audience.

Take the Level Up Challenge to dig deeper and enhance your skills:

- **Level I:** Create an event flyer (real or imaginary) using an image that you find online and the tools you learned in this chapter.
- **Level II:** Create a flyer with a very different feeling than what you've created in this chapter. Use different fonts, styles, and effects. Explore and experiment with the tools.
- **Level III:** Create a flyer for someone at your school, work, or organization. Learn to work with your clients and help develop a flyer that represents *their* goals.

CHAPTER OBJECTIVES

Chapter Learning Objectives

- Work with multiple images in the Photoshop workspace.
- Make effective selections and masks and use them to blend images.
- Modify the canvas to extend your image area.
- Use color adjustment tools to make blended images believable.
- Learn to use the content-aware move and extend feature.
- Save files to be used effectively in other Photoshop projects.

Chapter ACA Objectives

DOMAIN 3.0
UNDERSTANDING ADOBE PHOTOSHOP

3.6 Demonstrate knowledge of layers and masks.

DOMAIN 4.0
CREATING DIGITAL IMAGES USING ADOBE PHOTOSHOP

4.2 Import assets into a project.

4.3 Make, manage, and manipulate selections.

4.4 Transform images.

4.5 Create and manage layers and masks.

4.6 Use basic retouching techniques—including color correction, blending, cloning, and filters—to manipulate a digital image.

DOMAIN 5.0
PUBLISHING DIGITAL IMAGES USING ADOBE PHOTOSHOP

5.2 Export or save digital images to various file formats.

CHAPTER 5

Myths and Monsters

In this chapter, you will create something completely new. The most amazing images I've seen in my life are Photoshop creations. Whether it's a monster for a movie poster or a mythical creature for a book cover, we've all seen amazing images that looked *real*. This project will involve creating a mythical creature, refining it, and turning it into desktop and phone wallpaper.

In this chapter, you're going to create an imaginary creature by **compositing** multiple images into one. This is a popular Photoshop activity—the skills you learn in this example will easily transfer to any compositing project. The primary skills in this project will be making selections and combining layers with masks—skills you've been introduced to already that you'll now be taking to a new level.

***Video 5.1** Myths and Monsters*

To complete this project, you should be familiar with the Photoshop basics covered in the previous chapters. If you find yourself struggling, watch the videos for complete instructions. The steps presented in this and remaining chapters are intended to be a reference that you can use to quickly refer to the techniques introduced in these projects.

★ ACA Objective 4.2

Create a Mystical Animal

▶ **Video 5.2** Gather Your Images

The best way to learn some great compositing secrets is to jump in and create a really strange creature: one that started as photos of two very different animals. To follow this specific project, use the files **BieberBull.jpg** and **PBlion-721836.jpg** from the **Chapter 5 downloads** folder.

The first time you try, I advise using the provided photographs. But as you gain confidence, feel free to select your own images and follow the same steps. (To use the cool tricks for perfecting hair masks, it's best that your animal has hair or fur.)

> **TIP** *When considering which images to use for your own project, pay attention to the direction that animals are looking. For example, if you have one animal looking forward, make sure the second animal is also looking forward. If one is looking off to the side, choose a second animal with his head tilted at a similar angle (remember that you can always flip the image).*

Your first step is to open both of the images at once. You'll see one is a bull and one is a lion. To do this in the Open dialog box, Ctrl-click (Windows) or Command-click (Mac OS) to select multiple files.

★ ACA Objective 4.3

Grab the Bull by the Horns

▶ **Video 5.3** Grab the Bull by the Horns

You're actually going to grab the horns off the bull to place on the lion, as shown in **Figure 5.1**. (Remember, click a tab at the top of the document window to control which image displays.) Use any selection tool that's comfortable for this, but the most efficient is the Quick Selection tool. In your selection, be sure to grab some of the hair. (You will be able to experiment with a couple of ways to use these horns once they are placed in the lion image.)

Figure 5.1 You'll be combining two ordinary images into a mythical creature.

Once you have your selection, you should refine the edge before you copy it to the other image. This helps perfect your selection before moving the pixels from one image to another.

You can also click on the "Refine Edge..." button in the Option bar to open the Refine Edge dialog box.

To refine the selection:

1 Choose Select > Refine Edge (**Figure 5.2**).

2 In the Refine Edge dialog box, adjust the edge using the preview in the Photoshop interface to determine the settings. In this case, the following settings look good (**Figure 5.3**):

- Smooth: **60**
- Contrast: **40%**

3 Click OK.

TIP *In some images, the subject is isolated and there is no background. The easiest way to create a selection in this situation is to select the background, inverse the selection, and then copy and paste into your document.*

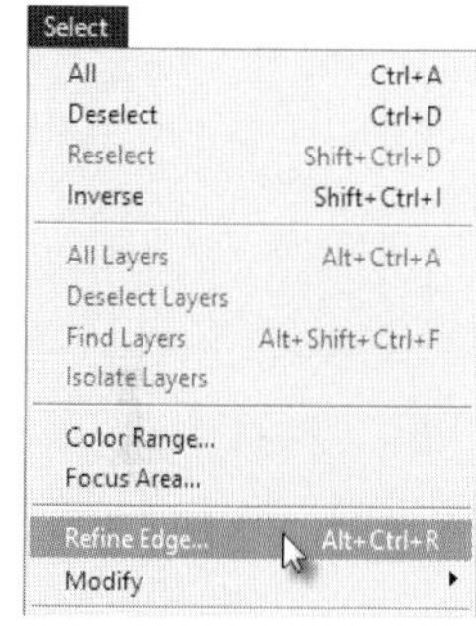

Figure 5.2 Choose Select > Refine Edge to adjust the edge of the selection.

Now that you have a clean selection on the horns, copy and paste the image into the document window containing your lion image (**Figure 5.4**). This will place them on a new layer in your document. Once the image is copied, you can close the document window you copied from—without saving any changes.

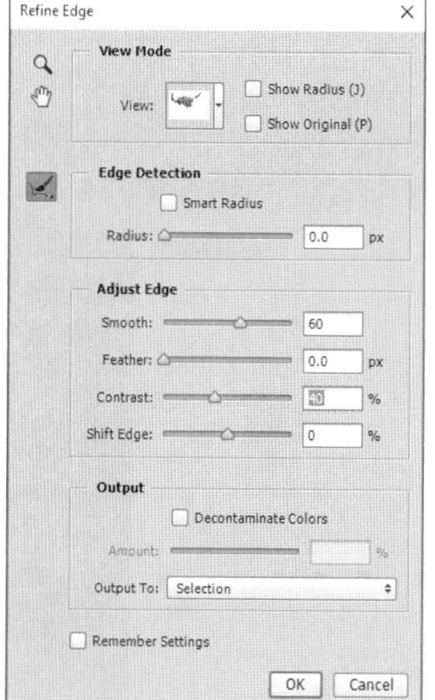

Figure 5.3 ◀ Change the Smooth and Contrast values in the Adjust Edge area of the Refine Edge dialog box.

Figure 5.4 ▲ After you initially paste in the horns, it's not a very believable creature.

Tweak the Horns

★ ACA Objective 4.4

Video 5.4 Transform Tricks

WARNING

Two methods enable you to rotate and flip an image, but they are very different. Don't confuse them! The Image > Image Rotation options affect the entire document and all layers. The Edit > Transform options affect only selected layers or selected pixels.

There's a problem with the horns: They're facing the wrong way. So let's cover some of the basic tools you can use to transform your images.

First, convert the horns layer to a smart object to be sure you can edit nondestructively (Layers panel menu > Convert To Smart Object). Then flip the horns horizontally by choosing Edit > Transform > Flip Horizontal.

Next, transform the horns by hand. You will use the Free Transform function to do this, as this tool allows you to visually modify and experiment with settings.

TIP

Shift-drag the mouse to constrain your transformation proportions.

To free transform a selection:

1. Choose Edit > Free Transform. You can also press Ctrl+T (Windows) or Command+T (Mac OS).

   Transform the horns so that they are positioned and sized correctly.

2. Once the horns are positioned and sized correctly, press Enter (Windows) or Return (Mac OS) to make the change. You can also click Commit ✓ in the Options bar to commit your changes.

Extend the Canvas

★ ACA Objective 4.4

Video 5.5 Open up the Canvas

If your images extend past the canvas, you can easily extend the canvas manually using the Crop tool. With the Crop tool selected, you can drag the canvas to the size you need, and press Enter (Windows) or Return (Mac OS) to commit the change. You can also use any of the methods you used to extend the canvas covered in Chapter 3. This image still needs work (**Figure 5.5**)!

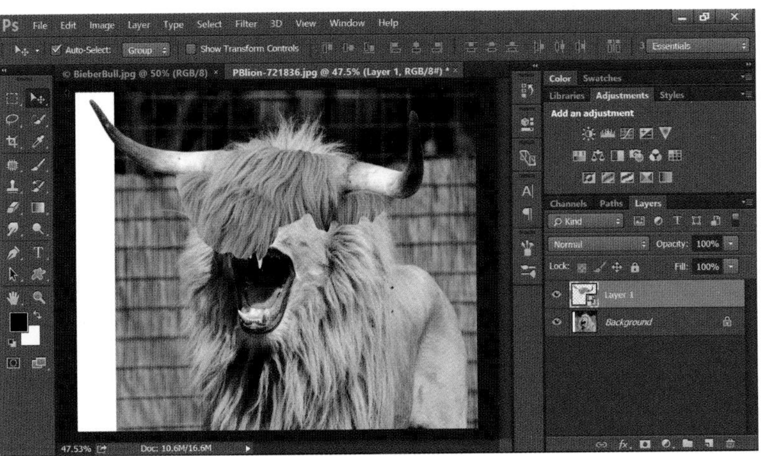

Figure 5.5 After the horns are in place and resized, the image still needs a lot of work.

TIP

You can also choose Image > Reveal All to show the part of the canvas that the horns extended.

Believable Blending

★ ACA Objective 4.6

Video 5.6 Smart Color Blending

Right now the horns don't look believable at all. The colors don't match, and the edges of the selection make it look like the horns are cut from a photo. Let's blend the colors and perfect the mask for a believable mix. There are a few ways to do this, but in this case use **Smart Filter** adjustments. These adjustments allow you to add all of the color adjustments (such as Hue/Saturation) from the Image menu as a smart filter. This means the adjustments are combined and affect only the specific layer you're working on.

Adjust with Smart Filters

To adjust the Hue/Saturation of a smart layer:

1. In the Layers panel, select the smart layer you want to affect.
2. Choose Image > Adjustments > Hue/Saturation (**Figure 5.6**).
3. In the Hue/Saturation dialog box, adjust the settings according to the image's needs.
4. To adjust a specific color channel, select it from the color channel menu and set the values for each channel accordingly (**Figure 5.7**).

   For the example image, the following settings seem appropriate:

   - Reds: Saturation **–12**
   - Yellows: Saturation **+15**

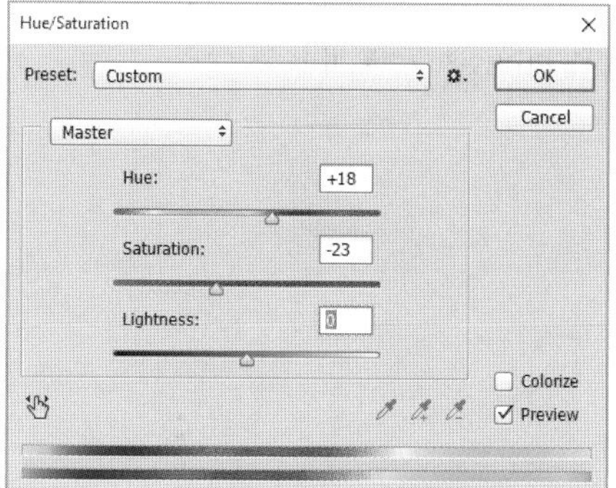

Figure 5.6 The Hue/Saturation dialog box

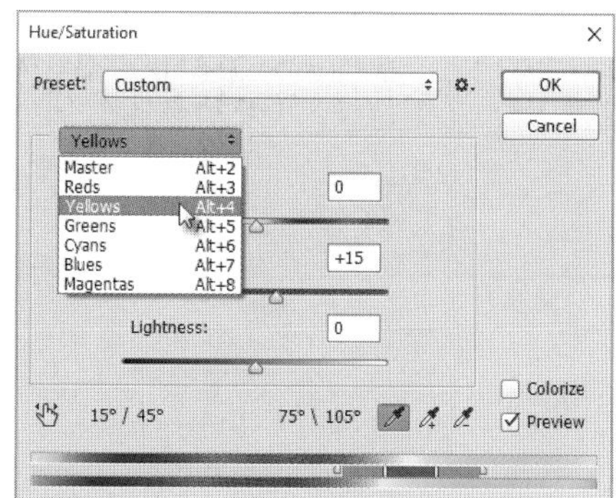

Figure 5.7 Choosing the Yellows channel in the Hue/Saturation dialog box

NOTE
When you add multiple adjustments to the same smart layer, they will stack under a single smart object, so you can edit the settings later of each individual adjustment.

5 Make any other adjustments you want to use on your layer.

Let's add a brightness contrast adjustment increasing Brightness by **15** (**Figure 5.8**).

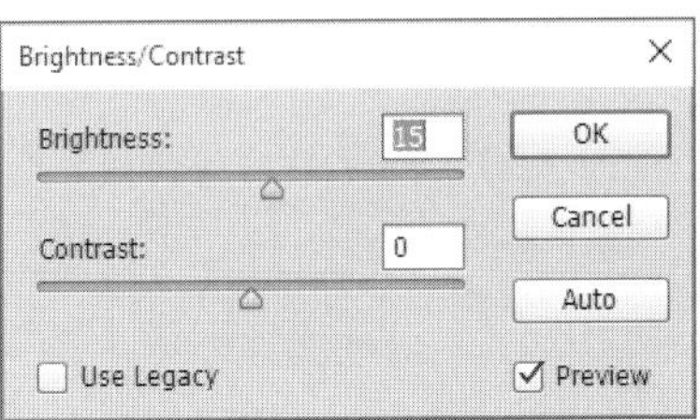

Figure 5.8 The Brightness/Contrast dialog box

The color matching isn't perfect, but it is very close (**Figure 5.9**). Because they are smart adjustments, you can come back and modify, add, or remove adjustments as needed. You will probably be editing the final image heavily, so work on the mask to keep your options open.

Figure 5.9 Though not complete, it's easy to see where this image is headed.

Save Your Progress

★ *ACA Objective 5.2*

Since you've worked a bit on this document, save your image as a PSD file with the name `HornLion.psd`. You have more to do, but you want to make sure that you have a saved layered Photoshop document with all your work so far. From here on out it's all just perfecting the effect.

Perfect Masks and Selections

★ ACA Objective 3.6

★ ACA Objective 4.3

★ ACA Objective 4.5

Video 5.7 Quick Mask Mastery

The image you have now is not believable, but you're actually pretty close. The only thing you need to do is perfect the blend of the hair and perhaps tweak the colors again. You're going to create this one image as a simple finished product, and then take it to the next level in the next chapter. Our goal here is to get the image looking like the lion really had horns when the photograph was taken.

Quick Mask Mastery

You may have noticed that the settings for masks and selections are very similar. As a matter of fact, the refine options of both are identical. A mask is essentially a paintable selection saved as a black-and-white image.

TIP

To quickly select everything on a layer, Ctrl-click (Windows) or Command-click (Mac OS) the thumbnail. This will automatically make a perfect selection of the layer's contents (minus the layer's transparency), which can then be used as a mask and/or modified.

Now add a mask to the horns layer. First rename this layer **horns** and add a mask.

To make a mask using the current layer's contents:

1. Press Ctrl (Windows) or Command (Mac OS) and point at the layer thumbnail. When the selection cursor displays, click to select the contents of the layer (**Figure 5.10**).
2. Click the Add Layer Mask icon in the Layers panel to create the mask.

   The mask is created on the active layer (**Figure 5.11**).

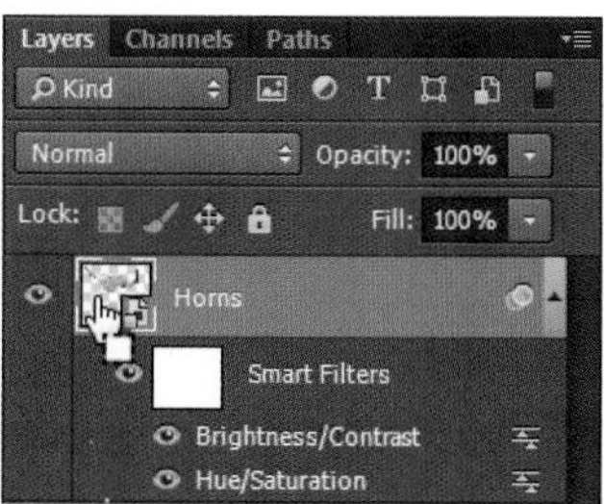

Figure 5.10 Click when the selection pointer is visible to select all the contents of the layer.

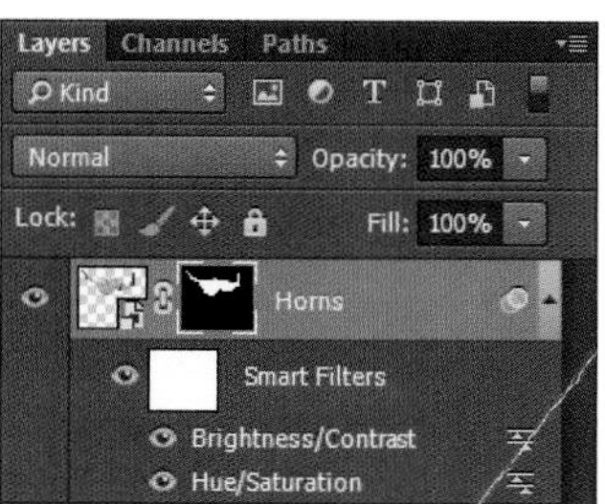

Figure 5.11 The mask is created on the active layer.

Now that you have a mask limited to the selection, you can edit the mask easily. Use a large, soft-sided brush to brush around the edges of the hair on this layer to blend in the hair to the lion. Use the same techniques you used in earlier projects; the video will guide you through this step.

PERFECT THE MASK IN QUICK MASK MODE

This image has an area or two where you might want to limit precisely what gets masked (hidden) from the layer. If this is the case, you can activate your selection and switch to Quick Mask mode to create a boundary of what can be edited in the mask.

TIP

Pressing Q on your keyboard will also enter or exit Quick Mask mode.

To enter Quick Mask mode:

1 Select an area you want to restrict editing to.

2 Enter Quick Mask mode by clicking Edit In Quick Mask Mode at the bottom of the Tools panel.

   To clearly illustrate the selection area, nonselected areas display in red.

NOTE

Quick selections and layer masks display in a similar way, with transparent indicating a selected area and semitransparent red indicating a nonselected area.

3 Edit your quick mask selection the same way you work on a layer mask (**Figure 5.12**).

Figure 5.12 Quick Mask mode shows your selection with a semitransparent red overlay to help perfect your selections.

4 When your quick mask is selected properly, click Edit In Standard Mode at the bottom of the Tools panel to exit Quick Mask mode.

This is an excellent way to select an area more precisely with the help of a semitransparent red overlay. After exiting Quick Mask mode, finish editing your selection.

Refine your selection and you're nearly done. You can see that the time taken to master this change is well worth it. The blend is much more believable at this point and the image looks quite realistic (**Figure 5.13**).

Figure 5.13 The lion's horns appear quite realistic, but the "Bieb-bowl" haircut is *so* 2010.

SAVE YOUR PROGRESS

It's a great time to save your progress before moving forward to finishing touches. You're going to fix the problem area on the right side, and then explore another amazing Photoshop trick that you should find fairly easy at this point.

Finishing Touches

The image is nearly complete, but there are some small issues that detract from it. After fixing the background, you'll use the editing tools you've already learned to clean up the dirt in the mane and tweak any other issues.

Content-Aware Move and Extend

ACA Objective 4.6

Video 5.8 *Content-Aware Move*

The background of this image is incomplete. Because you extended the canvas to fit the horns, it left a white area to the left. This is still the Background layer, and there's no need to convert it for this step. Instead, you'll use the **Content-Aware Move** tool that will allow you to reposition a selection and automatically fill in the hole left behind. In the Options bar, you will specify whether to use Move mode or Extend mode, which copies and moves the selection.

For this image, you're going to extend the background of the fence so that it fills the blank area on the right of our image. To extend an area using the Content-Aware Move tool in Extend mode:

1. Select a clean area of the image to extend. In this case, select the fence from the left edge of the background image up to the lion's whiskers.
2. Select the Content-Aware Move tool.

   The tool is located with the image repair tools (**Figure 5.14**).

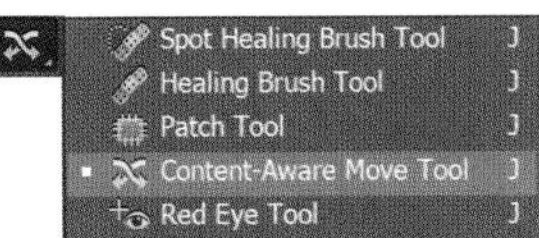

Figure 5.14 Select the Content-Aware Move tool.

3. In the Options bar, select Extend from the Mode menu.
4. Click inside the selection and drag it to the area you want to extend.

   Photoshop will evaluate the image and attempt to extend the background seamlessly (**Figure 5.15**).

If your selection doesn't move or extend the way you intended, undo the action by pressing Ctrl+Z (Windows) or Command+Z (Mac OS). Then, try adjusting the settings or reselecting your area. Many processes are going on behind the scenes with this tool, and sometimes just reselecting or adjusting the settings will render a great result.

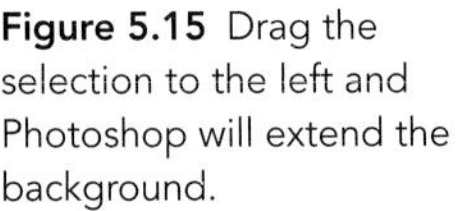

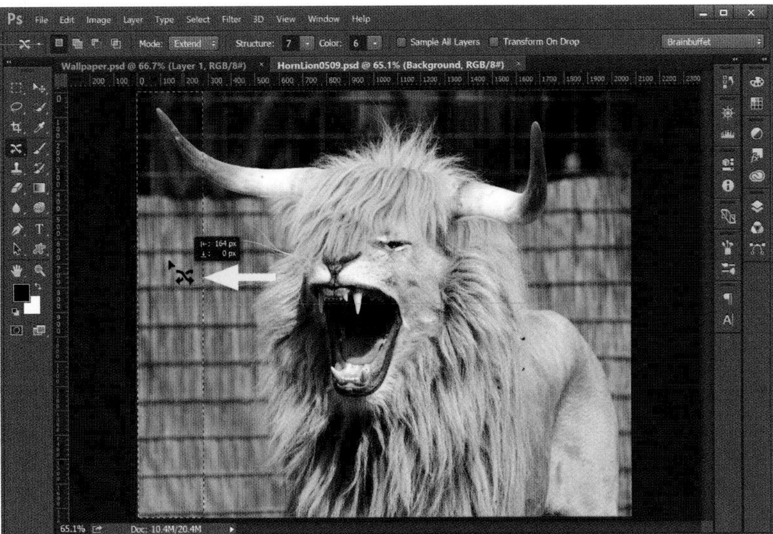

Figure 5.15 Drag the selection to the left and Photoshop will extend the background.

Content-Aware Move Tool Options

Let's discuss the options available in the options panel when using the Content-Aware Move tool (**Figure 5.16**).

- **Mode:** Select Move from the Mode menu to move the object and fill in the area. Select Extend from the Mode menu to copy the object without deleting the existing pixels.
- **Structure:** Specifies how closely the patch selection should reflect existing image patterns. Higher numbers restrict the pattern matching.
- **Color:** Specifies how much Photoshop should try to match colors. Higher numbers apply more color matching.
- **Sample All Layers:** Allows the Content-Aware Move tool to sample the entire document as viewed, rather than only sampling the selected layer.

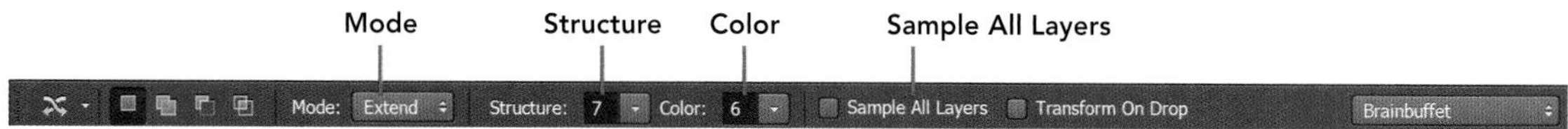

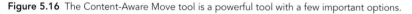

Figure 5.16 The Content-Aware Move tool is a powerful tool with a few important options.

Patch Things Up

Lastly, we're going to fix any problems in the image. If you ended up with whiskers copied in the fence, you can remove them with the Spot Healing Brush. However, in **Figure 5.17**, you can see that the damage is in the fence area and the Spot Healing Brush may not work well. That's great news because you can learn about another tool you can use for fixing problems in an image: the **Patch tool**.

Video 5.9 *Patching Things Up*

To use the Patch tool:

1. Select the Patch tool from the Tools panel.

   The Patch tool is nested with the image repair tools where you found the redeye and healing brush tools.

2. In the Options bar, select Content-Aware from the patch type menu.
3. Using the Patch tool, draw a selection over the damaged area you want to replace. In this case, select the area with the whisker.

NOTE

You can set the Patch tool to Normal mode so it does not blend automatically. Feel free to experiment with the Options bar settings, but Content-Aware mode will usually produce the best result.

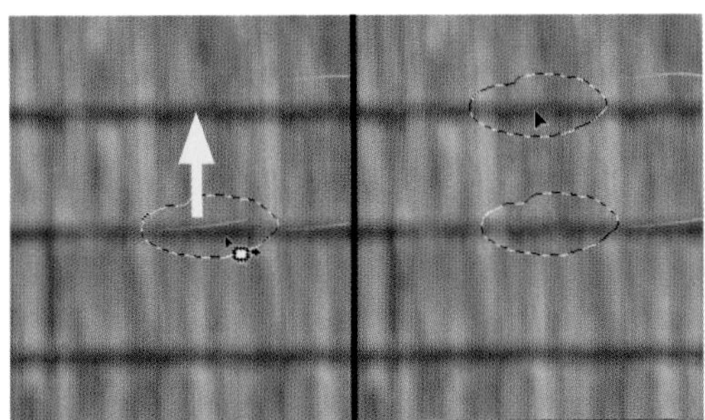

Figure 5.17 Drag the patch as shown.

4 Choose an area of the image that corresponds to the selection but is undamaged. Drag the selection to that area as shown in Figure 5.17.

When you're dragging the patch, a preview displays in the original location. Pay attention to patterns and try to match them to make your result closer to the desired outcome.

5 If the patch is not satisfactory, undo the action and try again. You can adjust the Structure, Color, and Sample All Layers options just as with the Content-Aware Move tool.

After fixing any more issues in your image, save the project—you're done! You just created an amazing new creature with very believable results (**Figure 5.18**). This was a really great project that's easy to repeat using different images. Try the Level Up Challenge at the end of this chapter to take it to the next level.

Figure 5.18 The final creature!

LEVEL UP CHALLENGE: CHERNOBYL ZOO

In this project, you created amazing results in a relatively short amount of time. The tools you learned to use are all you need to create very believable composite images. We would love to see what you've done. Visit us at *brainbuffet.com/peachpit* to connect with us online and see other student examples.

Video 5.10
Chernobyl Zoo

Take the Level Up Challenge and see if you can extend what you've learned into something new!

- **Level I:** Check out some other amazing composite images at *www.worth1000.com* and get inspired.
- **Level II:** Create another crazy animal using the tools you learned in this chapter. Post your result on social media and get bonus awesome points.
- **Level III:** Think of a new, creative way to use these compositing tools. Create an image that makes a statement or one that's just funny. Share the result on social media for bonus awesome points. Use the hashtag #ppbblearnPS and mention @brainbuffet to connect with us and other readers.

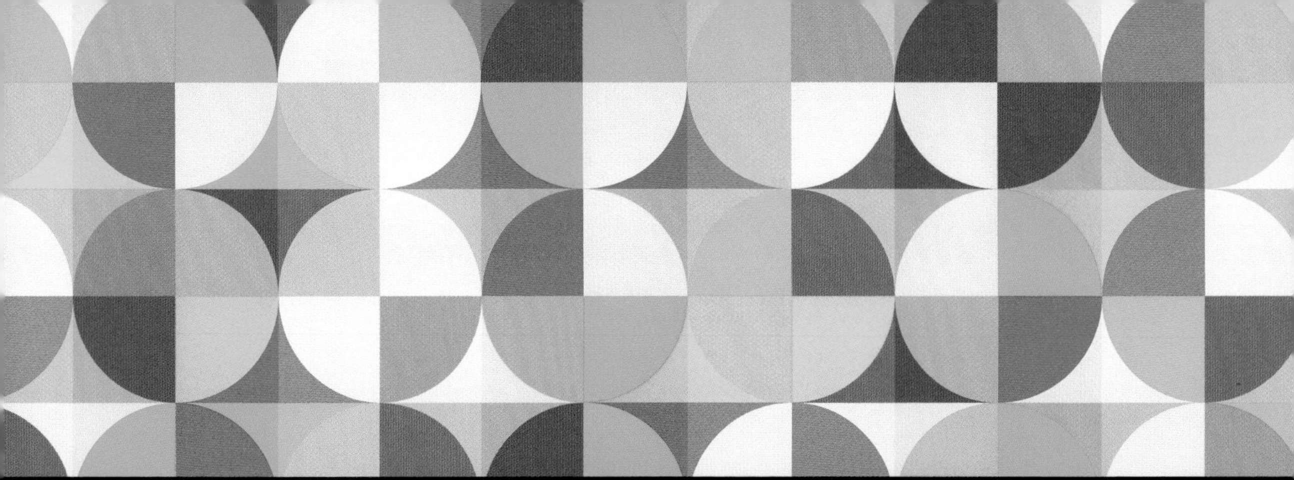

CHAPTER OBJECTIVES

Chapter Learning Objectives

- Create Photoshop documents with artboards.
- Use linked smart objects and modify linked smart objects while retaining the link.
- Master masks and creating custom brushes and presets.
- Use Photoshop libraries, such as colors, swatches, gradients, brushes, symbols, and patterns.
- Use Photoshop's warping tools.
- Explore the use of clipping masks with layers.
- Save selections.
- Create and use layer comps to compare different versions of an image.

Chapter ACA Objectives

DOMAIN 3.0
UNDERSTANDING ADOBE PHOTOSHOP

3.7 Manage colors, swatches, and gradients.

3.8 Manage brushes, symbols, graphic styles, and patterns.

DOMAIN 4.0
CREATING DIGITAL IMAGES USING ADOBE PHOTOSHOP

4.1 Create a new project.

4.2 Import assets into a project.

4.3 Make, manage, and manipulate selections.

4.4 Transform images.

4.5 Create and manage layers and masks.

4.6 Use basic retouching techniques—including color correction, blending, cloning, and filters—to manipulate a digital image.

4.7 Create a vector drawing, such as an icon, button, or layout.

DOMAIN 5.0
PUBLISHING DIGITAL IMAGES USING ADOBE PHOTOSHOP

5.2 Export or save digital images to various file formats.

CHAPTER 6

Digital Decorating

You've learned so much that most of the new tips and tricks in this chapter will build on the earlier projects. Like the last one, this chapter will be relatively short for the amount of information covered. Many of these ideas and concepts are fairly visual, so please check out the videos for the book. As a Photoshop designer, there are considerations and ways of working that are experimental, and it will greatly benefit you to listen to and watch the workflow and commentary. The biggest problem with a lot of Photoshop books is that they cover *what* to do, not *why*. Admittedly, it's tough to teach—the technical part is relatively easy. But the part that makes for a successful design career is everything that happens behind the tools—in the mind of the artist.

▶ ***Video 6.1*** *Digital Decorating*

This project is the capstone—your crowning achievement. We're going to cover a lot of previously covered concepts but go a little deeper. More than any other chapter, you should really experiment in this one. Much of what is being covered here is about creative experimentation. We'll provide fewer example values for the settings than before in hopes that you will experiment and tweak the values for your own image. As always, you're encouraged to experiment with your own images—it makes it a lot more fun when the image you create is truly yours.

The client in this scenario is a video game designer who is going to be giving away free downloads of desktop and phone wallpaper at a comic convention. You'll also use your fantasy animal from the last chapter—it will be in the game as well! The game is an action/fantasy game with a female main character that should appeal to gamers who like fast-paced games.

★ *ACA Objective 4.1*

Create a New Document

▶ ***Video 6.2*** *Set the Stage*

For the purposes of this tutorial, you're going to create an image that you can use as desktop wallpaper for a computer, and you'll then convert it for phone wallpaper at the end.

An advantage of designing for screen is that screen images are smaller, so if your computer doesn't have much horsepower, then designing for web sizes helps to not tax your system. Remember that if you want to design for paper, these won't work; you'll need to use much larger images—about four times larger!

Designing for the screen is great when you're learning since the files are already a great size to share because they're smaller. You can also use smaller images and the quality will be less of a concern. You will use the web preset when creating this document to explore another setting and also discover the presets for web and app development.

NOTE

The Web, Mobile App, Iconography, and Artboard document types will give you the option to start with an artboard.

To create a new web or screen document:

1 Choose File > New.

2 In the New Document dialog box, select Web from the Document Type menu.

3 Select Web (1920, 1080) from the Artboard Size menu for the artboard size.

4 Enter `Wallpaper` in the Name field for the document.

5 Click OK and your document will appear with an artboard (**Figure 6.1**).

Figure 6.1 By default, documents with an artboard will have a lighter-colored background, and the name of the artboard will appear above each artboard canvas and in your layer stack.

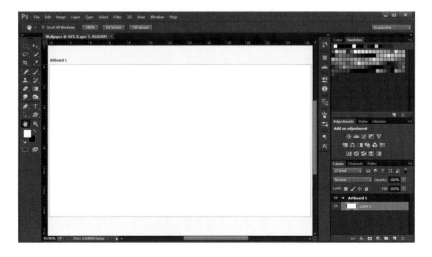

About Artboards

Artboards are a new feature in Adobe Photoshop CC 2015 that enable you to create multiple images in one document. In the past, you had to do this with multiple versions of the document, which made keeping track of files quite challenging. Now you can create multiple documents for a project—even with different sizes—all saved in one Photoshop document!

Video 6.3 *Artboards*

You can change the color of the background in an artboard document the same as any other background. Later on, you'll change it to dark gray like normal documents because the darker workspace will work better for the project.

NOTE
When you create an artboard document, the default layer created is not a background layer but a standard layer.

Artboards work just like layer groups, except they can reside on a different canvas within a single document. In an artboard document, layers that are not part of an artboard will not be clipped by that artboard canvas. You can easily resize artboards by entering values in the Options bar, dragging the artboard handles, or selecting the artboard in the Layers panel, and then selecting the Properties panel.

TIP *You can change the color of the canvas by right-clicking (Windows) or Control-clicking (Mac OS) in the canvas area and choosing a color from the context menu that appears.*

Smart Is as Smart Does

★ ACA Objective 4.2

We've discussed some of the advantages of smart objects, but there is one amazing feature that's difficult to demonstrate in all its glory in a book or on a single computer. This is the concept of a linked smart object. You can place a linked image into a document—even from another Adobe application—and it will automatically update in your Photoshop document when the original file is edited. This is a great feature for when you're working with a larger team. If the logo isn't perfect yet, for example, it's okay. Link the document with the logo, and when your coworker finishes editing, it will automatically update in your design.

Video 6.4 *Import Linked Smart Object*

To place a linked file in your document, you will use the same procedure that you used to place an embedded image earlier. Choose File > Place Linked and select the image. This image will now be automatically updated if the original file is modified.

Be sure to watch the video on this one for a demonstration of how linked smart objects work.

Mix Smart Objects and Raster Effects

▶ *Video 6.5 Raster Effects on Smart Objects*

This is a cool trick to help mix smart objects with raster effects: Create a group containing a smart object, then duplicate and rasterize the copy. This way you can keep the layers together and move the group around, but you still have the smart object linked and it can be updated.

Figure 6.2 By keeping smart objects and a rasterized copy in a group together, you can add raster effects to the copy and blend the effects together.

To mix raster effects with a smart object:

1. In the Layers panel, right-click (Windows) or Control-click (Mac OS) the smart object layer name and choose Group From Layers.
2. In the New Group From Layers dialog box, enter a name for the new layer. In this case, enter the name **Lion**.
3. Duplicate the smart object and rasterize the copy.
4. Use the raster effects on the copy of the smart layer (**Figure 6.2**).

Because the layers are in a group together, you can move them together, essentially adding the raster effects to the linked smart object (Figure 6.2). Of course, if the changes to the original layer affect an area that you edit in your copy, then they both may require more editing later.

Let's say you want to extend and shape only the lion's beard. The other team says that they might be working on the lion's horns later, so you want to have this linked to retain any changes. Since we're working on just the bottom of the image, we're probably safe!

★ *ACA Objective 4.6*

Attack of the Clones

▶ *Video 6.6 Attack of the Clones*

Before Photoshop had all the new amazing healing tools, edits were much more manual. They were still shockingly powerful, but you needed to take a little more time and pay closer attention. Today you have the healing brushes and Content-Aware Move that make it happen, but what about when you want more control? Sometimes you want to step back in time to use the older tools.

First, you need to move your copy of the lion down so that you can extend the lion's mane. Then you will use the **Clone Stamp** tool and **Patch tool** to modify the mane and blend it in with the lion.

Figure 6.3 Select the Clone Stamp tool.

To use the Clone Stamp tool:

1. On the Tools panel, select the Clone Stamp tool (**Figure 6.3**).

   Be sure to select the Clone Stamp tool and not the Pattern Stamp tool.

2 Pick a round brush and set the size and hardness for your brush:

- Size: **100**
- Hardness: **0**

3 Hold down Alt (Windows) or Option (Mac OS) as you drag to select your source area. The tool pointer becomes a target cursor .

4 Click the target cursor over the area you want to clone.

Wherever you click, Photoshop will use that as the starting point to copy the texture from the source to the destination.

5 Paint the cloned area over the destination area (**Figure 6.4**).

Pay attention to how the source location moves as your target destination moves.

Using a very low hardness on the Clone Stamp tool is almost always desirable. This will help your image blend naturally.

Figure 6.4 The Clone Stamp tool displays a plus sign where it samples from; it displays the brush cursor where it copies to.

As you can see, this tool is very effective, and it sometimes provides a better result than the automatic tools because it puts you totally in control. When using this tool, be aware of repeating patterns. If cloning over a large area, avoid cloning your cloned area and repeating identifiable image elements.

TIP

Sample often from different areas of the source image to avoid obvious repeating patterns that look fake.

PATCH THINGS UP

Another tool that is very similar when used in its traditional mode is the Patch tool. This tool lets you select an area and then drag this selection to replace parts of an image.

To use the Patch tool:

1. Select the Patch tool and set the Patch mode menu to Normal in the Options bar.
2. Select whether you want to drag the Source or the Destination by selecting the proper option in the Options bar (**Figure 6.5**).

Figure 6.5 Drag a selection with the Patch tool using source or destination.

   If you select Source you want to drag to the selection for the patch and have it be replaced. Selecting Destination means you want to drag the selection to the destination as a blended copy.

3. Make a selection with the Patch tool, and then drag the selection.

   Select Destination and drag a section of the beard to the top of the image, paying attention to the textures (**Figure 6.6**).

Figure 6.6 Using the Patch tool is a three-step process. Select your patch, drag to the other location, and the image will blend according to your setting.

These three steps have given us lots of extra mane to blend into the image. Now you're going to blend and isolate the lion for our final image.

SAVE YOUR PROGRESS

You've done a fair amount of work; save your work now to be safe before you move on.

Mask Mastery

ACA Objective 4.3

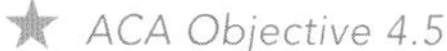

ACA Objective 4.5

Video 6.7 Mask Mastery

Now you're going to mask the lion so that you can get rid of the background and isolate the lion's head. Blend the lion's beard using a soft-edged brush and make it believable. If you need to make any edits to the work you've already done, use the tricks you just learned. Don't worry too much about the bottom and edge of the lion's mane as you'll soon edit those out (**Figure 6.7**).

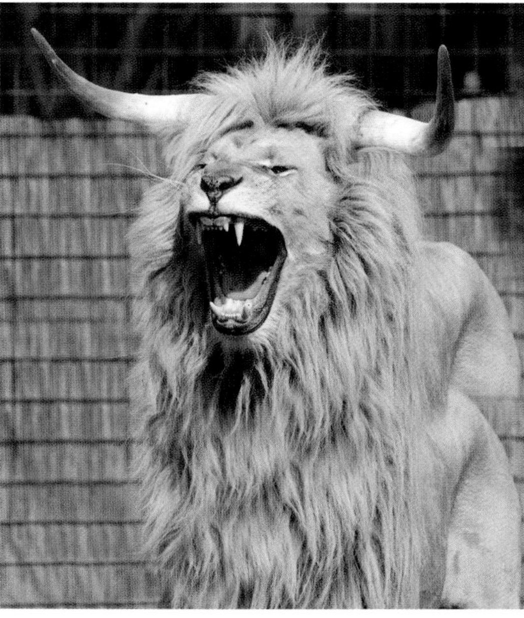

Figure 6.7 Get the lion's mane extended so that you have a lot of room to edit and perfect the mane when you remove the body and background next.

Close and Mask the Group

Be sure to leave this group together in the Layers panel so that you don't accidentally move the lion and the extended beard separately. You blended them, so you need them to stay together. Collapse the group so that you only see the group, not the layers contained within.

You can add masks to entire groups just like you can add masks to layers. You're going to learn to select with the Quick Selection tool, but use all the layer data to help the tool find the edges in all layers of the image. Then, you will create a mask that is applied to all layers (**Figure 6.8**).

To perform a quick select and mask a layer group:

1. Be sure the group is selected in the Layers panel.
2. Select the Quick Selection tool, and select Sample All Layers in the Options bar.

   Selecting Sample All Layers uses the edges in all of the visible layers to help make the selection.
3. Make a decent selection of the lion's mane and horns.

   Try to select the horns with a fair degree of accuracy, but don't worry too much about the hair. Just get a good selection around the lion's mane.
4. Click the mask icon in the Layers panel to apply the mask.

   The nonselected areas of the background will disappear.

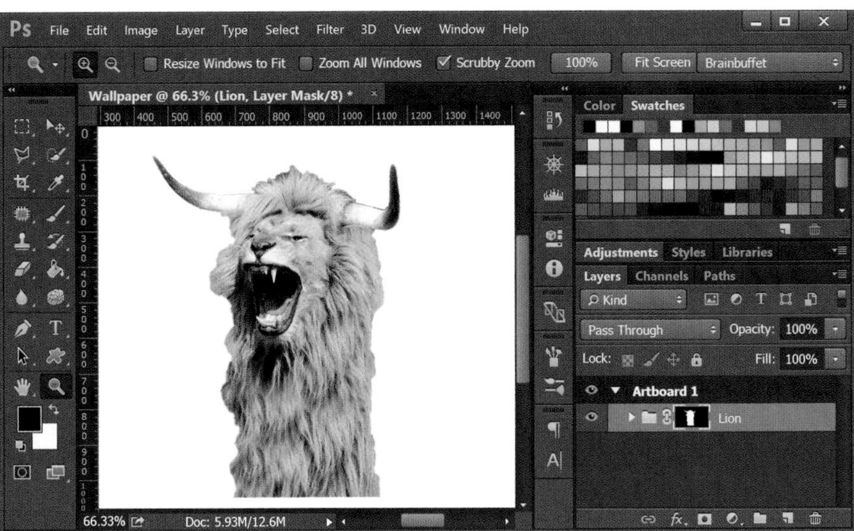

Figure 6.8 The lion image with the layer group masking all layers inside

Refine the Mask

▶ ***Video 6.8** Refine Your Masks*

You will work on the mane in a bit, but you can easily perfect the horns just as you did in the last chapter when you made the selection. This time, however, you will refine the edge *after* the mask is made.

To refine a mask:

1. Select the mask you want to refine.

   The corners are highlighted on the layer mask thumbnail.

2 Right-click (Windows) or Control-click (Mac OS) on the mask and select Refine Mask. Alternatively, you can choose Select > Refine Mask (**Figure 6.9**).

   The Refine Mask dialog box appears.

3 Refine the mask so that the horns look very sharp against the background (**Figure 6.10**). To do this, enter **100%** in the Contrast field.

4 Smooth, feather, and shift the edge until the horns get to a very defined selection with little to no feathering or edging visible. The hair will look terrible, but that's okay for now.

You should have a decent selection of the horns with clean edges. This is right where you want to be right now. You're going to learn some amazing tricks for brushes that will let us make this mask absolutely stunning!

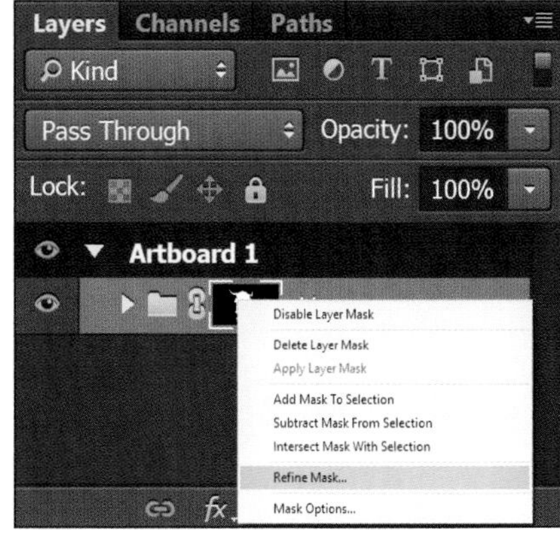

Figure 6.9 Choose Refine Mask from the context menu.

Figure 6.10 The Refine Mask dialog box

Add a Solid Fill Layer

There's something not quite right about that white background. Desktop wallpapers are best when they're dark, so the next step is to lay in a solid fill layer and create a black fill layer to work on.

NOTE

You can either create a solid fill layer or just fill an empty layer with black. I often just press D, then Alt+Delete (Windows) or Option+Delete (Mac OS) to quickly go to default colors and fill the layer with the foreground color.

Here's another great time-saving tip. Instead of going to the Layers menu, you can add a new solid fill layer by using the Adjustments menu within the Layers panel. Create a black solid fill layer and move it to the bottom layer (**Figure 6.11**).

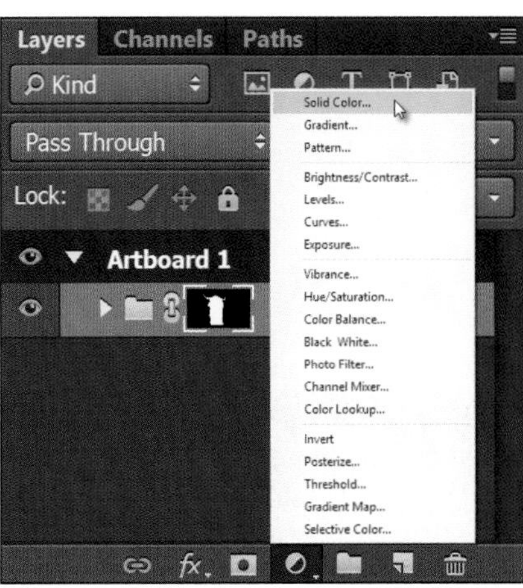

Figure 6.11 The Layers panel has a handy shortcut for making new solid fill layers.

★ *ACA Objective 3.8*

Brush Mastery

Video 6.9 *Brush Mastery*

You are familiar with some basic brush settings, and now you're going to crank it into high gear! When mastered, brushes are one of the most powerful features in Photoshop.

In this section, you will go beyond the basic round brush and use another brush shape. You will also play with the settings of the brush to create a mask that simulates the jagged edge of the lion's mane. You will be using this brush on the mask, but all brushes can be used on layers as well.

To customize your brush, do the following:

1 Select the Brush tool and the specific brush tip you want to use.

   You will be using the Grass brush (**Figure 6.12**).

2 Choose Window > Brush or click the Brush icon on the Options bar to open the Brush panel.

   The Brush panel opens (**Figure 6.13**).

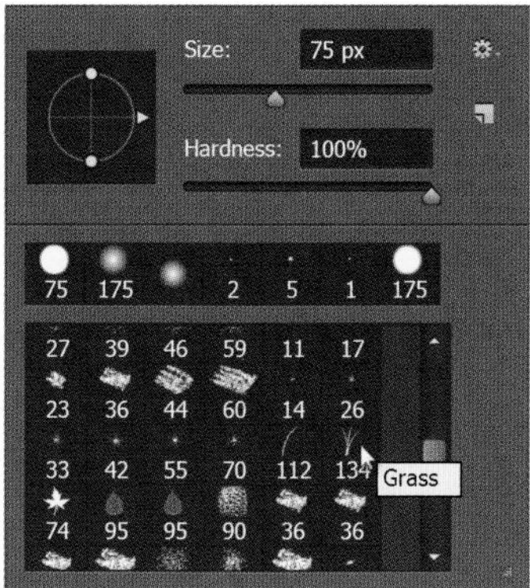

Figure 6.12 The Grass brush is a default brush in Photoshop.

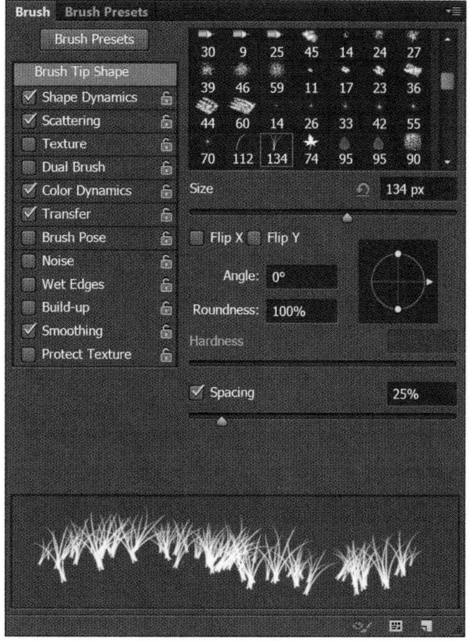

Figure 6.13 The Brush panel

3 Deselect Transfer and Color dynamics. Select Shape Dynamics to display its options.

The Shape Dynamics settings open (**Figure 6.14**). Here you can set the size, angle, and roundness settings for the brush. The settings might be:

- Size Jitter: **83%**
- Minimum Diameter: **3%**
- Angle Jitter: **10%**
- Roundness Jitter: **37%**
- Minimum Roundness: **25%**

4 Select Scattering to open its options (**Figure 6.15**):

- Scatter: **Both Axes**
- Count: **1**
- Count Jitter: **20%**

5 Close the Brush panel.

TIP

The preview at the bottom of the Brush panel gives you an idea of what the brush looks like.

Now you are going to work on making the top of the lion's mane. Slowly paint in the mask at the top of the mane using this brush to get the appearance of random hair (**Figure 6.16**).

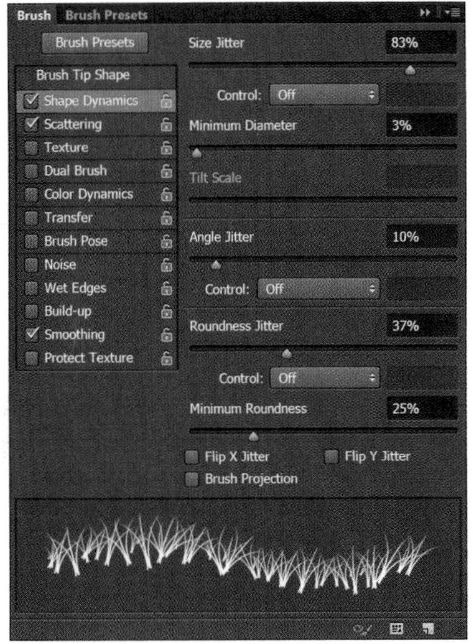

Figure 6.14 The Shape Dynamics settings in the Brush panel

Figure 6.15 Scattering options

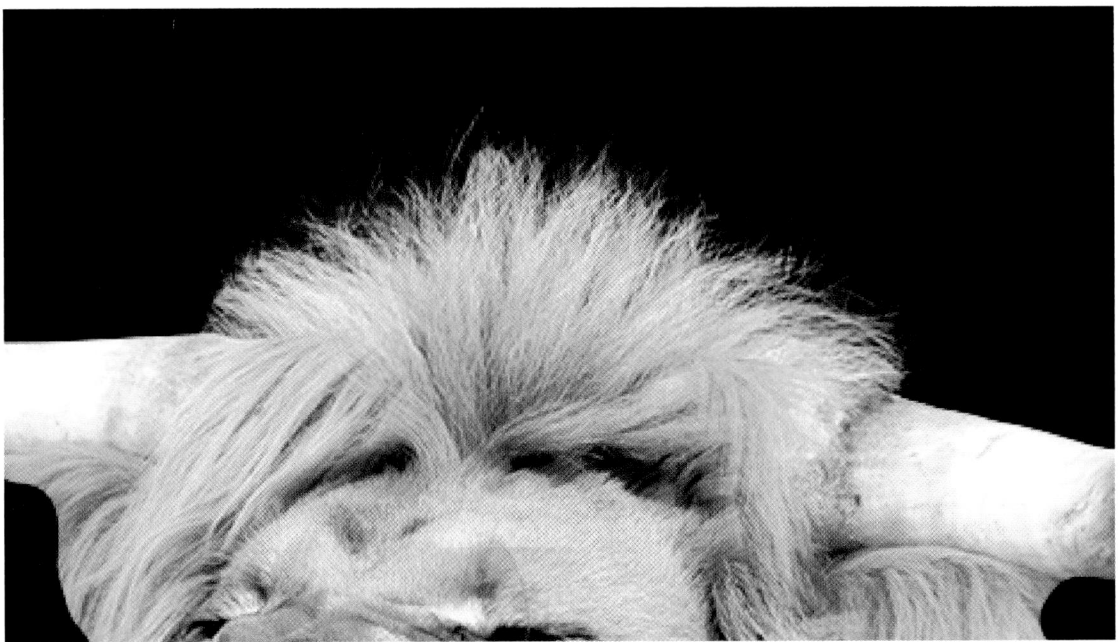

Figure 6.16 Brushing in the lion's mane with a properly set brush can yield believable results.

Once you're done with the top of the mane, you need to pay attention to the side of the mane. To do this, you need to adjust the brush rotation. Open the Brush panel again and select Brush Tip Shape at the top of the option list. Change the rotation by clicking the small arrow icon next to the angle setting, rotating the angle to make the Grass brush face to the right (**Figure 6.17**). Then paint in the mask on the right side of the mane. You might want to add a couple of brush strokes above the horn as well.

Now simply brush around the mane, adjusting the angle as necessary to get a natural effect. You're trying to get it to be a V-shaped mane with the random bristle edges we were just creating.

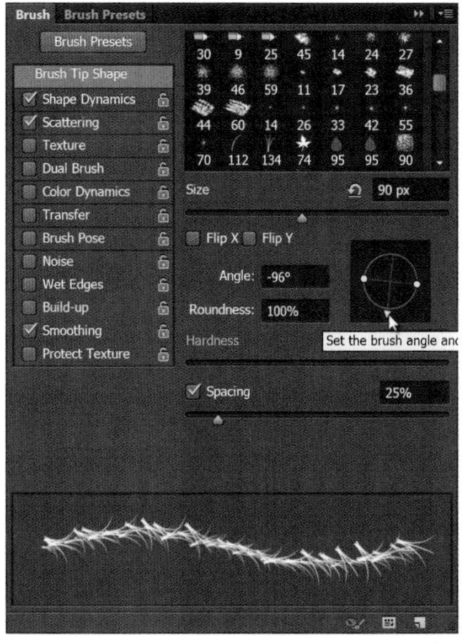

Figure 6.17 Adjust the brush's Angle to "turn" its direction.

Reuse and Save Brush Settings

You may need to switch back to the regular round brush to shape the mane. You'll note in the top of the Brush panel there is a brush preset picker. This will show your last few brush settings so you can select them again (**Figure 6.18**). Go ahead and save this brush as a new preset that you can always access.

To save a custom brush preset:

1. Open the Brush Presets panel, which is nested within the Brush panel.
2. Click the Create New Brush icon.
3. Give the brush preset a descriptive name and click OK to save it (**Figure 6.19**).

   You can now select this brush preset anytime you need it.

Video 6.10 Reuse and Save Brushes

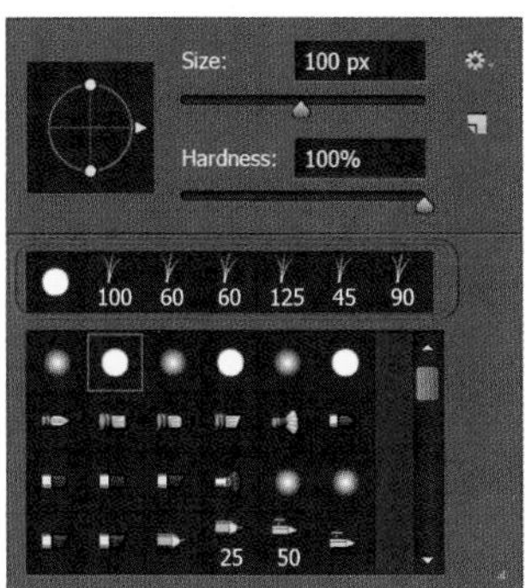

Figure 6.18 Recent brushes are listed at the top of the brush preset picker in the Brush panel.

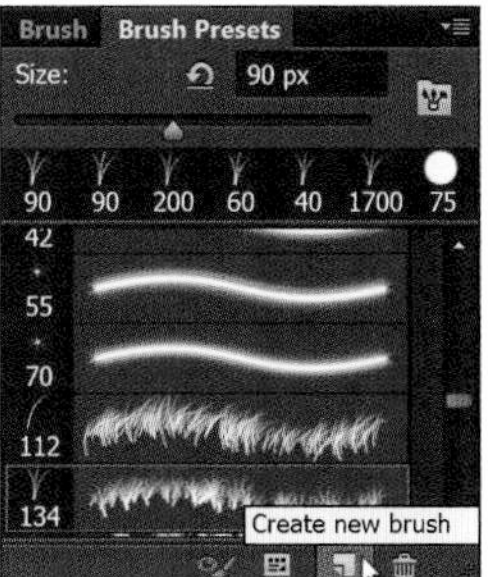

Figure 6.19 Creating a new brush preset

Figure 6.20 The final masked lion with the extended mane

Using this brush, perfect your lion's mane by shaping it and getting the edges to have believable edges. Try to get it looking something like **Figure 6.20**.

Save Your Progress!

Save your progress by pressing Ctrl+S (Windows) or Command+S (Mac OS) and then save a separate copy of the file as `Wallpaper2.psd`. You've done a fair amount of work on this file so far; by saving multiple versions, you'll have a separate file if the file somehow becomes corrupted. There's way too much work done here to risk losing it. This is a good habit to get into. Saving multiple versions and iterations also keeps a cool progression that you can reflect on later.

Bring In the Lead Character

▶ ***Video 6.11***
Masking Models

The next step is to bring in the photo of the actress who is the model for the lead character in the game. Because you may use this image in more than one place, open the document in its own window and just get an accurate mask to reuse later.

Open the image named `ToughGirl.jpg` in the Chapter 6 downloads folder. This opens the model image in a new document. Add a black solid fill layer and move it behind the model.

Next, mask out the image. Use the Quick Selection tool to select most of the figure, but don't worry about the strands of hair that are blowing from the fan—just get the basic selection and add a mask. It definitely needs work, which is a great reason to introduce a new tool that is specifically made for refining masks in situations like this.

To refine hair masks:

1. Right-click (Windows) or Control-click (Mac OS) on the mask thumbnail in the Layers panel and select Refine Mask from the context menu.
   The Refine Mask dialog box opens.
2. Use the context menu to set the View option to Reveal Layer.
3. In the Edge Detection area of the dialog box, select Smart Radius. Drag the slider to roughly 60% or enter a value in the field.
4. Using the Refine Radius tool, paint around her hair (**Figure 6.21**).

Figure 6.21 Paint over the area with the flyaway hair and Photoshop will search that area to perfect your selection.

5 Change the View to Preview the mask if you'd like, or just click OK to apply the refined mask (**Figure 6.22**).

Figure 6.22 Using the Refine Mask feature really helps perfect complex selections.

The mask did an amazing job on the hair, but it didn't do a very good job on the boots. Because the black boots on the black floor are similar in color, Photoshop tried to make those edges blend like it did the hair. We could paint it manually, but I have a cool trick to teach you for situations like this.

Fix Mixed Selections

Video 6.12
Blending Selection Tools

Change your background fill layer to white to really see the dirty edges of our selection. Select the Magnetic Lasso tool from the Tools panel .

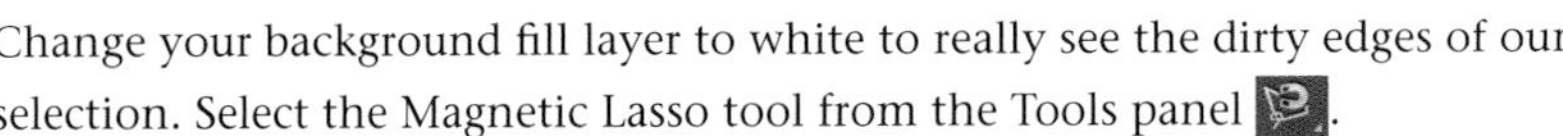

This tool tries to find edges in your image to follow. Carefully select around the figure's legs and boots, and then make a big finishing loop around the background as seen in **Figure 6.23**.

Once your selection is made, just click the mask and fill it with black. That will make the area you just selected invisible in your image. Problem solved!

Figure 6.23 ◀ Selecting the legs with the Magnetic Lasso tool

Save the Masked Model as a PSD File

You've done a lot of work on this image, so let's save this file as a Photoshop Document. This way, you will have it with the mask so that you can reuse the image later. Save the file as `ToughGirl.psd`.

★ *ACA Objective 5.2*

Copy and Paste the Loaded Mask

★ *ACA Objective 4.3*

▶ ***Video 6.13** Load, Copy, and Paste a Selection*

Because you have a great mask, you also have an accurate selection that you can reload at any time. Let's copy our selected model into our original web document.

To copy a loaded selection into a new document:

1. Ctrl-click the layer mask and it will load your selection (Command-click in Mac OS). Be sure that the layer thumbnail, not the layer mask thumbnail, is active.
2. Choose Edit > Copy and click the tab for your `Wallpaper2.psd` file.
3. Choose Edit > Paste and it will paste the ToughGirl into the `Wallpaper2.psd` file.
4. Convert your ToughGirl into a smart object to preserve the image quality once imported.
5. Choose Edit > Free Transform and resize your layer, holding Shift to keep it from distorting to fit the full figure into your document.

ADD THE GAME TITLE

Lastly, you're going to add the video game's name to the image. You can call the game whatever you want, but use a really heavy font so that there is a lot of room inside it to play with effects. I'm adding the title Brain Buffet to the image.

SAVE YOUR PROGRESS

Once the lead character is in your image, you can close the ToughGirl document. You already saved changes to the PSD file you created, so you do not need to save changes. Save your `Wallpaper2.psd` file to be sure this document is saved with both images in it (**Figure 6.24**).

Now, you just need to add some design elements to wrap it up.

Figure 6.24 The two main characters and the video game name in the document

Get Creative

▶ ***Video 6.14*** *Get Creative*

Now that you have the two main elements in the image, the rest is all exploration and experimentation. Don't be afraid to try new things. Grab your own images (yes, a smartphone camera is more than adequate) and just *try* something. We'll be going through some items just to teach you tricks, and you should really read the commentary and watch all the videos. The exact steps are not what's most important—it's all about thinking like an artist.

Look at your image now. It's technically fairly good, but boring. The spice is in the experimentation, so don't be shy. I'm shoving you out of the proverbial nest and encouraging you to assemble the tricks you've learned in your own way.

From now on, the instructions will provide fewer specific settings. This is partially to encourage you to explore, but also because you will need to set these options visually as it is impossible to make sure our layer positions will perfectly match. You're going to need to watch the videos from here on out to get the most out of the rest of this chapter.

Let's face it—it wouldn't be a very good chapter on getting creative if you are simply following directions given to you in a book, would it?

Warp Tour

★ *ACA Objective 4.4*

▶ ***Video 6.15*** *Warp Tour*

Let's explore a couple of fun ways you can manipulate objects in your image using warps. The basic **Warp** command lets you distort an object's shape using a grid. To experiment with it, choose Edit > Transform > Warp and distort your image. It's a bit more flexible than some of the other transformations, but it can still be fairly unwieldy. Once you've selected Warp, you can also select from the multiple premade warps from the Options bar—these can be fun, especially for quick text warps (**Figure 6.25**).

The Bend value has the most effect on your warp; experiment a bit and keep the warp if you like the effect.

Figure 6.25 The preset warps allow you to select common warp shapes for your objects.

For the real fun, explore the **Puppet Warp** feature. It allows you to reposition objects like you would a puppet. First determine where the pivot points are, and then alter your object.

Use Puppet Warp

To use the Puppet Warp feature:

1 Select the layer you want to warp.

2 Choose Edit > Puppet Warp.

The Puppet Warp activates on your layer.

TIP *To remove a pin, Alt-click on the pin you want to remove (Option-click in Mac OS).*

3 Place pins where you want to be able to move your object by clicking (**Figure 6.26**).

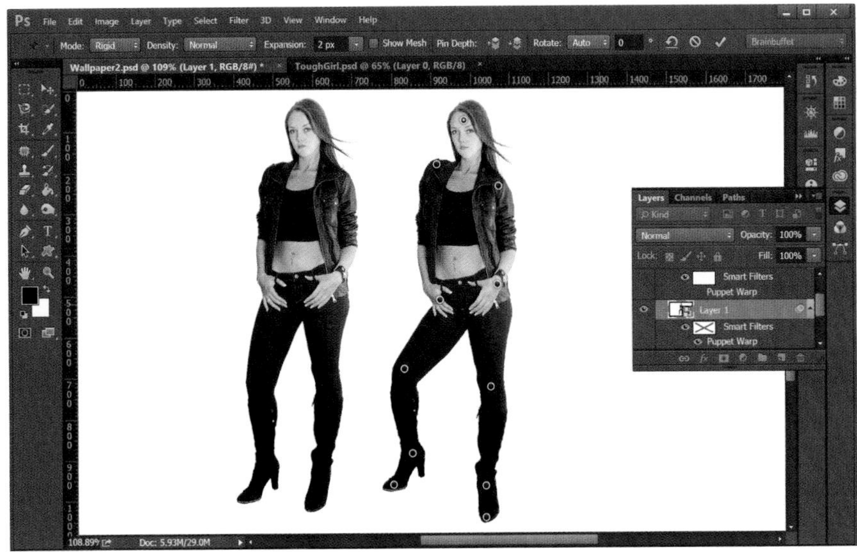

Figure 6.26 The original model on the left, and the warped model on the right using Puppet Warp. Note the position of the pins for our warped model.

TIP *You can't use Puppet Warp on a group, but you can convert a group to a smart object and then use Puppet Warp on that smart object. Cool trick!*

4 Reshape your object by moving the pins.

To more clearly see the image, deselect Show Mesh in the Options bar.

5 Click the Commit button to save your changes.

The Puppet Warp feature is awesome, there's no doubt about it—but it does take time and experience to master. Don't get frustrated; just play with it a little bit. You'll master the fine art of Puppet Warping in no time with practice!

Tweak the Text and Save

TIP *The question is always asked, "How often should I save?" The easy answer is save when you've done enough work that you don't want to lose it!*

The white color of the text was too bright and distracting with the darker colors, so you might select the text and change the color using the Character panel (**Figure 6.27**). You've done a lot of work to this point. Save your work, and then save a copy as `Wallpaper3.psd`. This will ensure that you can always go back to an earlier point, and that you can recover if file corruption occurs.

Figure 6.27 The darker text on the black background

Color Coordinated

★ *ACA Objective 3.7*

A couple of tricks in Photoshop help you modify colors and the tonal qualities of your image or layers. You can modify colors, add to them, or create gradients and effects using a variety of tools.

▶ ***Video 6.16*** *Replace Colors in an Image*

Replace Colors in an Image

At times, you may want to replace colors. The model is wearing dark blue jeans, but in the game the lead character fights in iconic maroon jeans. This can be handled easily with the **Replace Color** command in Photoshop. The problem is that it doesn't work on smart objects, only raster images.

Because you pasted this image in as a raster layer and then converted it, you can double-click the thumbnail for that layer and then replace the color on the raster object inside the smart layer. (If you were working on a regular raster layer, you would not need this additional step.)

To replace the color on the model:

1 Select the layer for which you want to replace colors and choose Image > Adjustments > Replace Color (**Figure 6.28**).

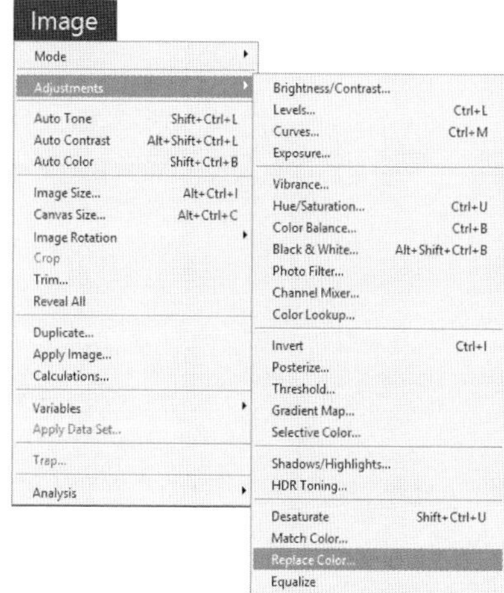

Figure 6.28 Choose Image > Adjustments > Replace Color.

TIP

Holding down the Shift key when sampling will add the new sampled area to your selection.

2 Using the Replace Color dialog box, sample the area you want to adjust and modify the hue, saturation, and lightness for the area (**Figure 6.29**).

If you're not happy with the sampling, just click again to reselect the area. Depending on your image and the sample, the settings will vary. Set this by eye.

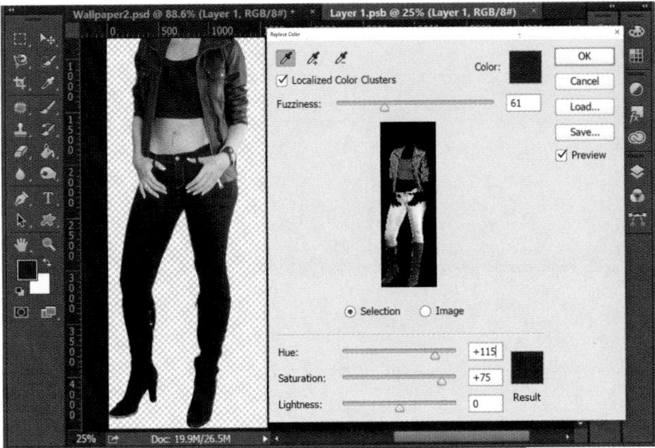

Figure 6.29 The Replace Color dialog box

3 When you are finished, click OK to replace the color in your selected area.

Great! The main character is wearing the right color jeans for fighting crime. Save and close your PSD file and you will be returned to your Wallpaper2 document with the colors of the jeans replaced. Because it was a smart object, it updates with the puppet warp automatically.

Get Clipped

Video 6.17 Get Clipped

Earlier in the book you learned about how to tweak the colors in layers using adjustment layers. Let's take a minute to discuss a couple of differences in the ways you can work with coloring layers and adjusting layer tonal qualities.

We've already seen the many adjustment layers you can add using the Adjustments panel. But when you use these adjustment layers on an image, it affects *all layers below it*. Here are a couple of tricks to get around that.

One option is that you can make the layer a smart object, and then apply a regular adjustment from the Adjustment menu. This makes the adjustment a part of the smart filter, and it will only affect that one layer. However, it will get grouped in with all your other smart effects and filters, so that may not be optimal.

The other option is to add an adjustment layer, but then make a clipping mask out of the layer beneath it. This is an amazing trick that can be used a lot of different ways—almost any layer can be made into a clipping mask.

To make a clipping mask:

1 In the Layers panel, place the layer you want to clip above the layer you want to clip it with.

  The layer on top will only appear where the bottom layer has content.

2 Hold Alt (Windows) or Option (Mac OS) and move the cursor between the layers until the clipping indicator appears.

  You can also select the Create Clipping Mask icon from the Layers menu, Layers panel, or the layer's context menu.

3 Click when the clipping indicator is visible to clip the lower layer (**Figure 6.30**).

Figure 6.30 The clipped layers are indicated with the clipping arrow to show that the clipping mask is only visible over the layer beneath.

TIP

When creating an adjustment layer, there is a shortcut to create a clipping mask at the bottom of the Adjustments panel while adjusting the image settings.

The layer will be indented with a clipping arrow preceding the thumbnail; it will only be visible above the lower layer's pixels. To remove the clipping mask, do the same thing in reverse. Alt-click between the affected layers to remove the clipping mask (Option-click in Mac OS).

Clip Images for Awesome Text

Keep in mind that clipping masks can be used on regular layers also—you can clip an image with another image to create textures inside of elements or create quick masking using other layers to accomplish various effects. Let's try that now. We're going to bring in a texture and clip it to our text.

NOTE

You don't need professional gear to have a blast with Photoshop! The texture in Sill3.jpg is an old, peeling windowsill photographed with a smartphone camera.

To clip a texture into text:

1 Copy and paste or place the image you'd like to clip with.

  To follow along, use `Sill3.jpg` from the Chapter 6 downloads folder.

2 Place your texture directly above your text layer in the Layers panel.

3 Right-click (Windows) or Control-click (Mac OS) the layer and select Create Clipping Mask from the context menu. Or Alt-click (Windows) or Option-click (Mac OS) between the layers as above.

TIP

To make your text and texture stay together, place them in a layer group.

4 Experiment with the blending mode and opacity of the texture layer in the Layers panel (**Figure 6.31**).

Remember that the color of the text will affect how the blending modes interact with the layer—experiment with changing the text color also.

This is purely trial and error (or as I like to call it, playing). Have fun experimenting and trying new things. Depending on what textures and colors you use, your results may be very different—that's okay. If you really want to get it just like our examples here in the book, be sure to watch the videos and follow along closely.

You can also experiment with applying a layer effect (such as an outer glow) to help your text layer stand out, particularly if it is hard to see on your black background. Few Photoshop effects can stand completely on their own, like colors in paint—you need to mix things to get a wide variety of effects.

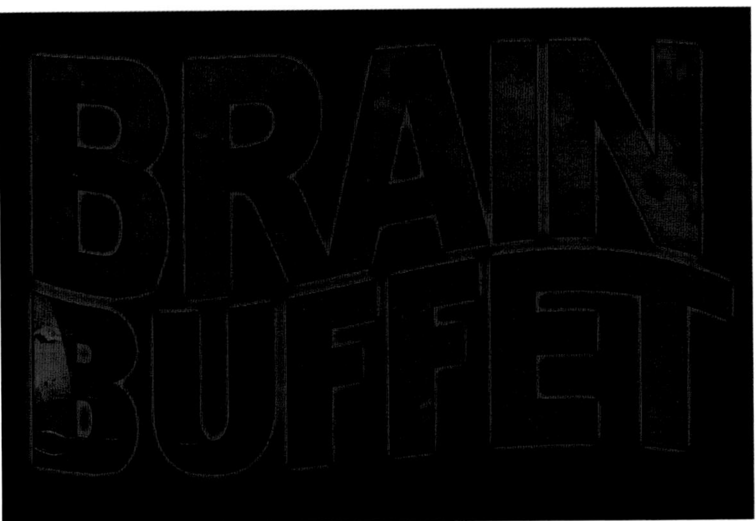

Figure 6.31 Our text with clipped textures, color adjustments, and layer effects

Save Your Progress

Save your progress before we move into the final stretch. If you're really happy with what you have now, then also save it as `Wallpaper4.psd` (or whatever number is next for you).

Shapes, Splatters, and Selections

Video 6.18 *Explore and Experiment*

This last section is where you learn some amazing "power tools" that professionals use all the time in their workflow. This introduction should help you grasp some of the ways you can think beyond the obvious with the Photoshop features. We've already covered almost everything you really need to know. Here, we're learning to use the common feature in uncommon ways to help expand your Photoshop toolbox.

Much like the last section, we're going to be moving into a lot of features that require visual input from your own image. Watching the videos that accompany this book is critical since the directions here are basically notes for reference. Not everything you need to know is included—just enough to help you remember what you learned in the videos. These instructions can provide a refresher when you come back to experiment with one of these tricks again.

Shape Layers

★ *ACA Objective 4.7*

Video 6.19 *Shape Layers*

Shape layers are special layers in Photoshop that are created with vectors just like text layers. Vector images are created with a series of lines and curves, so they never get pixelated. You will add a shape to the image, and learn about importing vector shapes from Adobe Illustrator. You're going to use the Custom Shape tool because it's use is the least obvious and the most cool to play with.

To add a shape to an image:

1. Select the Custom Shape tool from the nested Shape tools.

   By default, the Rectangle tool is on top of the nested tools.

2. Set the fill and stroke for your custom shape.

   In the Options bar, set the fill to Red and the stroke to none.

3. From the Options bar, click Custom Shape picker, then click the small gear in the upper-right corner and select the Grime Vector Pack from the category of shapes (**Figure 6.32**).

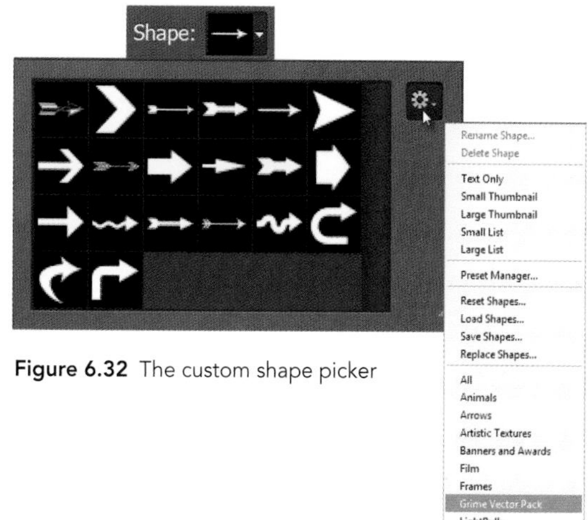

Figure 6.32 The custom shape picker

4 When the dialog box appears, specify whether you want to replace the current shapes (OK) or add them on to the shapes that are there (Append).

Replace the current shapes by clicking OK.

5 Select one of the circular grime shapes and add it to your image.

Click and drag the shape, holding Shift to constrain the shape proportions.

6 Press Enter (Windows) or Return (Mac OS) to place the shape on your image.

7 Using the Move tool, move the shape layer to the position you want. Place the layer just above your image background and adjust the size and opacity to fit your image (**Figure 6.33**).

The example image has a bright red that looked better adjusted down to 50% opacity, but depending on your image, your settings may vary.

TIP *Shape layers can also use layer effects and styles—try experimenting with them to add a little extra "wow" to your shapes!*

Figure 6.33 The image with the shape layer added

TIP *You can find shape files from a variety of online sources to download and add to Photoshop so that you can use them in your documents.*

Shape layers are really fun to play with, and when you learn the editing tools, they're incredibly powerful. An in-depth exploration isn't feasable here, but we suggest grabbing *Graphic Design and Illustration Using Adobe Illustrator* (from this series) to learn how to master vector art. An excellent designer needs to know both Photoshop and Illustrator.

Brush Bling

ACA Objective 3.8

Video 6.20 Brush Bling

You learned how to modify existing brushes earlier and created some believable masks using the Grass brush for creating a mask for the lion's mane. But what do you do when the brushes built in to Photoshop don't meet your needs? You make your own brushes.

TIP *Need tips on creating your own ink splatters? We have a free tutorial on how to use free Adobe apps to create your own. Check out our Photoshop page at* http://brainbuffet.com/adobe/photoshop/ *for tutorials on how to create custom brushes.*

The first thing you need to do is get the image ready. For this effect, let's create a very dark image. Open one of the splatter image documents in the Chapter 6 downloads folder in Photoshop. The following figures show the image named `IMG_1902.jpg`. Select a part of the splatter that you want to make into a brush and then choose Edit > Crop to reduce the image to just that area.

NOTE *I used the camera on my phone to take this shot. Not having a high-end camera is no excuse for not creating your own images and tools! I have very expensive cameras I could have used, but for a brush my phone was more than adequate.*

Brushes don't need to be really big—especially grunge/splatter brushes—so it's a good idea to shrink this image. To do this:

1. Choose Image > Image Size to open the Image Size dialog box.
2. Enter **1000** pixels for the largest dimension (Width or Height).
3. Select Bicubic Sharper (Reduction) from the Resample menu since you're reducing the image. Click OK (**Figure 6.34**).
4. Choose Image > Adjustments > Threshold.
5. Adjust the threshold so that the image is black and white and the splatter looks really clean, and then click OK.

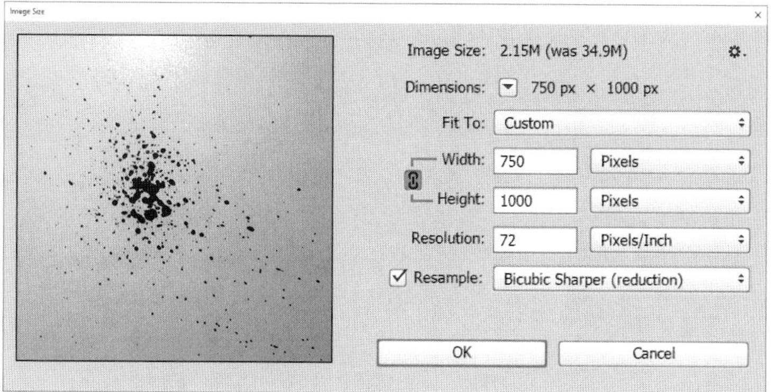

Figure 6.34 When reducing, resample using Bicubic Sharper to get the best result.

You should now have a very stark image that's pure black and white—no gray. You're now ready to make a brush out of this image (**Figure 6.35**).

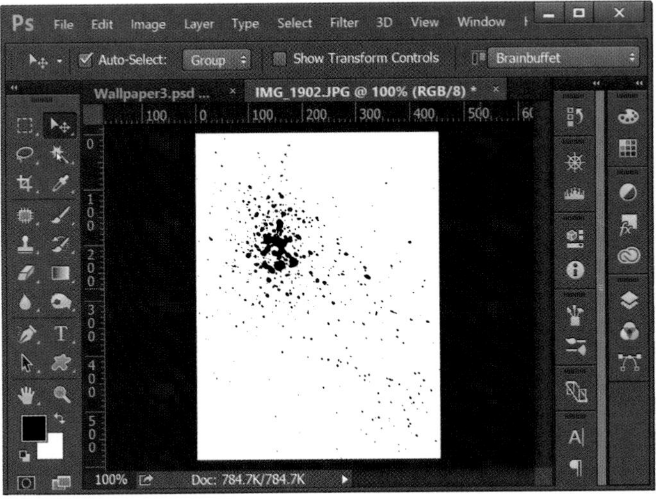

Figure 6.35 To create a good splatter brush, use the threshold adjustment to make sure your original image is pure black and white with no gray.

To make a brush out of your splatter image:

1. Choose Edit > Define Brush Preset.

   The Brush Name dialog box appears (**Figure 6.36**).

Figure 6.36 The Brush Name dialog box

2. Enter a descriptive name for the brush, and click OK.

   The brush is added to your active brush collection.

Now that your brush is created, you can use it in your images. Go ahead and try it out. You can close the splatter image document as you won't need it anymore. Click Don't Save when it asks if you want to save changes.

To use your brush:

1. Create a new layer above your shape layer and name it **Splatter**.
2. Select a vivid color.

   For example, a bright green. Drag to the top-right corner of the color picker and you'll have a vivid color.
3. Click once to add the splatter behind the model (**Figure 6.37**).

Figure 6.37 The green splatter behind our model

I know it's really cool—but *stop*! Don't get carried away adding splatters because there's an even better way. Remember how you used brush dynamics to get the lion's mane looking really natural and random? We can use those same tools, plus another setting we haven't discussed to make this brush amazing.

Brush Better

Video 6.21 Brush Better

Now you're going to create a brush that automatically rotates and distorts every time you click, similar to the lion's mane. This time you're going to add a new trick—randomizing color like you randomized the position earlier.

To create a colorful random brush:

1. With the brush tool selected, open the Brush panel. Choose Window > Brush or click the Brush Preset Picker icon in the Options bar.
2. Specify the settings for the Shape Dynamics and Color dynamics (**Figure 6.38**):
   - Size Jitter: **50%** (to randomize the size)
   - Minimum Diameter: **0**
   - Angle Jitter: **100%** (to make the splatters rotate to appear random)
   - Roundness Jitter: **75%** (this will squish some splatters to be thinner)
   - Minimum Roundness: **25%**

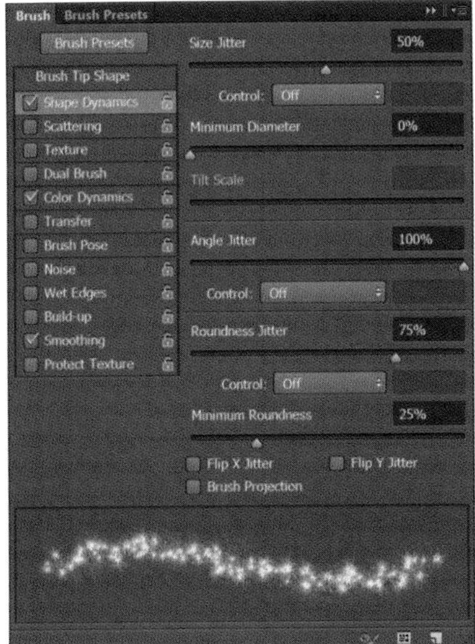

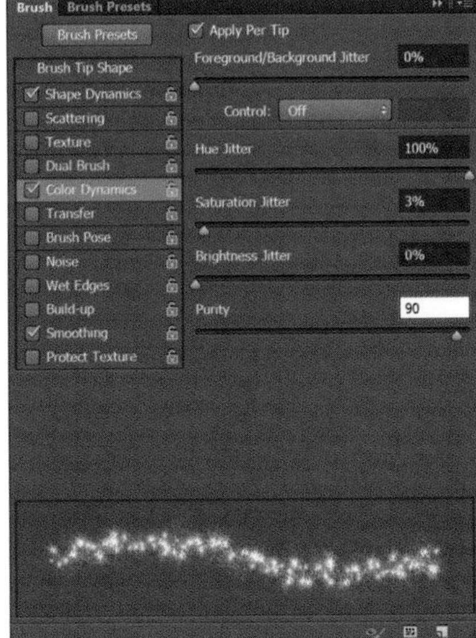

Figure 6.38 Settings for Shape Dynamics and Color Dynamics

Color Dynamics is where the colors get added and randomized. The important settings are:

- Foreground/Background Jitter: **0%**
- Hue Jitter: **100%** (to totally randomize the color)
- Purity: **90%** (to make the colors vivid)

Turn Brightness Jitter and Saturation Jitter down to keep the brush bright and saturated like your original color.

3 Click around the model and lion to see these settings in action.

Splatters will appear with each click, varying in color and shape. Click just a handful of splatters behind your model and lion—don't click and drag. This effect needs to be placed intentionally (**Figure 6.39**).

Be careful not to overdo it—but if you do you can always delete the layer and start over. It's tough not to go a little nuts with this brush the first time, so experiment on a new layer that you can delete later. Normally, I turn the layer opacity down to around 50% and then you get the splashes of color without overwhelming the image too much. You're going for subtle accents here, not glaring neon craziness.

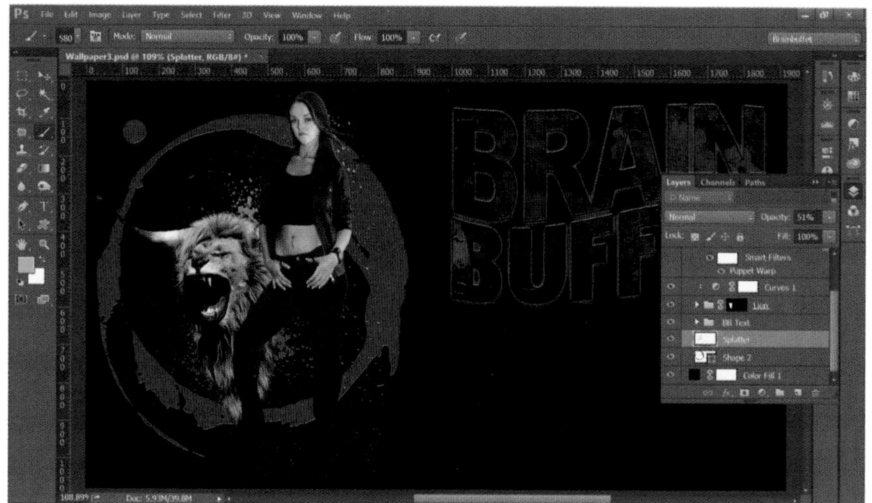

Figure 6.39 Splatters vary in color and shape with every click because of the dynamics of our custom brush.

LAYER COMPS

Video 6.22 *Layer Comps*

As is normal when working with art, as the project evolves, it can start to take its own direction. With this image, I'm not crazy about our herione's position. There is a better way to create more mystery and emphasis on her. In the past, I used to create multiple versions of the document using multiple files, but now I prefer to use layer comps, especially on smaller images.

Layer comps allow you to take a snapshot of the document and all of its layers in its current state. Then you can try changing things and save another comp when you have that idea completed. You can then easily swap between these two versions to compare them. This is especially helpful when working with clients, as you can show multiple versions of the image in a single document.

To create a layer comp:

1 Choose Window > Layer Comps to open the Layer Comps panel (**Figure 6.40**).

Figure 6.40 The Layer Comps panel

2 Click the Create New Layer Comp icon to create a new layer comp.

The New Layer Comp dialog box appears. Enter a name and descriptive comment, and be sure all three options for Visibility, Position, and Appearance are selected (**Figure 6.41**).

3 Click OK.

Your layer comp appears in the panel (**Figure 6.42**).

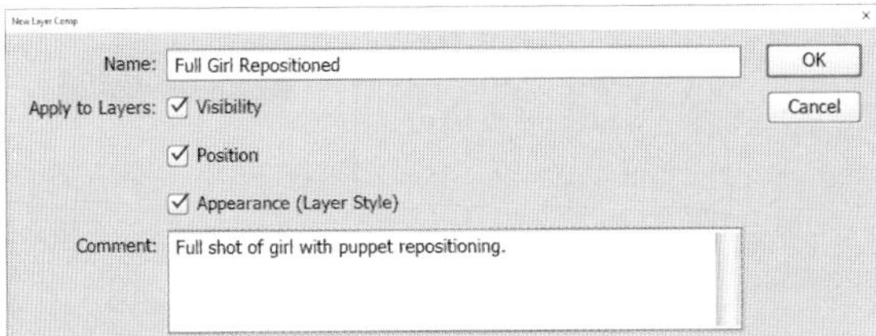

Figure 6.41 Select whether to include Visibility, Position, and Layer Styles in the New Layer Comp dialog box.

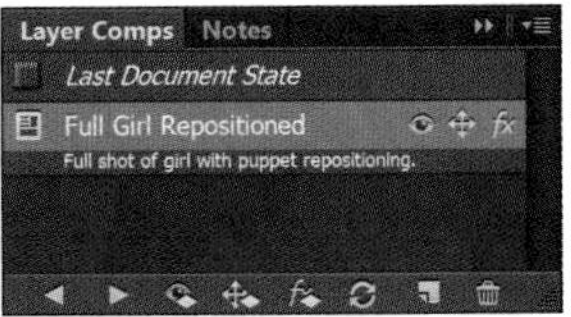

Figure 6.42 The Layer Comps panel showing the new comp

Now that you have this layout saved, you can try making some changes. Remember, you can always go back to this current position. Layer comps enable you to lock in a particular state that you can always go back to.

CLOSE UP, CLEAN UP

Video 6.23 Close Up, Clean Up

You're already familiar with these steps. Put the old ToughGirl layer and its adjustment in a new group and hide it. Then place an embedded copy of **ToughGirlCU.jpg** and mask the image. Add the Hue/Saturation adjustment layer set to colorize it with hue and lightness set to **0** and saturation to **40**. Clip the adjustment to the ToughGirlCU layer. Now Group your ToughGirlCU layer and its clipping mask and name it **GirlRed**.

If you managed all that without watching the video, very impressive! You learn quickly, grasshopper! And looking at this image, it looks better with this layout so far. Try tweaking just a few things and then you'll be ready to make this a wrap.

Selection Perfection

★ *ACA Objective 4.3*

Video 6.24 Selection Perfection

Making really great selections is critical to success. Now you'll learn some tricks that you can use with selections and masks. Remember that selections and masks are very closely related—in fact, all selections are temporary masks on your image that limit the area of the image you can edit.

You have worked diligently on some of your selections, namely the lion and the main character. Let's make sure that you have those selections saved to possibly use in creative ways later. You're going to lay this out as a number of steps, but each step is its own critical tip. Get familiar with these steps to master selections.

1. To load the selection of your model Ctrl-click (Windows) or Command-click (Mac OS) on the layer thumbnail. This is the fastest way to make a selection of everything on a mask or layer, and is a critical shortcut to remember. You'll use this one daily!
2. Second, choose Select > Save Selection. Saving a selection lets you save the selection to reuse later in your image. We'll explore a few ways to do this in a bit. When the Save Selection dialog box appears, enter **Model** in the Name field and click OK (**Figure 6.43**).

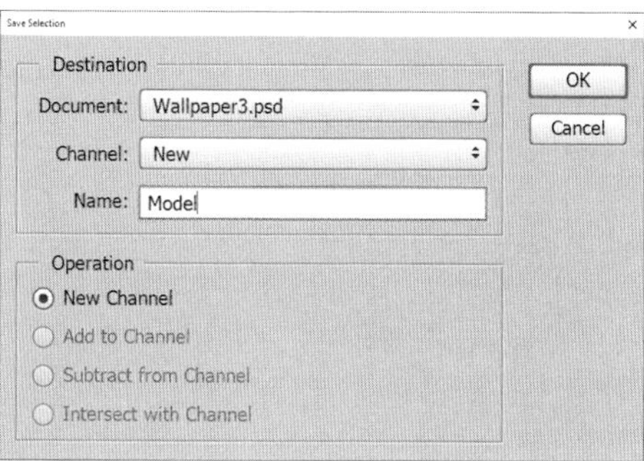

Figure 6.43 The Save Selection dialog box. Save your selections in a new channel and give them memorable names.

3. Save a selection for the lion by Ctrl-clicking (Windows) on the layer mask (Command-clicking in Mac OS). Remember that masks can always be loaded as selections using this method. Name your selection **Lion**.
4. Load the saved selections by choosing Select > Load Selection. All the saved selections in the document will appear in the Channel menu. Load the model selection (**Figure 6.44**).

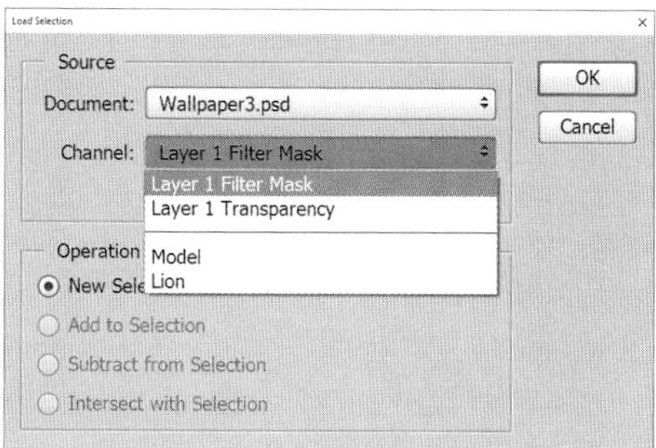

Figure 6.44 Saved selections for your document will appear in the Channel menu in the Load Selection dialog box.

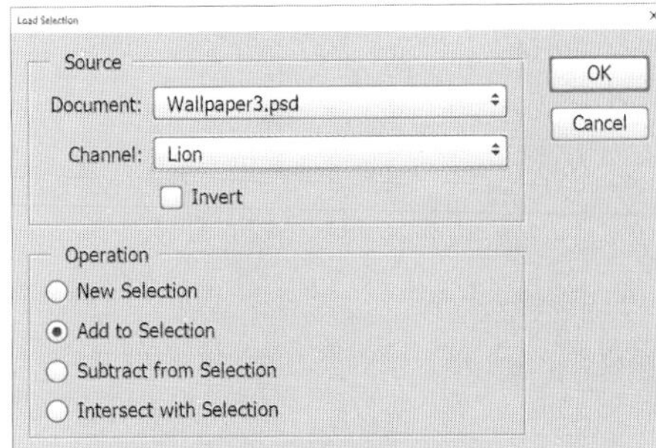

Figure 6.45 Loading layers with active selections gives you access to the operation options in the Load Selection dialog box.

5 Combine saved selections in multiple ways using the operation options in the Load Selection dialog box. This allows you to combine your selections in multiple ways. Load the lion selection using the Add To Selection option (**Figure 6.45**).

There are two other critical shortcuts. You can use Ctrl+Shift+I (Windows) or Command+Shift+I (Mac OS) to invert a selection, or you can choose Select > Inverse. To deselect, use Ctrl+D (Windows) or Command+D (Mac OS) or choose Select > Deselect.

STRIPED SELECTIONS

Video 6.25
Striped Selections

Here's a trick that I love to use, and it's a great shortcut. I often like to play with lines in my images—creating movement or feeling using lines can be a great way to introduce some direction to your image. I used to jump into Illustrator to create these looks, or laboriously work with creating selections using the rulers in Photoshop until I stumbled on this trick.

All you need to do is create a text layer with a bunch of capital letter I's. For this trick I almost always use Arial Black as the font, but any sans serif, super bold font will work. Create enough that it goes across your image. Set the tracking and font size so that it creates spaces between the letters the same thickness as the letters themselves. Now, stretch them very tall so that they look like evenly spaced bars as in (**Figure 6.46**).

Figure 6.46 Creating layers with text can be a great way to quickly create geometric selections.

Now Ctrl-click (Windows) or Command-click (Mac OS) the layer thumbnail to load these bars as a selection. Save that selection. I normally also turn them 45 degrees and save them again because I almost always use them in this orientation. However, you can always rotate an active selection later. After you have these selections, you can delete the layer or drag it below your background solid fill layer in case you might want to use it again later.

Duplicate your GirlRed group, and then load your 45Degree selection and create a mask of the group. Open the group and then modify the Hue and Saturation adjustment layer by double-clicking the thumbnail, and lowering the saturation to **0**. Next, apply a gradient overlay layer style with the preset Blue, Red, Yellow gradient selected. Hold Shift and then drag the group at a 45 degree angle following the lines you just created to shift sections of the girl similar to **Figure 6.47**.

Because this group is only going to be used for a slight effect, go ahead and merge the group. Then experiment with blending modes for the group (such as Screen) and erase the effect covering her face, just leaving a few of these elements in the image as in **Figure 6.48**.

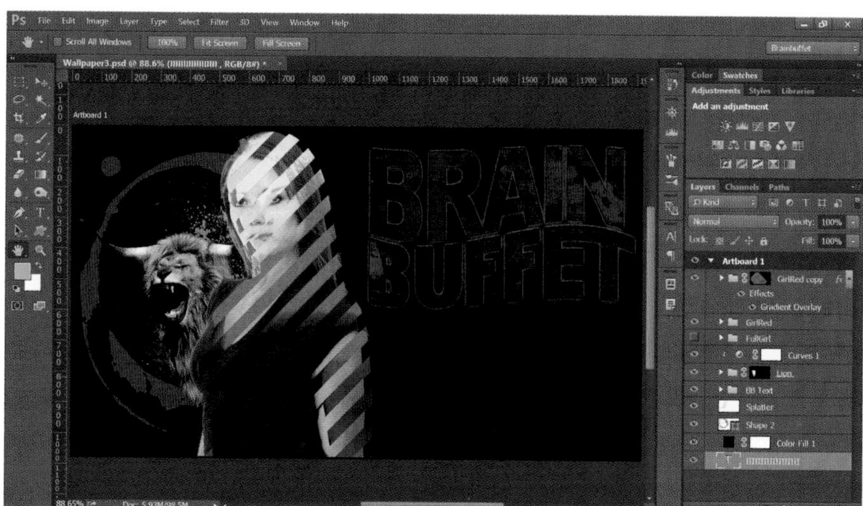

Figure 6.47 The result of the slant distort

Figure 6.48 You can erase parts of this diagonal selection to create an artistic offset effect.

SAVE THE FILE, SAVE A COMP

You've done a fair amount of work, so save your file and also save a comp at this point. Choose a name such as "Big Girl" and add a short description.

★ *ACA Objective 3.8*

Shatter the Heroine

Video 6.26
Shatter Selections

This is a great trick that's been popular in movie posters for the last few years. It's sometimes called the dispersion effect. It's also pretty easy to duplicate—so let's give it a quick go!

Duplicate your GirlRed layer group and name the top copy **GirlShatter**. Turn the opacity of the top layer down to about 50% so you can see where you're overlapping and move the GirlShatter layer to the right. Make sure the face is overlapping skin as in **Figure 6.49**. Your original and copy should look like they're cheek to cheek or a little more overlapped than that.

Now create a new blank layer and draw a random jagged shape with the Lasso tool, and fill this selection with black. Make a new brush out of this selection named **Shatter** (**Figure 6.50**). Delete the layer you made to create the brush.

Figure 6.49 Make sure the character overlaps skin on the face and arm.

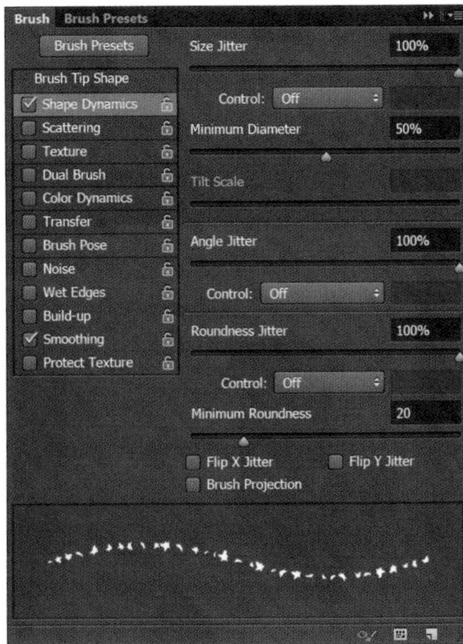

Figure 6.50 Creating a new brush from the random jagged shape

Modify your brush tip shape to have spacing of **150%** and turn on Shape Dynamics. Set the values for the boxes as seen in **Figure 6.51**.

Now, create a mask on your GirlRed layer and carefully paint away the image with your mask. Try to stay near the face areas where it will show up best, and don't go too far. Then make your GirlShatter layer visible, turn up the opacity, and mask the layer—but fill it with black to hide it all. Then change to a white brush and again lightly paint in some of the girl, focusing on the areas close to where you subtracted. Try to get it to look something like **Figure 6.52**. I tend to make the brush smaller as I move away from the dissolving object with this trick, and I just go back and forth between black and white on both masks to get things to look the way I want. It's really a matter of trial and error.

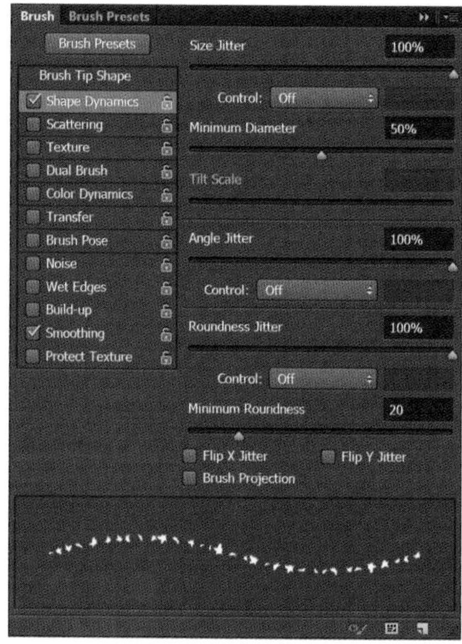

Figure 6.51 Setting up the Shape Dynamics to create a random dispersion brush

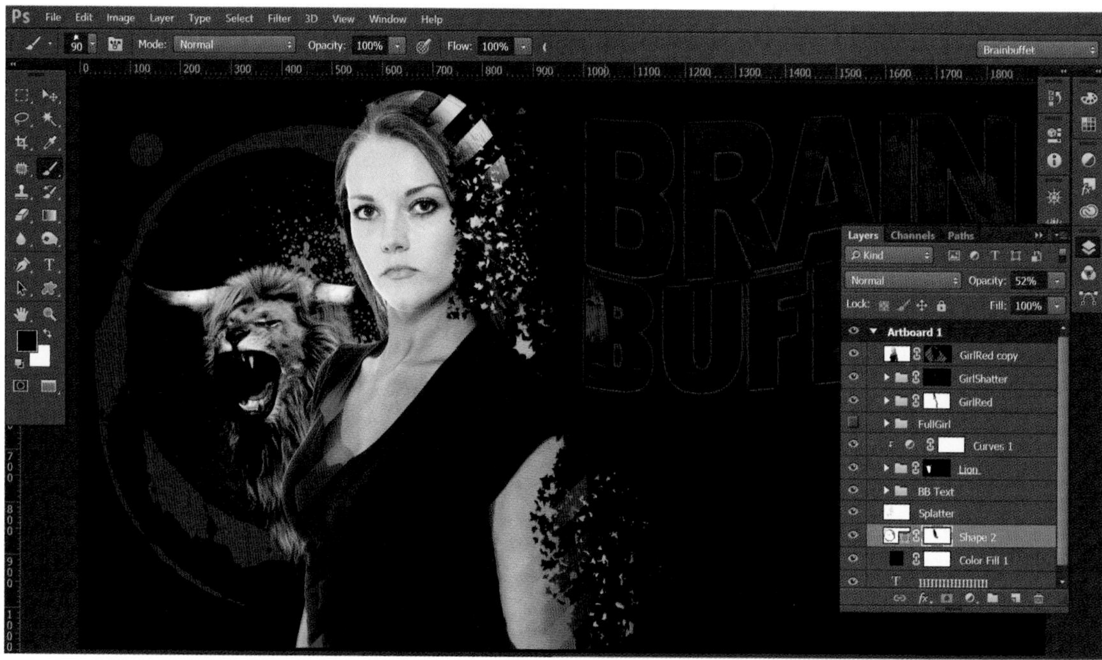

Figure 6.52 Using randomness in our custom brushes to make the model appear to be partially dissolving

★ ACA Objective 3.7

Gradient Goodness

▶ *Video 6.27 Gradient Goodness*

TIP

Find us at www.Brainbuffet.com and poke around the site for goodies. You'll find a lot there, and we're working on making it even better!

This is the very last trick we'll cover. I just learned this trick last week. I've been using Photoshop for more than 15 years, and I still learn new stuff all the time. That's a huge part of what makes Photoshop so amazing. It's kind of like getting a free expansion pack every time you learn a new trick. There are so many creative experiments you can try and amazing tricks to learn. Keep checking our site and follow us on Twitter—we use Twitter as much to bookmark ideas on the road as we do to share what we find!

You're going to create a new gradient with a little twist. Select the Gradient tool, and then double-click the gradient preview in the Options bar to open the Gradient Editor (**Figure 6.53**).

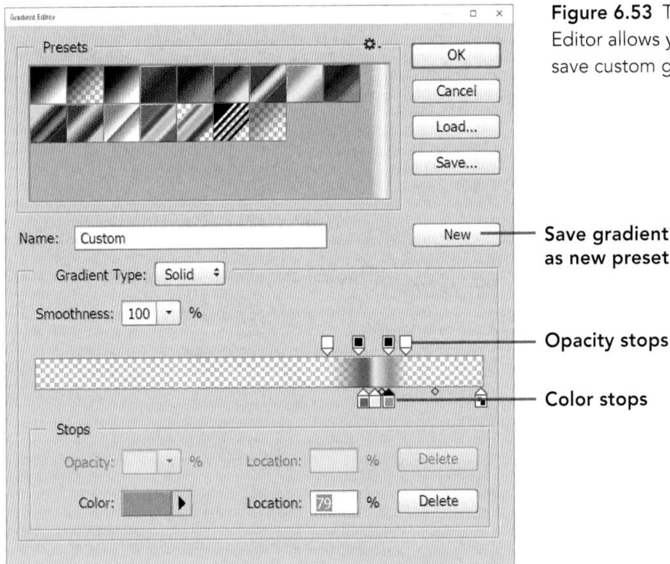

Figure 6.53 The Gradient Editor allows you to create and save custom gradient presets.

NOTE

If a color stop shows two small boxes, it is using the foreground or background color and will change when these are altered.

Above the Gradient bar, the opacity stops determine how visible that section of the gradient is. Like masks, black indicates transparent and white indicates opaque. Below the gradient bar are the color stops. Each stop indicates where a color will appear in the gradient, and you can customize each one.

Click in either area to add a stop, and drag a stop out of the area to remove it. To edit a stop, select it and then enter the desired color or opacity in the bottom of the Gradient dialog box. (Figure 6.53 shows a color stop selected.) Create a gradient similar to the one shown and click the New button to save the preset.

Click OK to close the Gradient Editor and create a new layer. You should still have the Gradient tool selected. Hold Shift and drag vertically on your document to create a gradient (**Figure 6.54**). Be sure to try the different gradient types for different effects—each has its own appeal. You can transform the gradients you create using the Free Transform function, and use a mask or just use the Eraser to sculpt your light. Be sure to experiment with blending modes and opacity for your layers as well.

Figure 6.54 I kept my gradients subtle, a diagonal straight beam in the back, and a round one behind the model. I erased sections and changed blending modes to my taste.

Final Tweaks

Video 6.28 Final Tweaks

You're done! Experiment a little more with position, blending modes, adjustment layers, and more. For **Figure 6.55** I did the following: I saved a comp and then rearranged all the layers related to the model into a single group and then enlarged her. I masked out the red in her eyes and added vibrance using a mask to make the effect only appear in her eyes. I added a clipped curve adjustment to her to increase contrast, masking out the eyes, and did a similar clipped curve adjustment on the lion. The video will walk through this experiment, but that's all it was—experimentation! You can always use layer comps to save versions of your file in different arrangements.

Figure 6.55 The final wallpaper created by combining all the tricks you've learned in the book

The Final Save

Save your file, and then save it as `WallpaperCOMPS.psd`. Also make a new layer comp with all these enhancements.

Check Out Your Comps

Open the Layer Comps panel to see all the previous versions you've made. Comps are a great way to show multiple versions of your document.

Quick Phone Wallpaper

▶ ***Video 6.29*** *Adding an Artboard*

You're going to make a quick cellphone wallpaper using these image elements. It's a fairly easy process that will only take a few minutes because you have the desktop wallpaper already.

To create a new artboard:

1. Select the Artboard tool nested with the Move tool.
2. In the Options bar, click the New Artboard icon to create a new artboard.
3. Click in your document workspace next to your existing artboard. The artboard will be created where you click.
4. In the Options bar, select the phone size you need from the Size menu. The artboard will change to reflect that size.

After your new artboard is created, you can select the items you want to copy, holding Shift to select multiple layers. After making the copies, drag the copies into your new artboard and just rearrange the elements to fit.

Artboards work in the Layers panel the same ways that groups do. The difference is that they exist in a different place in the interface, where all groups within an artboard must share the same area (**Figure 6.56**).

NOTE

If you have layers that don't reside in an artboard, it will not be constrained to the artboards. You can collapse your artboard layers to determine if anything exists outside your artboards and move them as necessary.

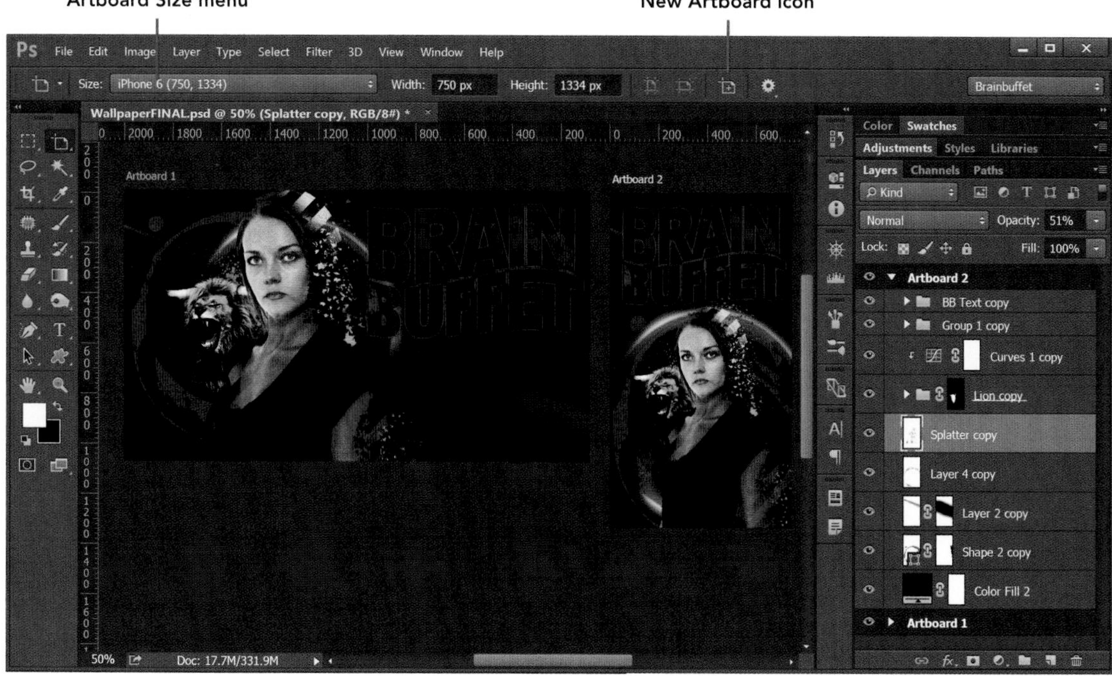

Figure 6.56 Multiple artboards allow you to create documents of different sizes for a project in one Photoshop file.

CHAPTER OBJECTIVES

Chapter Learning Objectives

- Understand important design considerations and concepts for printing using a home or office printer.
- Understand design constraints when designing for the web.
- Understand how to design and do preflight checks when preparing images for commercial printing.
- Understand how to best prepare images for import into other Adobe Creative Cloud apps.

Chapter ACA Objectives

DOMAIN 5
PUBLISHING DIGITAL IMAGES USING ADOBE PHOTOSHOP

5.1 Prepare images for export to web, print, and video.

5.2 Export or save digital images to various file formats.

CHAPTER 7

Publishing Awesome

We have come a long way! Did you imagine at the beginning that you'd get this far in this short amount of time? Amazing projects. I hope that you took on some of the challenges and used your own images to re-create or redesign your final work into something truly original and personal. That's the beauty of design! Taking something, reshaping it, or reusing the skill or tool to create something new. The act of creating something that has never been created before—it's a pretty cool feeling.

Video 7.1 Publishing Awesome

This is a good time to review the ways that you can export your creations into sharable formats. Whether printing on paper or sharing online, this chapter provides all you need to understand the basics of sharing your documents with others. Sharing for different purposes entails different steps, so I'll break it down into the different ways you can share. Some of this was mentioned quickly in other chapters, but it's all together here in this chapter, so you can easily refer to it when you need to produce an image in a specific way.

Print at Home or Work

ACA Objective 5.1

For most of us, printing at home or work and uploading to the web are the most common ways we'll publish or share our work. You can also do this as part of the workflow when working professionally to create quick composite sketches (comps) or previews for the client. Printing at home causes some confusion because home printers (and basic office printers) are calibrated to work with the RGB color space—that's the default color space for computers. Even though you're eventually printing to a device that uses CMYK inks, you send it to the printer as an RGB image.

NOTE

When designing to print to a home inkjet or laser printer, do not convert your images to CMYK. Most home and office printers are designed to work with RGB images.

There are some other really great shortcuts and tips for printing at home or the office that I will share with you in this section. Keep in mind that every printer is slightly different, and between manufacturers the differences are even greater. You might need to dig a little into your printer documentation if the default solutions don't work for you—but generally these standard practices should provide consistent high-quality prints from your home or office printer.

Quick Prints

***Video 7.2** Quick Prints*

To open the Print dialog box in Photoshop, choose File > Print (**Figure 7.1**). This enables you to set certain printing parameters that are ideal for printing at home. The following settings help print your images scaled to the printable area of the paper or in actual size.

- **Printer Setup**: In the first section of the Print dialog box, you can see the layout option that allows you to set the image to print in either landscape (horizontal) or portrait (vertical) orientation. In this case choose landscape.
- **Color Management**: This section has a couple of settings that can produce reliably good color. First, select Photoshop Manages Colors from the Color Handling menu. This allows the Photoshop internal color management system to handle color processing. This works especially well if you obtain the ICC color profile files for your printer. The next step is to select Relative Colorimetric from the Rendering Intent menu. The rendering intent specifies how colors will be managed, and Relative Colorimetric allows Photoshop to switch out-of-gamut colors to the closest match. This is the standard setting for printers in North America and Europe.
- **Position and Size:** This section of the Print dialog box allows you to specify the size that you'd like the final image printed. Most commonly, you'll print at 100% to get a sense of the actual size of the final image. Occasionally, you'll need to shrink or enlarge an image to fit the printable size of the paper. This is especially handy when the original image is too large to fit on one page. Selecting Scale To Fit Media will automatically scale the image to the printable size of the paper you have designated (whatever you have in your printer!).

NOTE

*The **gamut** of a device is the complete range of colors a device can produce.*

NOTE

In some industry exams, you may encounter a question that tells you to print the image. Go through the actions that would cause an image to be printed, including clicking the Print button.

After customizing the Print dialog box settings according to your needs, click Print to send the image to the printer. Print times will depend on your image and how much work Photoshop needs to do to prepare your image for the printer.

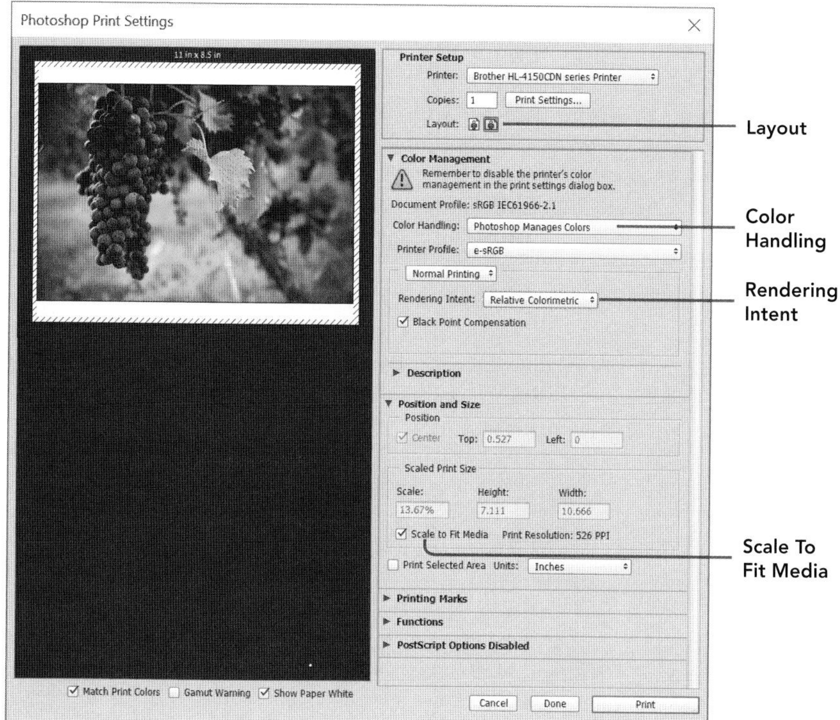

Figure 7.1 The Photoshop Print dialog box

Save for the Web

★ *ACA Objective 5.2*

Video 7.3 *Prepping Web Ready Images*

We have already addressed saving for the web in previous chapters, but it's presented here as a quick reference. I'll also address some of the minor concepts that we didn't go into detail about in earlier chapters.

First, be sure that your working color profile is sRGB. This is the standard for RGB images with Photoshop and is the best working space for the web. This is set by default when creating a print document in Photoshop, but ironically it is not set for the web presets. To ensure consistency in what you design in and what you see on the web, set your working space to sRGB when setting up the document as shown in **Figure 7.2**, and then you will convert to sRGB when saving.

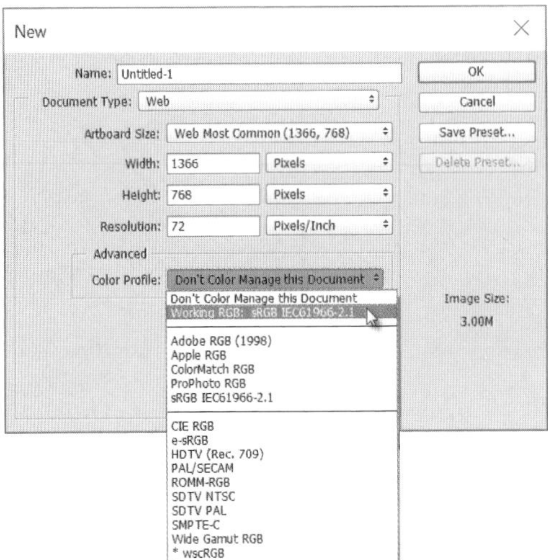

Figure 7.2 Set your color profile to Working RGB: sRGB when creating Photoshop documents to ensure consistency with saved document colors.

NOTE

To assign a profile to an existing document choose Edit > Assign Profile.

There is a long-standing misconception that web images need to be set to 72 pixels per inch (ppi) resolution. When dealing with web images, resolution does not matter. Digital images on digital displays will display images according to the number of pixels, not the resolution set when the image was created. Web images will display at the total image size set by the web page or the application, and the resolution in ppi will be set by the display device. If I look at the same web image on my phone and my monitor, they are different sizes. The "pixels per inch" at which an image is displayed will be determined by the resolution of the display screen, not the resolution in the image file.

Save Photos for the Web

Video 7.4 *Saving Photos for the Web*

Photographic images for the web should be saved in either JPEG or PNG-24 format. JPEG images are more common and are accepted by any website that accepts images. PNG-24 is a newer standard that has the advantage of allowing for true alpha transparency, which means that it allows pixels to be partially visible.

JPEG IMAGES

JPEG files are generally the best overall format to use for saving photographs for the web—they are typically the smallest file sizes and widely accepted. When saving for the web, the main consideration is the quality setting. You can use the 2-up view to compare different quality settings as we did earlier in the book. Let's go over some of the main considerations when saving as JPEG (**Figure 7.3**).

- **Quality Settings:** You can select a predefined quality setting from Low to Maximum, or you can manually set the quality using a numerical value from 0–100. You will generally need to set this visually based on your image and the intended use of the file.
- **Optimized:** Selecting this will create smaller files, but some older systems may have trouble opening the files. Try deselecting Optimized if your destination does not accept the file.
- **Embed Color Profile:** Deselect this unless you have a specific reason to use it. The best option is to convert the image to sRGB.
- **Convert To sRGB:** Select this option to ensure the most consistent color across devices.
- **Metadata:** Select an option from this menu to specify how much information is stripped from your final file. Use the minimum metadata you need for the file to help minimize file sizes.
- **Image Size:** Enter the final output size of the image in these fields. It's generally best practice to reduce the image in Photoshop beforehand, but if image quality is not critical, this normally works fine.

Once you have the options set properly for your image, click Save. Select the filename and destination using the standard system Save dialog box.

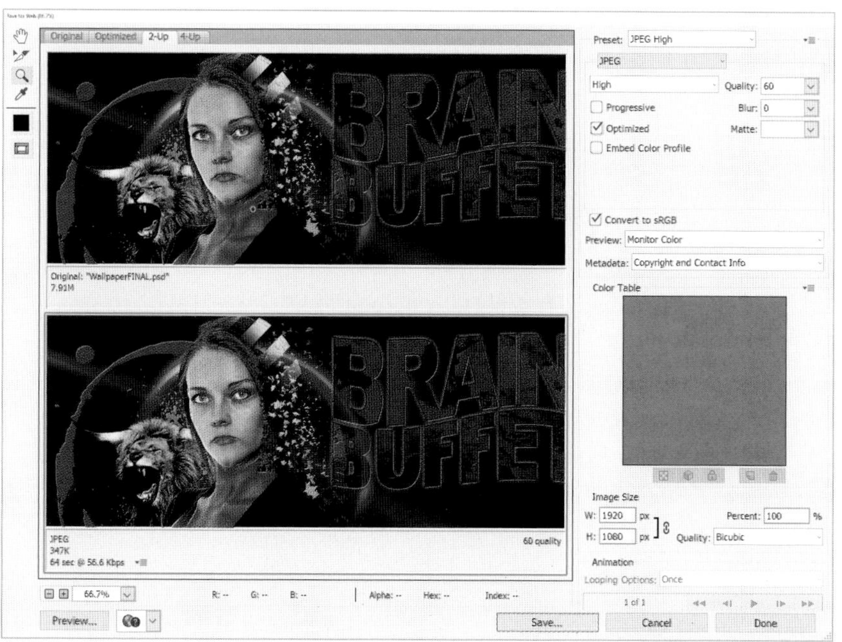

Figure 7.3 The Save For Web dialog box when the JPEG format is selected

PNG-24 IMAGES

PNG-24 is a relatively new image standard and has some advantages. The main advantage is that it allows for true alpha transparency. The image files tend to be larger than JPEG files, but they feature exceptionally high quality. The final images saved with PNG-24 files are generally equal to the highest levels of JPEG quality settings (**Figure 7.4**).

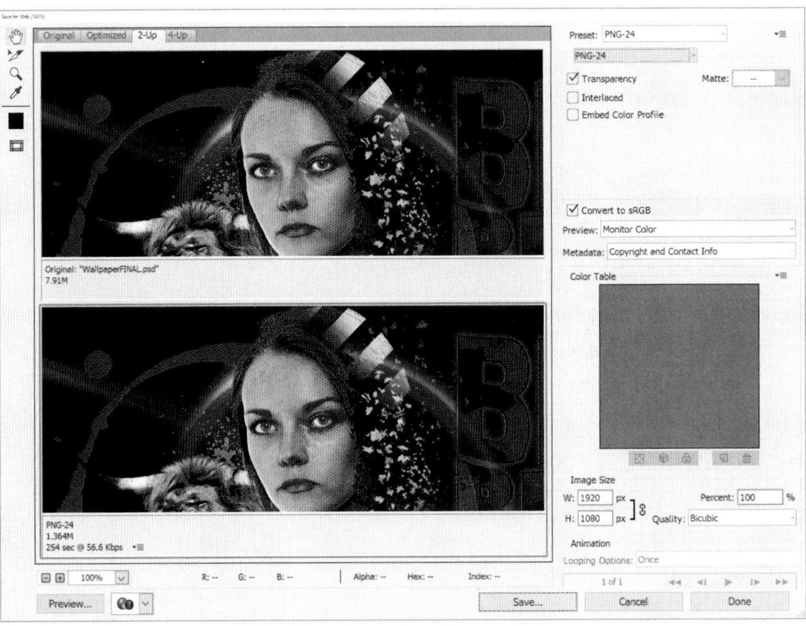

Figure 7.4 Saving PNG-24 images creates very high quality photographic images with small file sizes.

NOTE

PNG-24 images are actually 32 bit images that use 24 bits for color (allowing for millions of colors) and the additional 8 bits for creating the transparency information.

Creating PNG-24 images involves few settings, many of which are the same settings used for JPEG images (Figure 7.4).

- **Transparency:** Select this if the image has transparent pixels. The image size doesn't change either way. Generally it's best to just leave this on its default setting.
- **Embed Color Profile:** As always, when saving for the web, deselect this unless you have a specific reason to include it.
- **Convert To sRGB:** Select this to ensure the optimal color consistency on the web.
- **Image Size:** You can enter values in these fields to change the size of the exported image for a specific purpose. It's best practice to convert inside of Photoshop before exporting, but the quality is generally acceptable using this export resizing for most purposes.

As with all the Save For Web dialog box options, once you have the options set properly for your image, click Save. Select the filename and destination using the standard system Save dialog box.

Save Graphic Images for the Web

Video 7.5 Saving Graphic Images for the Web

Graphic images such as graphs, logos, and other images that have solid areas of color are best saved in indexed file formats such as PNG-8 and GIF. Though you may be more familiar with GIF images, PNG-8 is a newer format and is preferred by many web developers. Indexed image formats are not true color—they can hold a maximum of 256 colors. They create very small files with excellent quality as long as they're the right type of image. Both of the file formats we will be discussing support transparency based on an index color. This means that a specific color will be rendered transparent, and all other colors will be fully opaque.

SAVE AS PNG-8

To export a graphic image as a PNG-8 file, select PNG-8 from the menu at the top of the Save For Web dialog box. There are many options available for this file format, and we won't get into detail here, but I recommend you explore the options with your documents to get the best result for your images. I'll explain the basics here, and I encourage you to try a few different images to explore how this format is best used (**Figure 7.5**).

- **The Color Reduction Algorithm** menu allows you to select how Photoshop reduces the colors in the image.
- **The Colors** menu allows you to choose how many colors will be in your final image.
- **The Diffusion Algorithm Selector** menu lets you select the way that the colors will blend in your image.
- **Transparency:** Select this if the image will have a transparent color based on an Index color. You must choose the transparent color using the Color Table below this option.
- **Convert to sRGB:** Select this to ensure the optimal color consistency on the web.
- **Map Selected Color to Transparent:** After selecting the color you want to become transparent in the Color Table, click this icon to enable transparency for the image.

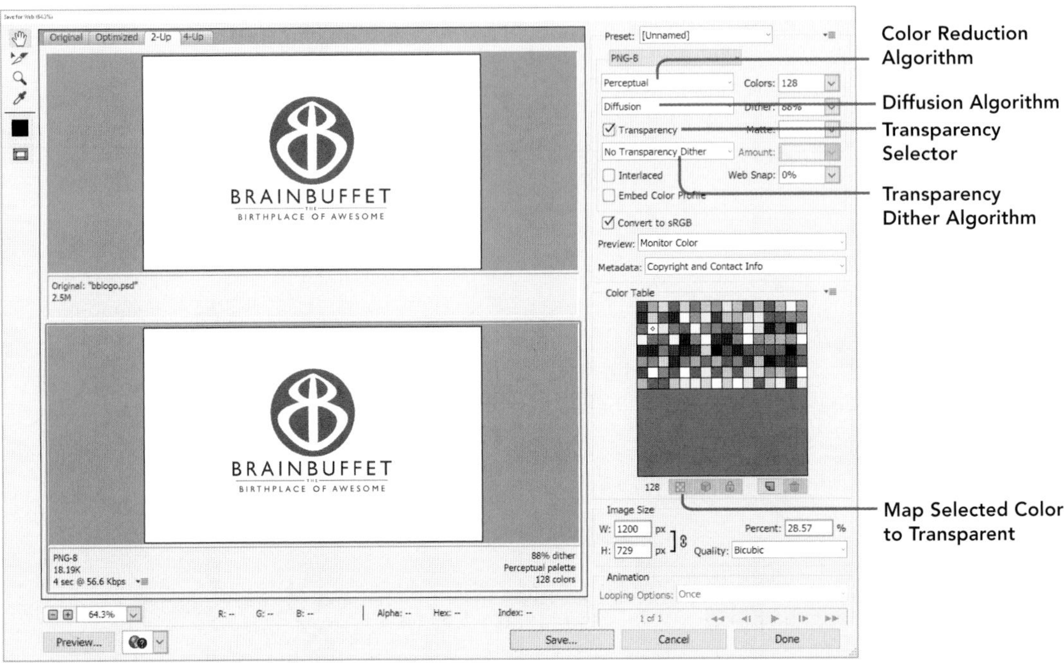

Figure 7.5 PNG-8 is the newest standard for indexed images.

- **Image Size:** Enter values in these fields to change the size of the exported image for a specific purpose. It's best practice to convert inside of Photoshop before exporting, but the quality is generally acceptable using this export resizing for most purposes.

As with all the Save For Web dialog box options, once you have set the options for your image, click Save. Select the filename and destination using the standard system Save dialog box.

SAVE AS GIF

Saving as GIF has the same settings to consider as PNG, so I won't go over those options here. Unless the destination system does not accept PNG-8 files, it's best to always use that format over GIF. However, the GIF format allows animations, and is the best for animated images on the web as it creates very small files. If you are saving full-motion video, it is best to export in MP4 format (but animation and video editing is beyond the scope of this book). You should know that Photoshop is a capable animation tool and video editor.

Determine Image Settings

Saving images for the web takes a little experimentation. Every image is different, and there are many different quality and size requirements for different web platforms where you might want to post your images. Therefore, you will need to experiment and explore which settings are best for your image.

We've covered the basics here, and everything that you need to know to get started has been explained. If you begin to design more for the web, you will learn the nuances and intricacies of the preferred formats for your work. Remember to use the multiple views in the Save For Web dialog box to compare different file formats and quality settings when unsure.

Design for Commercial Printing

★ *ACA Objective 5.1*

▶ ***Video 7.6***
Designing for Commercial Printing

In Chapter 4, we covered a lot of the concepts that you need to know for creating an image that will be printed professionally on an offset press. Here is a quick preflight checklist that you can use to easily determine what settings you should use when designing for CMYK.

1. **Design in RGB when creating images for commercial printing.** The final image that you send to the printer will need to be converted to CMYK, but it is best to keep your images in the RGB color mode while working because it is Photoshop's native color space. Working in RGB will give you the greatest access to Photoshop features and tools, and you can soft proof to have Photoshop show you what the image will look like after conversion.
2. **Set up soft proofing for your destination printer.** When you begin working with a specific printer, they may have a color profile that you can use to see onscreen a close approximation of what the final colors will look like. If a custom color profile is not available, you can use the standard working CMYK color profile and that should give you a pretty good idea of how the final image will look.
3. **View the image at the print size view often while working.** This will show you onscreen the approximate size of the final image and can help you determine the size that the design elements in your composition need to be. Remember to always show the client the image in print size view so that they get an idea of what size it will be when printed.

4. **Save a separate copy of your final image as a flattened document and convert the image to CMYK to send to the printer.** This will make the file size much smaller and will ensure that layers don't accidentally get turned on or off. This also gives you an opportunity to see the file exactly as it is sent to the printer in the proper color space. Saving this flattened CMYK version of the file as a separate image allows you to always return to your original RGB layer document to make any necessary changes.

These four steps give you a basic introduction to designing for print. In addition, every commercial printer will have a document that details exactly what that printer prefers with in terms of file formats. Most commercial printers accept PSD files, but some prefer TIFF images. TIFF images are very popular in the print industry because they are uncompressed and all professional printing software can open a TIFF image.

★ *ACA Objective 5.1*

Create Images for Use in Other Applications

Video 7.7 Designing for Use in Other Adobe Applications

When you're creating images that will be used in other Adobe applications, it is generally best practice to save the images as layered PSD files. The reason for this is that most other Adobe applications can accept these layers, and can even edit layer visibility if necessary for the design. There are a few best practices you can follow to help make your files easier to use by others.

Practice Good Layer Management

Properly naming your layers and organizing layers into groups can help other designers who use your file understand how it was constructed. This is an excellent practice even when you are the only person using your files—it can be very difficult to remember what you did and how you built your file when opening it later.

Save Text Entry for Illustrator and InDesign

Both Illustrator and InDesign have excellent tools for managing and formatting text—much better than Photoshop's built-in text editor. When designing images that will be used in Illustrator or InDesign, it is a best practice to save the text entry and typography for the other applications. If you do enter the text, never rasterize it so that it can still be manipulated with other tools when brought into external applications.

Communicate

When you begin to work with a team or other designers, it is best to ask questions about the workflow and how you can best create the images that are needed for the project. Find out what specific requirements they have, and if you don't understand feel free to ask for clarification. Many design problems can be solved with good communication. Get comfortable asking for clarification or specifications when you are working on a new project or with a new team. In Chapter 10 you will learn a lot more about project management and working with others. You will also get some good tips about being an effective team member on a design project.

Get to the Next Level

Video 7.8 Getting to the Next Level

We've covered everything that you need to know to get started with Photoshop. But to get successful in the industry requires more than just technical knowledge of the software. The next three chapters will really give you a head start with understanding how to become more creative, how to work well in a design environment, and some of the insider lingo that you might hear while working in different areas of the design industry. In many ways the next three chapters are the most important for a design career. Learning how to use Photoshop and being a Photoshop professional are really two different things—the first seven chapters have helped you learn how to use Photoshop, but the next three will help you begin to think and act like a Photoshop professional.

CHAPTER OBJECTIVES

Chapter Learning Objectives

- Understand trends and standards in industries related to Photoshop.
- Understand terms related to digital imaging and photography.
- Understand industry trends and standards related to web publishing.
- Understand industry trends and standards related to the commercial printing industry.

Chapter ACA Objectives

DOMAIN 2.0
UNDERSTANDING DIGITAL IMAGES

2.1 Understand key terminology related to digital images.

2.5 Demonstrate knowledge of image resolution, image size, and image file format for web, video, and print.

CHAPTER 8

Working with Insiders

When starting out in your design career and getting comfortable working in the industry, you're going to discover that there is a lot of jargon—industry-specific vocabulary that you'll be expected to understand. This short chapter is designed to help you with the industry-specific terms you'll need to know. Some of them may have been covered in earlier chapters, but I'm writing this chapter to provide you with a handy "cheat sheet" for use when translating from "designer speak" to English.

Most industries also have specializations and jargon related to those specializations. Because Photoshop is commonly used in so many areas of visual design, you'll come across many niche terms while working on design projects. Don't let this frustrate you—just get comfortable asking questions when you don't understand exactly what's needed from you as a designer.

▶ ***Video 8.1*** *Working with Insiders*

To keep this chapter short so it serves as a quick reference, I'm intentionally creating small sections with critical terms listed alphabetically. Note that there is a glossary for this book as well, but this section relates to the specific Adobe Certified Associate Objectives 2.1 and 2.5, which were not covered in depth in earlier chapters.

Insider Terminology

★ ACA Objective 2.1

Not only does every industry have specific jargon, but the specializations inside these industries have their own jargon as well. Photoshop merges with print design, photography, film, 3D, video game design, and more. Few applications are so deeply ingrained and so critical to the workflow in these industries as Photoshop.

Key Terms for Digital Imaging

Video 8.2 *Industry Terms for Digital Images*

This section covers all terms related to digital images in general, whether used for print, web, or video.

Bitmap: An image created by a grid of pixels with each pixel assigned a color and, in some file formats, a transparency value.

dpi: Stands for dots per inch and refers to the resolution of an image when *printed*.

Path: Often related to vector images, a specific path created by a vector to define a shape or line. Paths technically have no dimension, so a stroke must be added to make it visible.

Pixel: A single dot that makes up a raster image. Pixel is short for "picture element."

ppi: Stands for pixels per inch and is a setting that affects only printed images. Higher ppi affords more detail in printed images.

Raster: Originally described an image created by scan lines on CRT monitors, but today it is basically synonymous with bitmap.

Rasterize: To convert an image of another type into a raster/bitmap image.

Resolution: A measurement of the number of pixels in a given space—either in an inch (ppi) or total pixels (such as 1920x1080).

Render: To convert a nonraster image or effect into a raster image.

Stroke: The thickness of the visual representation of a path.

Transparency: An area of an image that is not visible. When exporting a file, transparency is only supported by certain file formats.

Vector: A series of points connected by lines and curves determined by mathematical equations. Vector images built from these points are resolution independent. This means they can scale infinitely with no loss of quality.

Key Terms in Photography

Photoshop is obviously closely aligned with photography. Photography is its own art form, and you will be working with photographers in this industry. Learning some of the terms used in photography will help.

Video 8.3 Industry Terms in Photography

Blown-out: Images that have no detail in the brightest (pure white) areas due to overexposure.

Bokeh: An out-of-focus effect created by lenses and apertures, especially when referring to the circular blur from lights that are out of focus.

Crop sensor: A term to describe cameras with a sensor smaller than the 35mm standard; these cameras will appear to have a zoomed-in effect with standard lenses.

Depth of field (DoF): Describes the depth of the focal plane of a subject within an image (**Figure 8.1**). A shallow DoF will only show a small part of a subject in focus while a deep DoF will show the whole image in focus.

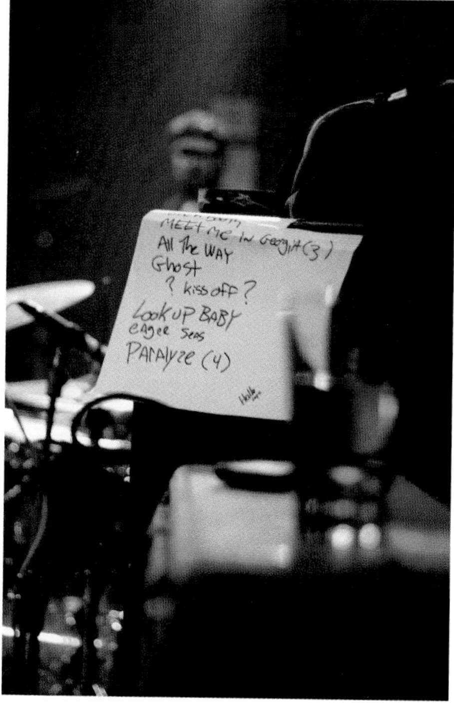

Figure 8.1 A "short" depth of field has a narrow area in focus.

Fill light: A light used on the darker side of a subject in a photo to make it appear more dimensional.

Grain: The term used to describe sensor noise (a stippled look) in images shot with low light.

High key: An image that has very few dark pixels, resulting in a light and bright image; this can be a desirable artistic effect.

Low key: An image that has very few light pixels, resulting in a very dark and moody image; this can be a desirable artistic effect for some images.

Megapixels: Describes the number of pixels in millions that a device can capture. Among devices with the similar image sensors, megapixels provide higher image detail.

Zoom: A function of the camera lens that enlarges image elements on the sensor of a camera—digital zoom simulates this effect.

Images and Industries

★ ACA Objective 2.5

Each industry has its own needs and standards for digital images. Some of this information is sprinkled around the chapters, but I wanted to gather this industry-specific information here for you as it relates to images for each industry. Keep in mind that there may be slight differences from region to region even within the same industry. This is not uncommon, where certain names for certain things become popular in a particular area that is uncommon in other regions.

The most important thing to remember is that you need to always be comfortable asking for clarification if you don't understand something. Sometimes you can even learn something new about the industry because of the terms people choose to use to describe things. You start to be able to recognize who has a print orientation and who has a digital orientation.

▶ **Video 8.4** Print Industry Standards

Keep in mind that I'm not trying to create an industry reference manual here. I just want you to understand some of the most common terms that are widely accepted and understood, even if another term might be used in a particular region.

Figure 8.2 Each plate and a commercial press lays down one color, resulting in a full-color image.

Images for Print

The print industry has specific methods for creating images as well as specific processes (**Figure 8.2**). When we discuss the print industry, we're referring to images created for the CMYK four-color process printing on offset presses. There is no need to get into the technical details of how these images are created, but you should know that the print industry generally needs larger images than all other industries. It's always a good idea to get specifications from your printer.

FILE FORMAT

TIFF images are a common format for the print industry. It is a very high quality, lossless file format.

If you're working with a team that also uses Adobe tools or software, it may be best to provide your original Photoshop (PSD) files. As we learned earlier, these files can be placed into other Adobe applications as smart objects or linked files, and the layers and elements within the image can be manipulated individually. Adobe InDesign is the most popular application in the world for page layout and design, and you will find in the print industry you are often creating files to be placed in InDesign layouts.

IMAGE RESOLUTION

It is most common to have files designed at 300dpi for printing. This is a standard resolution for offset printing, and resolution is critical when dealing with print.

COLOR MODE

The standard color mode for process printing is CMYK. There are four "plates" on an offset press that lay down each color on the paper (Figure 8.2).

Images for the Web

Working in the web industry is a very interesting specialty. With all of the emerging technology and constantly evolving standards, it can be very difficult to keep track of what is preferred and current when you are working on projects (**Figure 8.3**). This makes working with the web challenging sometimes, but it can also be really exciting, as new ways of working are created every year.

Video 8.5 Web Design Industry Standards

Figure 8.3 Different screen sizes display the web page differently, often requiring multiple versions of the same image.

FILE FORMATS

The most common file formats for the web are JPEG, PNG, and GIF. Each has its own advantages and disadvantages, which we have touched on lightly in earlier chapters, but I wanted to summarize them here and add all of the industry-specific concerns for each file format.

- **JPEG** is the most common standard for the web. It stands for Joint Photographers Expert Group, and as the name implies it's an excellent format for photography. It is a "lossy" file format, meaning that in order to create smaller files, it discards information that is not easily discerned by the human eye. JPEGs are excellent for photographs and textures, but create "artifacts" in solid areas of color. Therefore, it is not an ideal format for graphic images with strong solids.
- **PNG** is a relatively new file format that is very flexible. PNG files were originally created to replace GIF when there was speculation that the GIF format might be restricted. PNG files can be 24-bit images that work great for photos, or 8-bit images that work great for logos, text, and graphs. PNG files can also be set to include transparency on the 24-bit images, creating a true alpha transparency channel. This means that an image can contain pixels that are only partially transparent, creating a very realistic fade.
- **GIF** images are indexed (limited) color images that are best used for logos, text, and simple graphics. GIF images were once very popular on the web, but have been replaced in many cases with PNG files. GIF files have recently experienced a surge in popularity because of their ability to contain multiple frames that will act as an animation. GIF files are incredibly small, but do not allow you to reproduce photographic images very well or reproduce images with more than 256 colors.

IMAGE RESOLUTION: THE 72 PPI MYTH

According to a popular myth, images for the web should always be created at 72ppi. The truth is, ppi has no effect on the way that images appear when posted online. Images are displayed online in pixels, and the resolution of your screen will determine how many pixels per inch will be displayed, not the image PPI setting. An image that is 900 pixels wide will take up 900 pixels on any standard screen; a setting of 300ppi or 72ppi will simply be ignored.

This is a very popular misconception, so it is often considered best practice to create images for the web at 72ppi. If the client or an employer requires that you create all of your web images at this resolution, just do it. It is such a widely held belief that even after proving it onscreen, some web professionals will still argue the point.

The most important thing for you to understand as a Photoshop professional is that for the web, you will always be creating images by using pixel resolution measurements (1024x768), not using ruler dimensions and dpi (4x6 inches at 300dpi).

COLOR MODE

Images for the web are always created in RGB color mode, no matter what the file format.

Images for Video

In addition to file formats, image resolution, and color mode, video requires an understanding of a concept called Action Safe Area and Title Safe Area (**Figure 8.4**). As you might guess, these are areas where it's safe to place action (or important parts of the image) in the shot or titles.

Video 8.6 *Video Industry Standards*

The reason these areas exist is that different televisions are capable of display different amounts of the screen. This is not as much a problem with today's LCD screens as it used to be with CRT screens, but it's standard practice to be sure that your titles and visual elements fall within these two zones.

Figure 8.4 Different screen sizes require images to be scaled differently, and you will often need to create multiple versions of the image for different displays.

FILE FORMATS

When you're creating images for insertion into video, you will generally stick to the same file formats that you use for the web. If your video team is working in Adobe Premier Pro, then it will be best to save your images as PSD files.

- **JPEG** files in a resolution similar to the final processed video are very common when creating title slides for video. This is probably the most popular format for photographic images that will be inserted into video. The file format is common and the images are small.
- **GIF** and **PNG** files are also very popular when creating graphics that need transparency. As discussed earlier, PNG is a very flexible format and is gaining popularity. These images are especially popular for creating bottom thirds, which are the graphics that are superimposed over a video to show a title. This is often seen in the news and in sports to show statistics or headlines.

Adobe Premiere is a very popular package for editing video, and Adobe After Effects is an industry standard for creating special effects in video. Both of these applications accept Photoshop documents directly, so be sure to always save your PSD files.

COLOR MODE

You will always create images in RGB when creating for video.

Wrapping Things Up

Photoshop has a very interesting place in industries other than print, web, and video. Photoshop's new abilities to work with 3D objects opens up the whole area of 3D printing and engineering. Photoshop is also popular in the video game industry for creating textures. Special niche industries, such as the signage industry, have special file formats or requirements that Photoshop can handle.

The most important thing to remember when working with an insider in a particular industry is that it is important to have an open mind and be willing to learn how to best serve those clients. As a Photoshop designer, you will not be required to become an expert in every industry, but you do need to be open to learning enough that you can open doors of opportunity to work in areas where other Photoshop designers fear to tread. Just like the application, working in an industry will constantly evolve and you need to be ready for the changes. Being open-minded and willing to learn new things will take you further than trying to master everything about a specific industry. In most industries related to Photoshop, things change so fast you really never can become an expert.

Your most important skill as a Photoshop designer overall will be learning to adapt and adjust to change. Learn to enjoy the fact that things change all the time—and that there's always an opportunity to understand a little bit more about how film, web pages, and printed materials are created.

CHAPTER OBJECTIVES

Chapter Learning Objectives

- Hone your creativity.
- Prepare your mind for design.
- Apply the design hierarchy.
- Discover the elements of art.
- Understand the element of shape.
- Learn how color works.
- Explore typography.
- Understand the principles of design.

Chapter ACA Objectives

DOMAIN 2.0
UNDERSTANDING DIGITAL IMAGES

2.2 Demonstrate knowledge of basic principles and best practices employed in the visual design industry.

2.3 Demonstrate knowledge of typography and its use in visual design.

2.4 Demonstrate knowledge of color and its use in digital images.

CHAPTER 9

Leveling Up with Design

Now that you have a good grasp on the tools in Adobe Photoshop, you'll start learning how best to use them. Much like any other skill, understanding how a tool works and becoming a master craftsperson are two completely different levels of achievement. In many ways, they're distinct ways of thinking about the tools you've learned to use.

***Video 9.1** Design School: Introduction*

As an example, think about carpenters. Their initial level of learning covers tools such as a saw, hammer, and drill. They learn how to use the tools correctly and when to apply specific techniques, including cutting with or against the grain and joining the wood at the joints. Using the right techniques, carpenters can theoretically build anything.

★ *ACA Objective 2.2*

You're now at the point at which the only way to get better is to practice and to learn the thought processes that a master craftsperson goes through to create amazing, creative, and unique work. The beauty of this stage is that it's when you start to become an artist. Being good at using any tool is not just about knowing how it works and what it does. It's knowing *when* to use it and what techniques to apply to create something new.

Creativity Is a Skill

▶ *Video 9.2* *Design School: Creativity Is a Skill*

We discussed creativity in the introduction to this book, and I'd like to share a little more about it. Let's look back at the highly scientific and statistically accurate diagram that I used before to illustrate the point (**Figure 9.1**).

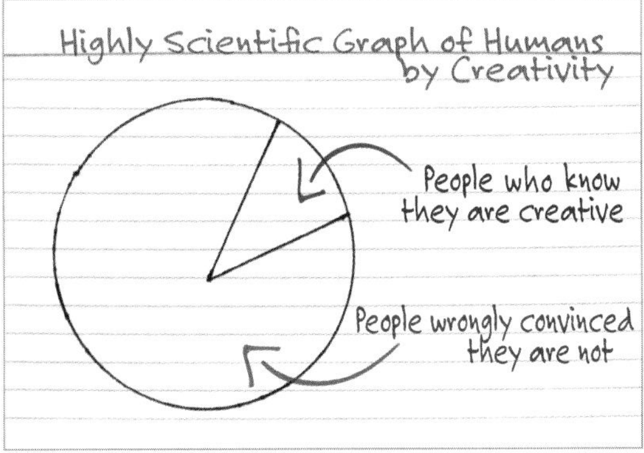

Figure 9.1 Graph of human creativity

Okay, so perhaps the diagram isn't *exactly* statistically accurate and maybe my methods weren't scientific, but it's still true. Creativity is a skill that you can learn and improve with practice. But there's only one way to guarantee that you'll never be more creative than you are now: giving up.

The biggest creative problem some people have is that they give up. Some give up before even making their first effort. Others give up after their fifth effort or after 15 minutes of not creating a masterpiece. Nobody creates a 15-minute masterpiece. A big difference between a great artist and a terrible artist is that a great artist has tried and failed, made some adjustments, and tried again. The next try may also lead to failure, but the artist pushes forward. The artist isn't deterred by bumping into a problem because it's all part of the learning and creative process.

Of course, you can't know how far you can take your creative skills until you start practicing and expanding those skills. But if you never use them, they'll only grow weaker. Remember that every effort, every new attempt, and every goof-up builds strength.

Getting a Creative Workout

This chapter is about developing your creative skills and flexing your creative muscles. It's about turning the craft of being a visual designer into a natural ability. Even if you take the big step of becoming an Adobe Certified Associate, you need to realize that passing the test is just getting through the tryouts. When you get that credential, it's like being picked to be on a professional football team. It's certainly something to be proud of, but the real goal is the *Super Bowl!* You have a lot more work ahead, but it's fun and rewarding work.

This book introduces you to exercises that help you explore and enhance the skills you already have. Getting beyond the basics of creativity and design is just a matter of applying your existing skills in ways you've never tried. That's all there is to creativity.

Prepping Your Mind

Preparing your mind is the most important part of increasing your creative skills. For most of us, it's also the hardest because today's culture is so focused on instant success and efficiency that people learn to fear the essence of creativity: failure.

Failure—and more specifically, the ability to take failure in stride—is the key ingredient in developing your artistic skillset. This is especially true if you're a beginner and aren't entirely happy with your current abilities. Just face that you're a design baby—and start acting like one!

Yes, I just encouraged you to act like a baby. But I mean an actual infant, not a grown person who is throwing a fit. Babies are fearless and resilient when they fail. They keep trying. They don't give up. Most of the time, they don't even realize that they're failing because they haven't yet learned that concept.

That's what you need to tap into. In art, there are no failures—there are only quitters. Tap into your inner infant! Try and fail, and try and fail, and try and fail. Eventually, you'll take your first step. You may quickly fail again on your second step, but don't give up. Babies don't know that they've failed. They just know that they got *a little bit closer*. They know what every true artist knows and what the rest of us need to remember but have forgotten along the way: *Failure is the path.*

The Design Hierarchy

★ *ACA Objective 2.2*

Video 9.3 *Design School: The Design Hierarchy*

Most of us recognize art when we see it, but nobody can agree on how to create it. In an attempt to provide a framework, artists have developed a list of elements, the building blocks of art, and principles, the essential rules or assembly instructions of art. While every artist understands the importance of the elements and principles of art, there is no official list of those elements and principles that all artists agree on. This can be incredibly frustrating. How can you study and learn about something that nobody can fully identify?

Celebrate this fact—the lack of an "official" list means that you can't be wrong. A sculptor and a painter see and approach their art in different ways. A movie producer approaches her art differently than a costume designer approaches his. But all of these artistic people still study and embrace some elements and principles to guide their art.

Applying the Design Hierarchy

The design hierarchy shown in **Figure 9.2** is one way to understand and think about the artistic elements and principles. This isn't the *ultimate* approach to understanding and interacting with the artistic elements and principles. (An "ultimate" approach probably doesn't exist.) It is more of an organized starting place that might help you focus your design skills.

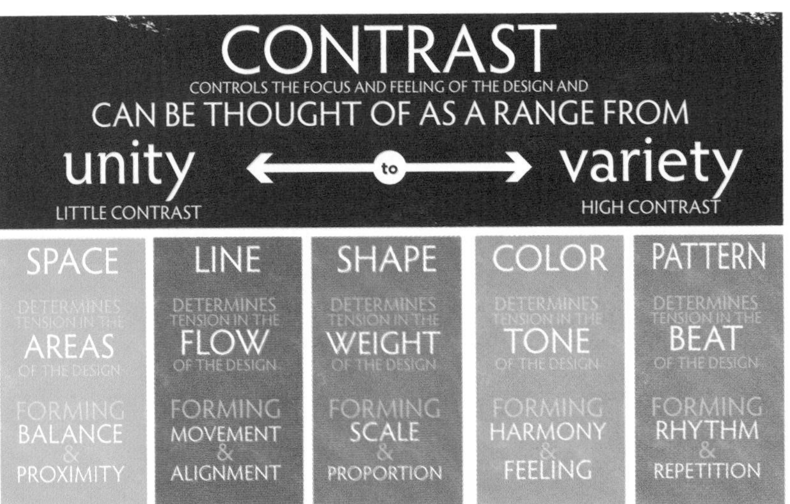

Figure 9.2 The design hierarchy

Design, unlike art, generally has a purpose. It's often about creating or accomplishing something specific, rather than simply enjoying or exploring an artistic impulse. A design task might require that you advertise a product, communicate an idea, or promote a cause or specific issue. I find it much easier to think about artistic elements and principles in terms of design, and you can use a design task as a framework on which to "hang" your creative quest when those vague artistic elements and principles seem confusing or muddled.

Thinking through these building blocks can also serve as a great little exercise when you're looking at a piece of work that you're not happy with but can't quite figure out why. Sometimes, just rolling through the following elements and principles in your mind can be an excellent creative checklist.

START WITH A FOCAL POINT

The **focal point** is what your design is all about. In an advertisement, it's your "call to action" phrase that will motivate the consumer. For a cause, it's the primary message that your cause is trying to get across. In visual design, it could be the navigation elements or the major interactive elements. It's the primary idea that you want people to take with them, like the title of a book or a chapter. It's the "sales pitch" of your design.

The focal point should be the most memorable aspect of the design. In a symmetrical or radial design, center the focal point for the most emphasis. In an asymmetrical design, let it fall on one of the natural focal points, which you'll learn about shortly when you study space.

Critical Question: *Do people know where to look in my design?*

CREATE FOCAL POINTS USING CONTRAST

Contrast creates a focal point by generating "tension" in the image (**Figure 9.3**). Place one red golf ball in a pile of 10,000 white golf balls, and you'll notice it immediately. The most dramatic way to create contrast is to vary the most common characteristic of the elements in the design. If you have a number of multicolored circles that are the same size, then varying the size of one circle, regardless of its color, will create a contrast that draws the eye. Keep the shape the same size, but make it a star instead of a circle to generate the same tension.

Figure 9.3 A focal point is created with contrast: Make one thing different and it stands out.

Establishing unity in a design is essential to allowing you to create tension. Without a degree of unity, you cannot create a focal point and the eye struggles to find something to focus on. Design is about forcing a focal point to be where you want it. When too many different, unrelated elements are present in your design it makes chaos, and the viewer will not know where to look.

Critical Question: *Does my design lack sufficient contrast to see the important features clearly?*

RANGING FROM UNITY TO VARIETY

Figure 9.4 Keep the contrast in your image low toward the unity side unless you're trying to make something stand out.

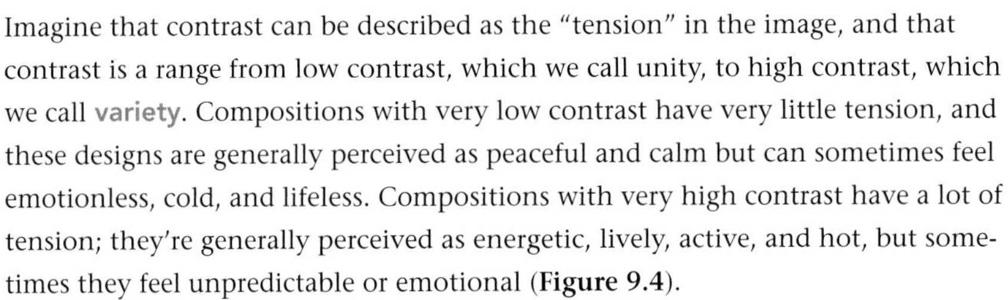

Imagine that contrast can be described as the "tension" in the image, and that contrast is a range from low contrast, which we call unity, to high contrast, which we call **variety**. Compositions with very low contrast have very little tension, and these designs are generally perceived as peaceful and calm but can sometimes feel emotionless, cold, and lifeless. Compositions with very high contrast have a lot of tension; they're generally perceived as energetic, lively, active, and hot, but sometimes they feel unpredictable or emotional (**Figure 9.4**).

A FRAMEWORK FOR CONNECTING THE DOTS

The following framework connects artistic elements and principles to help you at the onset of the creative journey. They're good starting points. Remember that with any design, you're not trying to *define* the artistic elements and principles as much as trying to *embrace* and apply them. As with every study of the artistic elements and principles, you won't arrive at a destination. Rather, you'll embark on a journey. These connections should help you make sense of the elements and principles long enough to find your way to understand and apply them.

- **Create balance and proximity by arranging the elements in your compositional space:** Tension develops among the various areas of your composition; unify the design with symmetry and equal spacing, or vary it using asymmetry and grouping elements.

Critical Question: *Does my design use space to help communicate relationships?*

- **Create movement and alignment by arranging your elements along lines:** Tension is created with the direction or flow of your composition; unify the design with strict alignment or movement along straight or flowing lines, or vary it with random, chaotic movements away from any single line or flow.

Critical Question: *Does my design use lines to communicate order and flow?*

- **Create scale and proportion by carefully designing shapes in your composition:** Tension is created among the sizes of elements in your composition; unify the design with similar or related sizes of elements, or vary it with a mix of unrelated sizes. Keep in mind that a paragraph has a shape, and a group of elements has a shape. Look at areas as well as objects in your design.

Critical Question: *Does my design consider the message sent by the size of shapes I create?*

- **Create themes and feeling by using typography, colors, and values in your composition:** Tension is created among elements of different type, value, or color. Unify the design with related type, colors, and values, or vary it with clashing colors or extreme difference in values or type.

Critical Question: *Does my design consider the message sent by the typography, color, and value I used?*

- **Use repetition and rhythm to create patterns and texture in your compositions:** Tension is created among elements with different texture or patterns. You can unify design with simple repetition to produce predictable patterns and rhythms, or vary it using complex, irregular, or chaotic patterns and rhythms.

Critical Question: *Does my design consider the message sent by the patterns and textures I designed?*

WRAPPING UP THE DESIGN HIERARCHY

If you're familiar with the basic artistic elements and principles, this hierarchy might be a framework you can use. But the goal of art is to continually explore the elements and principles. The next section covers them all, along with some challenges designed to help you dig a little deeper.

The Elements of Art

★ *ACA Objective 2.2*

▶ ***Video 9.4*** *Design School: The Elements of Art*

The **elements of art** (**Figure 9.5**) are the building blocks of creative works. Think of them as the "nouns" of design. The elements are space, line, shape, form, texture, value, color, and type. Many traditional artists leave type off the list, but for graphic designers it is a critical part of how we look at design (and besides that, type is really fun to play with).

Figure 9.5 The elements of art

the elements of art
line
line: the path of a moving point
shape
shape: the contour of a flat object
type
type: the visual depiction of language
form
form: a 3D object that has depth
texture
texture: the tactile quality of a surface
space
space: the internal/external areas of an object
color
color: the chromatic quality of an object
value
value: an object's brightness/darkness

The Element of Space

Space is the first element of art to consider. It also happens to be one of the most abused, overlooked, neglected, and underrated elements in design. You can look at and consider space in multiple ways.

***Video 9.5** Design School: The Element of Space*

SPACE AS YOUR CANVAS

The most basic way to look at space is as your canvas or working area. In Photoshop, you start a new document and specify its dimensions to create your space. Sometimes the dimensions are specified and provided to you, such as when you're designing for a specific project size or screen resolution. But sometimes you can create a fun way to work by giving yourself an uncommon space to design in.

LEVEL UP: A PENNY IN SPACE

Here's a fun challenge:

1. Grab a piece of blank paper, and simply place a coin on it. Don't pick a random place to put it; *design* the spot where it should go.
2. Look at the paper with the coin on it and get a sense for the "feeling" it creates.
3. Fold the paper any way you want, except directly in half, so that you have a differently shaped space, and repeat the process.

Can you see how simply using different sizes and dimensions of space—with the exact same content—can change the way your art "feels"?

And did it enter your mind to fold the paper in a way that wasn't rectangular? Not all spaces have 90-degree corners. Think outside the box...*literally*!

SPACE AS A CREATIVE TOOL

Another important way to look at space is as a design element (**Figure 9.6**). The inability to use space well is an obvious sign of a new designer. A crowded design practically *screams* "newbie"! It takes a while to use space well, and it requires some practice. Start learning to use space as a creative element and you'll see a drastic increase in the artistic feel of your designs.

TIP

Using layer masks in Photoshop is a great way to experiment with space. You can create a mask by painting or by using a selection to create a shape for your images.

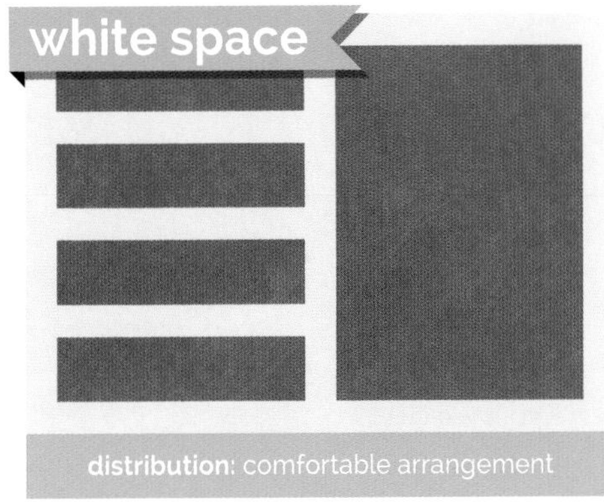

Figure 9.6 Use space to create comfortable arrangements of elements for your design.

When used properly, space can provide the following benefits to your designs:

- **Creating emphasis or focus:** When you have space around an object, it tends to give it emphasis. Crowding things makes them seem less important.
- **Creating feeling:** Space can be used to create a feeling of loneliness, isolation, or exclusivity. It can also be used to create a feeling of seriousness or gravitas.
- **Creating visual rest:** Sometimes space is needed to simply create some visual "breathing room" so that the other elements in your design can speak as intended.

THE RULE OF THIRDS

TIP

Beginning designers center everything, which can contribute to a static look and boring feeling. One way to get started with the rule of thirds is to simply stop centering things. You'll notice that you tend to move elements quite naturally to a focal point suggested by the rule of thirds.

The **rule of thirds** (**Figure 9.7**) is critical in photography and video, and it also applies to all visual arts. To visualize it, think of the rule of thirds like a tic-tac-toe board overlaid onto your design. Two horizontal and two vertical divisions create nine equal boxes on your design. The basic rule is that major elements of your design should fall on the dividing lines, and the areas of emphasis for the design should fall on the intersections. Using this rule in your designs creates compositions that have much more interest, tension, and visual strength.

Figure 9.7 Use the rule of thirds to determine where major elements should fall to create a visually appealing layout.

NEGATIVE SPACE

In the design industry, people use the term **negative space**, or "white space," to refer to blank areas in the design, even if you're working on a colored background. Negative space (**Figure 9.8**) is one of my favorite creative uses of the element of space. It can be fun to explore using negative space to create clever logos or designs.

Figure 9.8 Negative space

TIP

You can see an awesome collection of updated examples of negative space online at www.brainbuffet.com/design/negative-space.

Sometimes you can place a boring idea in negative space to get moving in a new, creative direction. It can be tough for beginners to even "see" negative space, but once you look for it, you'll start to see creative uses of it everywhere. Begin to use it, and your design skills will jump up a level.

From here on out, the elements get much easier to understand because we can think of them as things (whereas we tend to think of space as the absence of things, or "nothing"). Learn to use space well. The ability to do so is the mark of an experienced and talented artist.

NOTE

For many people, the terms negative space and white space are interchangeable. If you're unclear about what someone is asking for, seek clarification. Art and design are not entirely technical, accurate, and organized processes, so you'll need to get used to lots of "mushy" terms that are used in multiple ways.

LEVEL UP: SKETCHING NOTHING

This simple exercise will help you start to see negative space and learn how to create it.

Place a chair on a table, and then sketch everything you see *except* the chair. Don't worry if your sketch is messy—this is not about your artistic skill; it's about learning to see. Just focus on learning to see the space around things rather than the things themselves. When you're done, you'll have a chair-shaped hole in your drawing. Notice that the space where you drew nothing has the most visual impact. Space is powerful!

The Element of Line

▶ *Video 9.6 Design School: The Element of Line*

The meaning of **line** is pretty obvious. Although technical definitions such as "a point moving through a space" exist, we are all aware of what a line is. A line is exactly what you think it is: a mark with a beginning and an end (**Figure 9.9**). Don't overthink the basics. We're going to dig deeper than that, but let's start with the basic idea and then build the new understanding on it.

Figure 9.9 The element of line

LEVEL UP: LINE 'EM UP!

See how many ways you can think about the concept of a line. You'll explore more of these ideas later in this chapter, but first let's see how many different kinds of lines you can draw.

Here are some quick ideas to get you started:

- **Level I:** Short, long, straight, wavy, zigzag, geometric, organic
- **Level II:** Angry, lonely, worried, excited, overjoyed
- **Level III:** Opposition, contrast, politics, infinity

Try to create as many different kinds of lines as you can and find a word to describe each one. There are no wrong answers here; this is art.

Remember, you're just drawing lines, not *pictures*. So to indicate sadness, don't draw an upside down "u." The goal is to draw a line that, in itself, represents sadness. It's a little challenging as you move away from descriptions and closer to abstract ideas, but that's the point. The best artists learn to "hint" at feelings and concepts in their art. Explore!

COMMON LINE DESCRIPTORS

The following adjectives are often associated with lines, and thinking about the ways lines are used or drawn can help you determine the meaning that your lines are giving to your design.

- **Direction** (**Figure 9.10**): A common way to describe lines is to express the direction in which they travel. Lines can be horizontal, vertical, or diagonal. Sometimes the way a line is drawn can even express movement in a particular direction. Think about this and make sure that the lines of your art are moving in the directions you want. **Vertical** lines tend to express power and elevation whereas **horizontal** lines tend to express calm and balance. **Diagonal** lines often express growth or decline, and imply movement or change.
- **Weight** (**Figure 9.11**): Another common descriptor is the weight of a line, which describes its thickness. Heavy or thick lines generally represent importance and strength, and they tend to feel more masculine. Light or thin lines generally communicate delicacy and elegance, and they tend to represent femininity. Using a variable line width implies natural, artistic, flowing feelings and often suggests an intentional grace or natural beauty.

TIP

Having a hard time remembering horizontal and vertical directions? "Horizontal" (like the horizon) has a crossbar in the capital "H" that is a horizontal line itself. Vertical starts with the letter "V," which is an arrow pointing down.

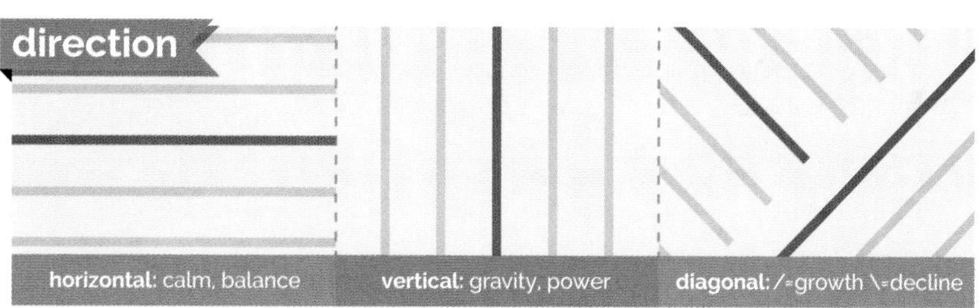

Figure 9.10 Line direction

Figure 9.11 Line weight

- **Style** (**Figure 9.12**): A line style is an effect, such as a double line or dotted line. Words used to describe popular line effects *include varying-width, hand drawn*, and *implied*. **Varying-width** lines are useful for expressing flow and grace. **Hand-drawn** lines look as if they were created with traditional media such as paints, charcoal, or chalk. **Implied** lines are lines that don't really exist—like dotted or dashed lines, or the lines we create when we line up at the grocery checkout. **These implied lines are powerful tools for designers; individual things can feel unified or grouped together when they are aligned.**
- **Flow**: We've created this word for the category that is related to the energy conveyed by lines and shapes. **Geometric** lines tend to be straight and have sharp angles; they look manmade and intentional. Geometric lines communicate strength, power, and precision when used in design. **Curved** lines express fluidity, beauty and grace. **Organic** lines are usually irregular, and imperfect—the kind of lines you find in nature or as the result of random processes. Organic lines represent nature, movement, and elegance. **Chaotic** lines look like scribble and feel very unpredictable and frantic. They convey a sense of urgency, fear, or explosive energy (**Figure 9.13**).

  If you look at the leftmost line of these paragraphs, you can see a "line" formed by the beginning of each line of type. Pay attention to the implied lines you create using the design elements in your artwork. Think of creative ways to use and suggest lines, and pay attention to what you might be saying with them. Make sure that the message all your lines send matches the intent of your work.

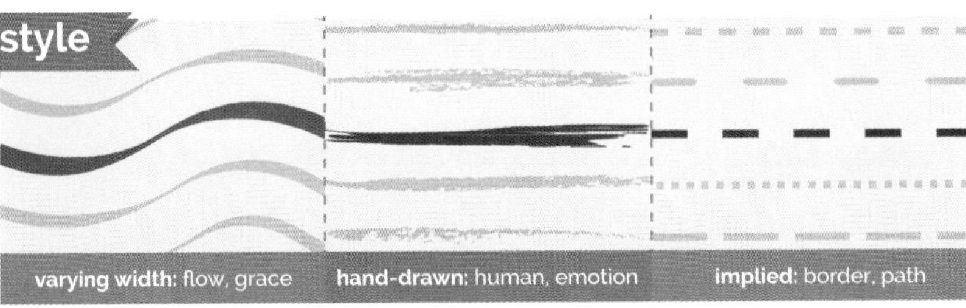

Figure 9.12 Line style

Figure 9.13 Line flow

The Element of Shape

The next element needs little introduction: Shapes are boundaries created by closed lines. **Shape** (**Figure 9.14**) can be defined as an area enclosed or defined by an outline. We're familiar with shapes such as circles, squares, and triangles, but there are many more shapes than that. Those specific shapes are created in geometry, but what about the shape of a hand or cloud? These are shapes too, and we often use the same descriptors for shapes as we do lines.

***Video 9.7** Design School: The Element of Shape*

Figure 9.14 The element of shape

COMMON SHAPE DESCRIPTORS

The next element needs little introduction: Shapes are boundaries created by closed lines. Shape (**Figure 9.15**) can be defined as an area enclosed or defined by an outline. We're familiar with shapes such as circles, squares, and triangles, but there are many more shapes than that. Those specific shapes are created in geometry, but what about the shape of a hand or cloud? These are shapes too, and we often use the same descriptors for shapes as we do lines.

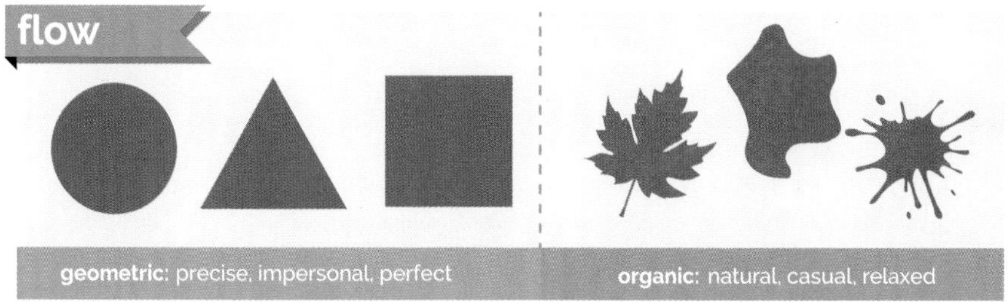

Figure 9.15 Shape flow

REPRESENTATIVE SHAPES

A **pictograph** (or **pictogram**) is a graphic symbol that represents something in the real world (**Figure 9.16**). Computer icons are pictographs that often suggest the function they represent (like a trash can icon to delete a file). Other examples of pictographs are the human silhouettes often used to indicate men's and women's restrooms. They're not *accurate* representations of the real objects, but they are *clear* representations of them. **Ideographs** (or **ideograms**) are images that represent an idea. A heart shape represents love, a lightning bolt represents electricity, or a question mark represents being puzzled. Representative shapes are helpful in communicating across language barriers and can be valuable when you are designing for multicultural and multilingual audiences.

Figure 9.16 Representative shapes

LEVEL UP: SHAPING UP!

This exercise is designed to get you experimenting with shapes. I've provided the same list of words you used to inspire line drawings.

- **Level I:** Short, long, straight, wavy, zigzag, geometric, organic
- **Level II:** Angry, lonely, worried, excited, overjoyed
- **Level III:** Opposition, contrast, politics, infinity

Draw shapes that represent these same words. Try to avoid any common representative graphics—that's too easy. Develop new shapes or just try to create shapes that seem to represent emotions or ideas that aren't normally communicated using shapes.

This is also a fun exercise to do with a friend. Have your friend pick a word for you to draw, or draw something and see how your friend describes it. You'll learn a lot about the different ways that people understand and express ideas. Remember, there are no wrong answers. Just explore, see what happens, and have fun with it.

The Element of Form

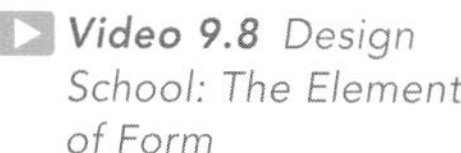
Video 9.8 Design School: The Element of Form

Form (**Figure 9.17**) describes three-dimensional objects or, at least, objects that look 3D. The best way to visualize form clearly is to consider that circles, squares, and triangles are shapes, whereas spheres, cubes, and pyramids are forms. Like shapes, forms are basically divided into geometric and organic types. Geometric forms, such as a cube, are common to us. We are also familiar with organic forms such as the human form or the form of a peanut. When you work with 3D in applications, these forms are often referred to as "solids."

Figure 9.17 Form

3D LIGHTING

In art and design, we place a special focus on the techniques that make images appear 3D in a 2D work of art. You have some standard elements to consider when you want to create a feeling of depth and form. **Figure 9.18** explains the standard elements of a 3D drawing.

- **Highlight:** The area of a form directly facing the light; appears lightest.
- **Object shadow:** The area of the form that is facing away from the light source; appears darkest.
- **Cast shadow:** The shadow cast on the ground and on any objects that are in the shadow of the form. One thing to remember is that shadows fade as they get farther from the form casting the shadow. Be sure to take this into account as you're creating shadow effects in your art.
- **Light source:** The perceived location of the lighting in relation to the form.
- **Reflected highlight:** The area of the form that is lit by reflections from the ground or other objects in the scene. This particular element of drawing a 3D object is most often ignored but provides believable lighting on the object.

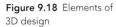

Figure 9.18 Elements of 3D design

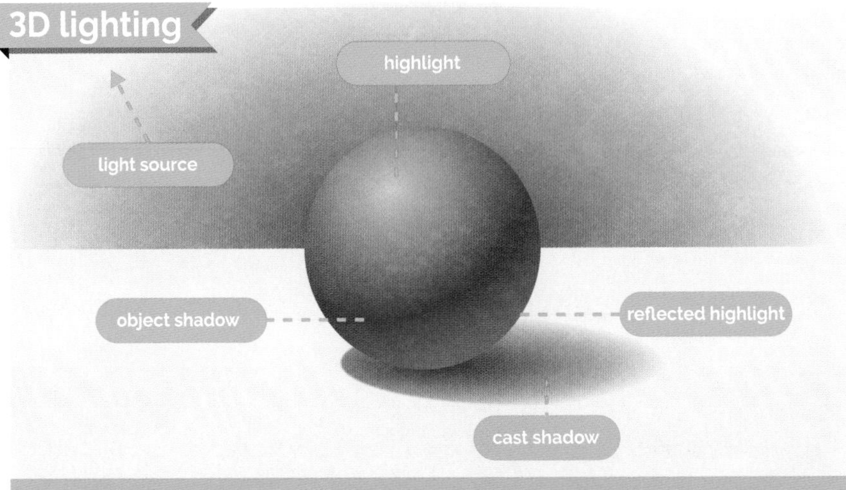

LEVEL UP: FORMING UP

This is a standard art exercise. You might ask a friend in an art class or an art teacher to help with this one, or find a tutorial online. You'll draw a sphere with lighting and shadow on a flat plane. Imagine a cue ball on a white table. Be sure to include the elements mentioned in this section and shown in the example of 3D lighting.

Your sketch might not be great. In fact, it may be horrible. If it's your first time and it looks better than you could do in kindergarten, you're doing well. Although you've got digital tools to help with this stuff, learning to draw and doodle activates a different part of your brain, and you want to wake up that part. I'm more concerned with you learning the ideas than mastering 3D drawing on paper.

Focus on learning how things *look* and how to represent them in art and design. And look at some real 3D objects in the light. Put a tennis ball on the sidewalk and just stare at it. It's amazing how much of the real world you never pay attention to! Art is more about learning to *see* than learning to draw or create.

The Elements of Pattern and Texture

Pattern (**Figure 9.19**) can be defined as a repetitive sequence of colors, shapes, or values. Pattern is technically a different concept from texture, but in graphic design it's often regarded as the same thing. Let's face it: all of our "textures" are just ink on paper or pixels. Any repetitive texture might also be considered a pattern. (Think of "diamond plate" or "tile" textures. They're just a pattern of Xs or squares.)

Video 9.9 Design School: The Elements of Pattern and Texture

Texture (**Figure 9.20**) can describe an actual, tactile texture in real objects or the appearance of texture in a 2D image. It's important to use texture to communicate feeling and authenticity in your art or designs. If you want to depict something elegant, soft, or comfortable, you could use a texture that resembles fabric or clouds. To represent strength or power, you might choose textures that represent stone or metal. And you could represent casual, informal, or nostalgic feelings using a texture that represents weathered wood or worn paint.

As you work more as a designer, you'll start to notice the nuances and subtle differences between textures and patterns. For now, just think of them as the visual qualities of your shapes and forms that can't be described by color and/or value alone.

Figure 9.19 Pattern and texture

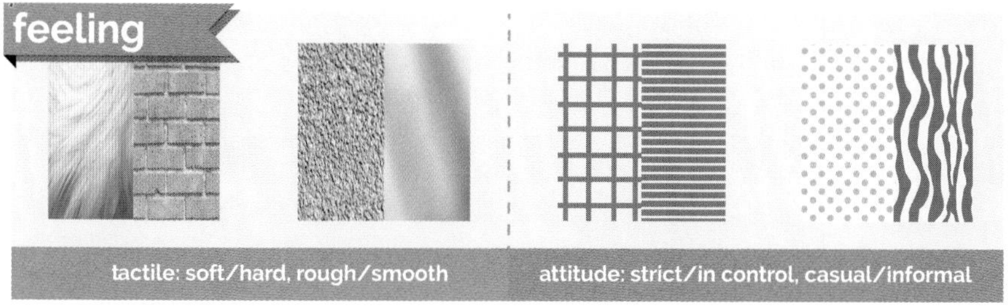

Figure 9.20 Texture and feeling

LEVEL UP: TEXTURE TANGLE

Texture is a valuable design tool. The goal of this exercise is to experiment with texture and patterns. Remember that it takes practice to create things on paper the way you visualize them in your head, but that's the life of an artist. It's never perfect; it's just art.

1 Grab a sheet of paper and a fine point pen.
2 Draw a line that crosses over itself at least once, forming a loop that goes from one edge of the paper to another. That loop is your first "texture pit."
3 In that loop, create a texture by just repeating a pattern.
4 Create another area and fill it with a different pattern or texture.

That's it! When your paper is full, you have leveled up.

- **Level I:** Use only geometric textures and patterns.
- **Level II:** Attempt to create areas that look like textures of materials, plants, or animals. You might need to switch to pencil to be able to shade the areas well.
- **Level III:** Introduce color. Try adding color to your designs and see how that works.

The Element of Value

Video 9.10 Design School: The Element of Value

Value (**Figure 9.21**) describes the lightness or darkness of an object. Together with color, value represents all of the visible spectrum. You can think of value as a gradient that goes from black to white. But remember that value applies to color as well, and you can have a spectrum that fades from black, through a color, and then to white. This also introduces the idea of a "red black" or a "blue black" that introduces a hint of color to your blacks. You'll explore that concept later in this chapter.

value
Values range from light to dark through gray and through all colors.

Figure 9.21 Value

Professionals in the art and design industry often use the term value, but clients rarely use it. Clients will just ask you to lighten or darken a graphic or text, or sometimes use tint, shade, or tone in place of value. Technically, these terms are different, but many people use tone, shade, tint, and value interchangeably. As always, when clients use a term and you're not exactly sure what they mean, ask for clarification. Sometimes clients don't know exactly what they mean, so asking ensures that everyone is on the same page.

The Element of Color

★ *ACA Objective 2.4*

Video 9.11 *Design School: The Element of Color*

When you think about it, **color** is hard to define. How would you define color without using examples of colors? Check out its definition in a dictionary and you'll find that defining color doesn't help you understand it. Color is best *experienced* and *explored*.

We have so many ways to think about color and so many concepts to dig into that exploring color is a lifelong pursuit for most artists and designers. Color theory is

LEVEL UP: VALUE VISION

Value is an interesting element to work with, and you've already experimented with it. Remember the "Forming Up" sidebar? That was a great exercise in controlling your pencil to draw a believable sphere. Honestly, there's no better exercise for learning to control your pencil and properly use value than to create 3D forms. But this experiment is going to take you a little further.

Pencils afford you the ability to create different values pretty easily, but what about a pen?

The challenge is to create a set of values while experimenting with monochromatic (no gray) textures. Learn about hatching, cross-hatching, and stippling, all created using a fine point marker. I prefer to use the thin-line Sharpies or an ultra-fine roller ball (.05 or less). Experiment with making different values using purely black and white duotone (no gray) methods.

- **Level I:** Create three levels of gray across a spectrum.
- **Level II:** Generate seven layers of gray across a gradient using mixed methods.
- **Level III:** Generate a 3D sphere using purely duotone methods.

a deep and complex study. You'll explore the basics here, but remember that this is just the on-ramp to understanding color. Grasp these concepts and you'll still have a lot more to learn.

Color psychology is a relatively new discipline and an interesting study that focuses on the emotional and behavioral effects that colors have on people. The colors you choose really do matter. For our purposes, we'll define color as the perceived hue, lightness, and saturation of an object or light.

HOW COLOR WORKS

Color is created in two ways: combining light to create additive color and subtracting light to create subtractive color (**Figure 9.22**). In Photoshop, the color mode you select will define how the color is created.

Additive color is created by combining light. This is how your monitor works, and the most common color mode for additive color is RGB. The letters RGB stand for red, green, blue, which are the three colors used to create digital images. Monitors and electronic devices are dark when turned off, and you create colors by adding light to the screen.

Subtractive color is created by subtracting light. This is the color system you learned in early art classes in which red, blue, and yellow were the primary colors. For print, we use CMYK, which is cyan, magenta, yellow, and black. We start with a white surface (the paper) that reflects all the light back to us. Then we subtract color by using paints or inks that limit the light that is reflected back to the viewer.

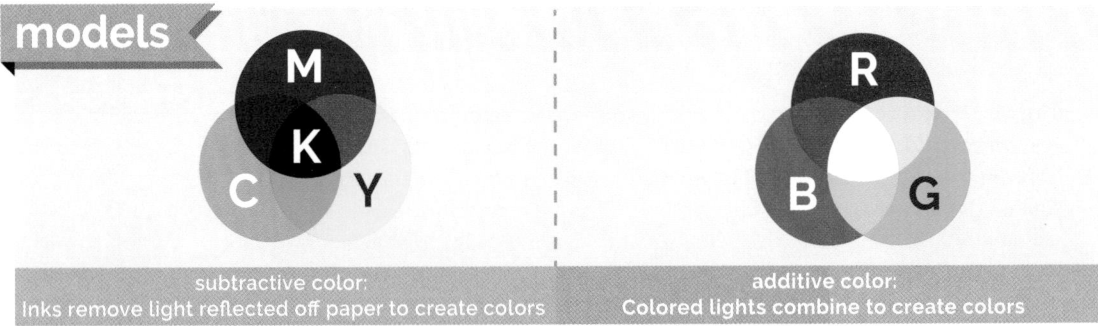

Figure 9.22 Subtractive and additive color

THE COLOR WHEEL

Sir Isaac Newton first invented the color wheel (**Figure 9.23**) in the mid-17th century. The color wheel offers a way to display and build all the colors possible using paint. It's a common exercise in beginning art classes to create a color wheel when learning to mix and experiment with colors. In digital imaging, it's not as important to go through this exercise, but if you have a chance, give it a try. It's interesting to see how all of the colors can mix to obtain the infinite colors and shades the human eye can perceive.

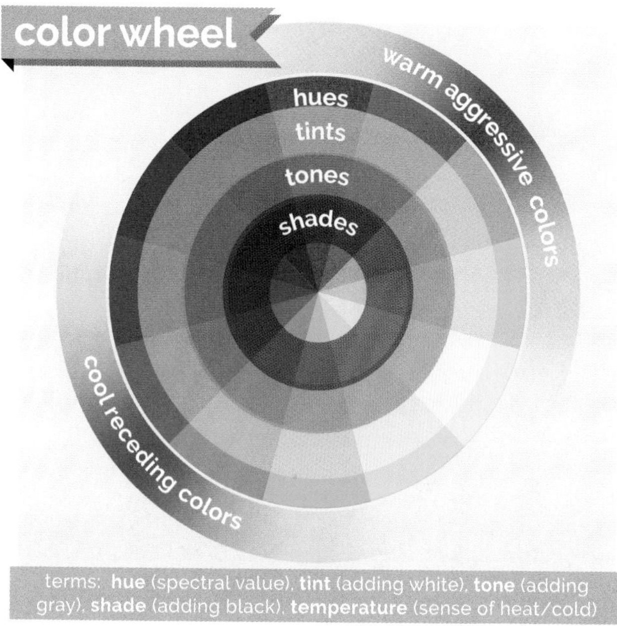

Figure 9.23 The color wheel

The color wheel is important because many color theories we use are named after their relative positions on the color wheel. They're a lot easier to remember if we use the color wheel to illustrate.

The first thing to realize is that some colors are classified as **primary colors**. These colors can be combined to create every other color in the visible spectrum. For subtractive color used in traditional art, the primary colors are red, blue, and yellow. For additive colors, the primary colors are red, blue, and green.

The colors that are created when you combine primary colors are called **secondary colors** because you can create them only by applying a second step of mixing the colors. When we mix secondary and primary colors, we get another set of colors known as **tertiary colors**. **Figure 9.24** illustrates how these colors are built.

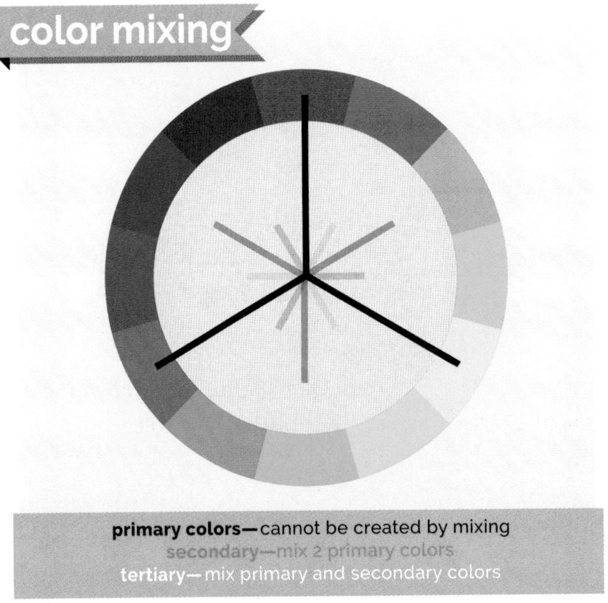

color mixing
primary colors—cannot be created by mixing
secondary—mix 2 primary colors
tertiary—mix primary and secondary colors

Figure 9.24 How secondary and tertiary colors are built

LEVEL UP: ROLLIN' WITH COLOR

Creating a color wheel is a staple project in art classes. Any experienced traditional artist or art teacher can help you with this task. You can find a ton of information about this online, but this is a valuable project to help you get in touch with color and understand how colors are related.

- **Level I:** Create a traditional color wheel using paint on paper.
- **Level II:** Create a CMYK color wheel in Photoshop.

BASIC COLOR RULES

Color rules (also called **color harmonies**) are a great way to start picking colors for your design projects. The color rules (**Figure 9.25**) are all named for their relative locations on the color wheel. When you're choosing colors and exploring other

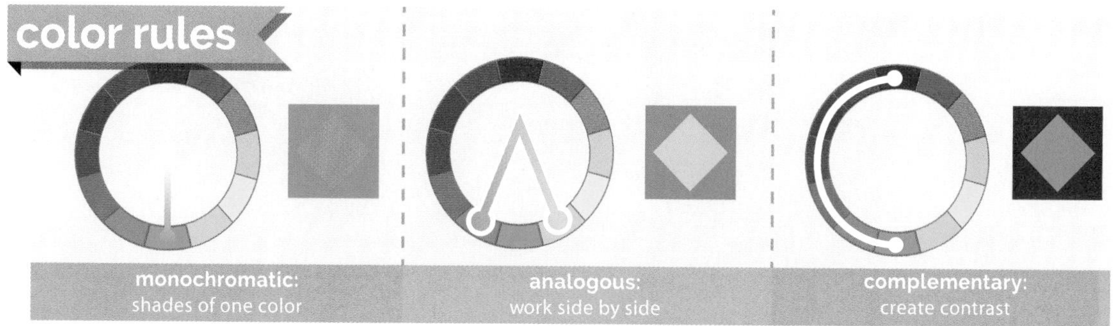

Figure 9.25 Color rules

ways to join colors to create contrast or harmony, these color rules are where you should begin. We're going to cover some of the basic color rules and the impressions they tend to communicate.

The three most common ways of thinking about colors (and, really, the basis of all color rules) are monochromatic, analogous, and complementary color schemes.

- **Monochromatic:** Monochromatic colors, as you've probably guessed, are based only on different shades and tints of the same color. They tend to communicate a relaxed and peaceful feeling, and you'll create little contrast or energy in art using these colors.
- **Analogous:** If you want to add a little more variation while maintaining a calm feeling, consider analogous colors. Analogous colors sit side by side on the color wheel, and they tend to create gentle and relaxing color schemes. Analogous colors don't usually stand out from each other; they seem to work together and can almost disappear together when overlaid.
- **Complementary:** Complementary colors are opposite each other on the color wheel. Complementary color combinations are high in contrast and normally very vibrant, so use with caution. When overused, complementary color can be very "loud" and can easily cross over into visually obnoxious if you're not careful. You can remember this rule with the alliterative phrase "Complementary colors create contrast."

If you want to explore color combinations, visit *http://color.adobe.com* and explore the Adobe Color CC website (**Figure 9.26**). It's an amazing way to browse other people's color collections, or grab colors from an image you like and create a color set to use for your projects. When you register with your free Adobe ID, you can save the color themes you find or create and bring them into your Adobe apps to use and share with others.

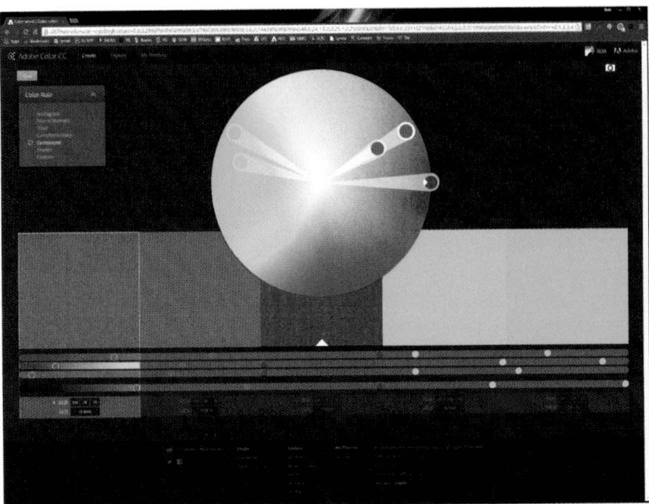

Figure 9.26 Use the Adobe Color CC website to explore color harmonies and save combinations to your Creative Cloud account.

Figure 9.27 The Adobe Capture app lets you capture colors from photos you've taken or grab them live using the camera.

Adobe Color is also part of a free app for iOS and Android. Open the Adobe Capture CC app (**Figure 9.27**) and select Colors, open an image or point your phone camera at something, and create a color theme. Experiment with creating custom themes from your favorite blanket, a sunset, your goldfish, or your crazy uncle's tie-dyed concert shirt from Woodstock.

COLOR ASSOCIATIONS

We tend to associate different things with different colors. Whether this is learned behavior or instinct can be debated. But as a designer you must learn to recognize and properly use the right color for the right message. Again, this isn't a science, and you'll need to consider more than this chart when developing your color-picking strategies. But understanding colors and their associations (**Figure 9.28**) can be useful to produce the right "feel" in your images. You can evoke interesting feelings and contrasts by capitalizing on these associations in your interactive design work.

Figure 9.28 Color associations

The Element of Type

Type (**Figure 9.29**) is generally not considered a traditional element of art, but it can be a critical part of your work as a designer. Typefaces carry a lot of emotional meaning, and choosing the proper typefaces for a job is a skill that every designer needs (yet many don't have). Like color, this area of design is so deep and has so many aspects that entire books and college courses are focused only on typography. We can't reduce it to simple rules such as "Use three typefaces, maximum. When in doubt use Helvetica. And never use Chiller." (Even though that's not a bad starting point!)

Figure 9.29 The element of type

★ *ACA Objective 2.3*

Video 9.12 *Design School: The Element of Type*

Working with type is often like being a marriage counselor or matchmaker. Every typeface has a personality and you need to carefully match the type in your design work so it has a compatible relationship with the overall feeling of the piece. The typefaces you use also need to work together. It takes time and experience to master this balance, but over time you can become a skillful typeface matchmaker. Most artists have a few fonts they tend to lean on heavily, and that's okay—especially at the beginning.

TIP
Check online at www.brainbuffet.com/design/typography for a list of fonts and typography-based resources to help you dig a little deeper with this concept.

LEVEL UP: PUZZLING TYPOGRAPHY

A popular jigsaw puzzle style right now (often available in bookstores) has a strong typographic focus that lists "Family Rules" or "Life Lessons" in various fonts. However, any puzzle with lots of larger text in multiple typefaces will work great. As you're doing the puzzle, notice the subtle differences between fonts and the letterforms of each font. You'll learn to pay attention to the subtle differences between the different styles of type.

- **Level I:** Do a puzzle like this with a group of friends and discuss your observations.
- **Level II:** Do a puzzle like this by yourself.

TYPOGRAPHY

Typography is the art of using letterforms and type arrangement to help the language communicate a message. As mentioned earlier, type can be its own topic of study and can easily get overwhelming. We'll skim the surface here but hope that as you move forward in your design, you'll dig a little deeper. Let's get some vocabulary out of the way first.

Technically, a **typeface** (**Figure 9.30**) is the letterform set that makes up the type. Helvetica, Arial, Garamond, and Chiller are examples of typefaces. In brief, it's the "look" of the letters. **Fonts** are the whole collection of the typeface in each of its sizes and styles. So 12 pt. Arial Narrow and 12 pt. Arial Bold are different *fonts* of the same *typeface*. The same is true for two different sizes of the same typeface.

Figure 9.30 Many of today's typography terms were created in the days of movable type and have changed as publishing technology has evolved.

From now on, let's use the term font, because that's also the name of the file you'll install when you add typefaces to your computer, and it's the most common term. Few people will bother splitting hairs in these differences that really don't exist anymore for computer-generated type.

TYPE CLASSIFICATIONS

There are many different ways to classify typefaces, but we'll rely on the Adobe Typekit classifications for the purpose of this chapter. Generally, people divide fonts into two main categories of type that should be used for large areas of type: serif and sans-serif (**Figure 9.31**).

- **Serif fonts** are often associated with typewritten documents and most printed books. Generally, serif fonts are considered to be easier to read in larger paragraphs of text. Because so many books use serif fonts and early typewriters produced them, serif text often feels a bit more traditional, intelligent, and classy.
- **Sans serif fonts** do not include serifs. "Sans" is a French word that migrated to English and simply means "without." Sans serif fonts are often used for headlines and titles for their strong, stable, modern feel. Sans serif fonts are also preferred for large areas of text for reading on websites and screen reading.

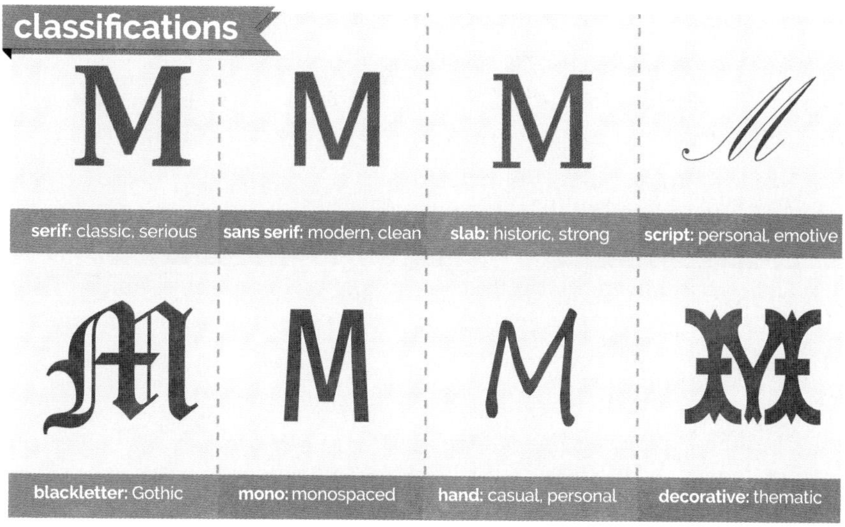

Figure 9.31 Serif and sans serif fonts

Beyond these basic types of text we use in our documents, designers use other typefaces that are not appropriate for large areas of type because they're not easy to read in a long paragraph. Most designers consider the following fonts to be "decorative" for that reason.

- **Slab serif fonts** (also called Egyptian, block serif, or square serif) are a more squared-off version of a typical serif font. These fonts bridge the gap between serif and sans serif fonts and generally feel a bit more machine-built. The simple design tends to make them feel a bit rougher than their serif counterparts.
- **Script fonts** (also called formal or calligraphical) have an elegant feeling. These fonts are great to use for invitations to formal events, such as weddings, and in designs where you want to convey a feeling of beauty, grace, and/or feminine dignity. If you are designing for a spa, for a beauty shop, or for products or services, script fonts will carry a feeling of relaxed and elegant beauty.
- **Blackletter fonts** (also called old English, Gothic, or textura) feature an overly ornate style and are often used to title formal documents such as certificates, diplomas, or degrees, as well as old German Bibles and heavy metal bands. It conveys a feeling of rich and sophisticated gravitas, often hinting at a long history of tradition and reliability.
- **Monospaced fonts** (also called fixed-width or nonproportional) use the same amount of horizontal space for each letter. Typically, fonts use a variable spacing technique called kerning. (You'll learn more about kerning later in this chapter.) Monospaced fonts, in contrast, use the same width for every character. Monospaced fonts are good to use when you're trying to make something look impersonal, machine-generated, or retro-geeky because typewriters and early computers used monospaced fonts.
- **Handwritten fonts** (also called hand fonts) simulate handwriting. They are popular for adding a personalized, casual, or human touch to your designs and are often used on junk mail to try to trick you into opening that "Special limited time offer just for you!" (don't fall for it). Handwritten fonts are prefect for communicating casual and friendly feelings, but they can be tough to read in a larger block of text.
- **Decorative fonts** (also called ornamental, novelty, or display) don't fall into any of the other categories. They also tend to convey specific feelings. Decorative fonts should be used sparingly and very intentionally. Never use a novelty font just because you think it looks cool; that's a typical newbie move. Make sure you are striving to convey something very specific when using decorative fonts.

TIP

Want to create a font based on your own handwriting? Go to www.myscriptfont.com to create a font from your handwriting for free.

- **Dingbat fonts** (also called wingdings) are a special type of font that doesn't have an alphabet but instead consists of a collection of shapes or objects.

NOTE

Each character of a font, whether it's a letter, number, symbol, or swash, is called a ***glyph****.*

TYPE TALK

You'll need to learn a lot of jargon concerning type when working in the design industry. Some of it is commonly used in discussion about design, and some of it will help you discuss fonts when you're trying to find the perfect typeface for your design.

TYPOGRAPHIC ANATOMY

Figure 9.32 illustrates many of the anatomical terms used when discussing typography. Software has no settings for these options, so we won't go into detail about them. When you start to study typography and learn these terms, you will more easily discern the differences between typefaces. It's easiest to understand these terms by simply looking at the illustration. You will hear these terms in the industry, and when you're looking for a specific font, knowing these terms will allow you to more easily describe what you're looking for. Let's face it: you can't get too far professionally if you're always using words like "doohickey" and "little hangy-downy thingy." These terms are descriptive like ascenders and descenders; anthropomorphic like arms, shoulders, and tails; or architectural like counters and finials.

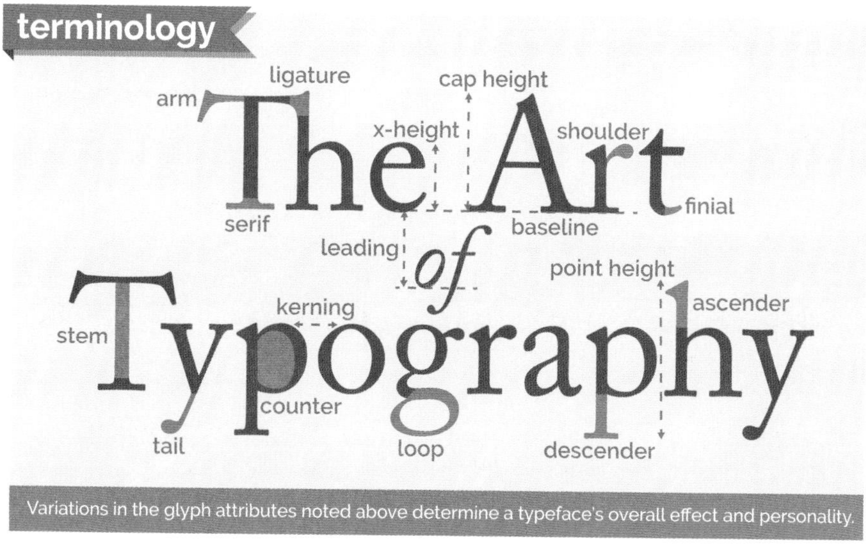

Figure 9.32 Many key typographical terms are illustrated in this image.

THE HOLY TRINITY OF TYPOGRAPHY

Three main concepts of typography exist: kerning, leading, and tracking, known as "The Holy Trinity of Design" (**Figure 9.33**). As a designer, you need to master these concepts. The terms defined here affect the ways that the letters are spaced from each other vertically or horizontally.

- **Kerning** is the space between specific letter pairs. For example, the first two letters in the word "Too" are closer than the first two letters in the word "The" because the letter "o" can tuck under the crossbar of the "T." A high-quality font file will have a good set of kerning pairs for specific letter combinations, but for some professional work (and with poorly designed fonts) you might need to get in there and tweak the kerning. Adjusting the kerning between specific letters can help you perfect your type presentation in logos and headlines.
- **Tracking** is the overall space between all the letters in a block of text. It allows you to compress or expand the space between the letters as a whole, rather than just between specific pairs as you do with kerning. Adjusting tracking can greatly affect the feeling that text conveys. Experiment with tracking to help create various feelings in headlines and titles.
- **Leading** is the amount of space between the baselines of two lines of text. The **baseline** is the imaginary line that text sits on. Whereas word processing applications tend to limit you to single and double-line spacing, professional design software lets you manipulate the leading to set a specific distance between multiple lines of text. Doing so can create great-looking space in a design or even overlap with your paragraph text. Experiment with this option in your work. You can change the mood of text by adjusting only the leading of a paragraph.

Figure 9.33 Kerning, tracking, and leading

SIZE, SCALE, AND SMALL CAPS

The terms that appear in **Figure 9.34** are available in the character panel of the interface for most Adobe design applications. However, even though Premiere Pro does not include certain aspects discussed here, you should still familiarize yourself with them.

- **Type size** is traditionally the height from the highest ascender to the lowest descender in a font, expressed in **points** (1/72 of an inch). Today, it's more of a guideline than a firm definition, so most designers set the appropriate type size by eye. Different fonts of the same point size can appear to be much different in physical size if the ascenders and descenders are different from each other.
- **Vertical** and **horizontal scale** are terms that describe the function of stretching letters and distorting the typeface geometry. Because they distort the typeface, use them with caution. They should be used only when you are trying to express a specific feeling and should not be used in blocks of type because readability can suffer with either of these adjustments.
- **All caps** and **small caps** are similar in that they both use only the uppercase letterforms for each letter, but **ALL CAPS** makes all the letters the same size, whereas SMALL CAPS sets the letters that would normally be capitalized at a larger size. Small caps tend to increase readability compared to all caps, but both cap formats should be avoided in large blocks of text because they are more difficult to read than standard text.
- **Ligatures** and **swashes** are special alternative settings offered with some fonts to combine letters or add stylized touches to certain letter combinations or letters. For example, when the "Th" combination touches in a headline, you can replace it with a single ligature that looks much better. Swashes add flowing and elegant endings to letters with ascenders and descenders. Both of these are normally reserved for type that is expressing an especially elegant or artistic feel.

TIP

Higher-end typefaces may provide a small caps face that is much nicer than using the setting in software. If this is critical for your design, look for a font that supports this feature.

NOTE

The settings for ligatures and swashes are available in the OpenType panel of most Adobe design apps but not in the character panel. These rarely used features can lend creative expression to fonts that support it.

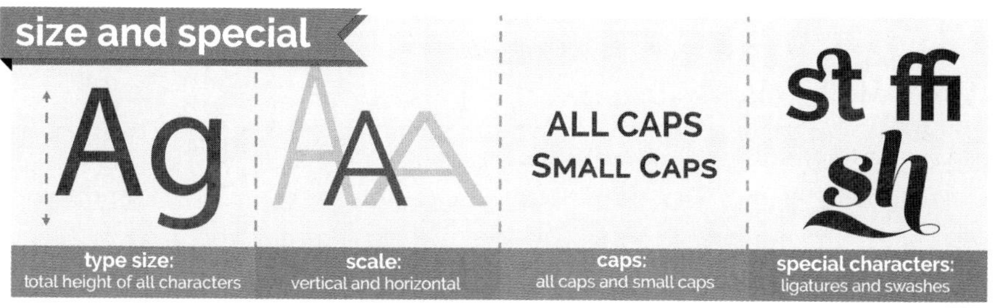

Figure 9.34 Size and special characters

LEVEL UP: GAMES OF A CERTAIN TYPE

You can find a lot of great online resources for exploring typography, and you can also find some that are not that great but are worth visiting at least once or twice. A frequently updated list of typographic resources is available at *www.brainbuffet.com/design/typography*, and we hope you'll take the time to explore some of them to dig a little deeper into your understanding of type and typography.

- **Level I:** Experiment with at least three typographic games online.
- **Level II:** Achieve a high score on at least one typographic game online.
- **Level III:** Achieve a high score on five or more typographic games online.

PARAGRAPH SETTINGS

Paragraph settings affect an entire paragraph, rather than selected words (**Figure 9.35**). These options adjust the **alignment** of the paragraph: left, centered, or right. **Justified** text aligns a straight edge on both edges of the paragraph with the ability to dictate how the last line is aligned. **Indent** settings let you choose how far the entire paragraph is indented on each side or in just its first line. **Paragraph spacing** settings are similar to leading, but apply to paragraphs—instead of lines of type within them—and you also can set the space above or below paragraphs. **Hyphenation** allows you to determine if and when words should be split with hyphenation.

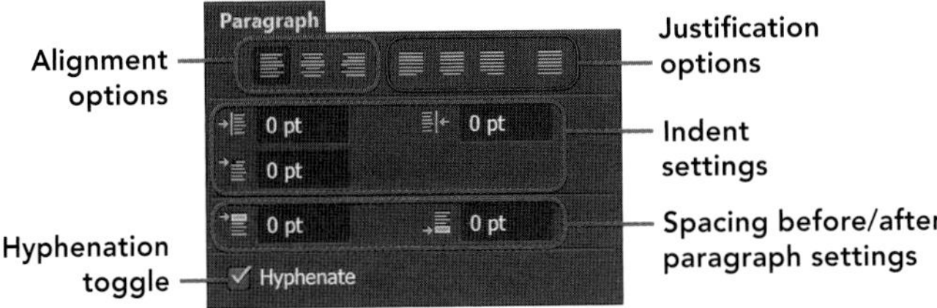

Figure 9.35 The icons for the paragraph settings are quite helpful in illustrating the function of each setting.

Wrapping Up the Elements

As you've seen in this chapter, the elements are the building blocks or the raw materials of design. But what turns these elements into art is applying the principles of design to the way you arrange these elements on your workspace. In the next section, you'll explore these principles, which are a framework that help you arrange your work in an artistic way.

The Principles of Design

Much like the elements of design, different artists and schools of thought will generate different ideas about what makes up the principles of design (**Figure 9.36**). For a young artist, this can be frustrating. Sometimes you just want someone to tell you the answer.

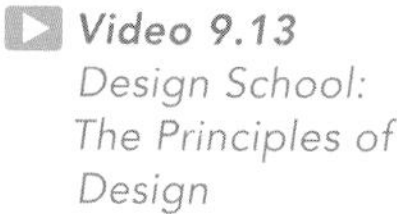

Video 9.13
Design School: The Principles of Design

Figure 9.36 Principles of design

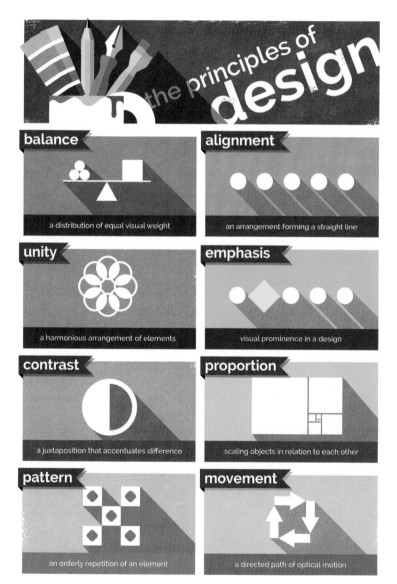

But after you understand the principles, you'll appreciate that no one can point to a universal list of artistic principles. If there's no correct answer, there's also no *wrong* answer either. Creatively, you always have another way to approach your art, and becoming an artist doesn't mean that you learn to see any one approach. Becoming an artist means that you learn to *see*.

Until you explore **design principles**, you will not be ready to understand them. Therefore, definitions are not as helpful as hands-on work. But truly grasping the principles and experiencing them is the only way to grow as an artist. This is the beginning of a lifelong exploration of beauty and creativity.

The bottom line is this: Don't get hung up on names or descriptions. Try to engage with each idea as a loosely formed concept that remains fluid and flexible rather than defining boundaries. By studying principles, you're trying to do just the opposite—moving in directions that have no boundaries. The goal of all good art and design is to explore new ways to use the elements and principles, and not to repeat what's been done in the past. You'll examine these principles to start your understanding of something, not to limit it.

The Principles of Emphasis or Focal Point

Video 9.14 *Design School: The Principle of Emphasis*

Emphasis (**Figure 9.37**) describes the focal point to which the eye is naturally and initially drawn in a design. Some art has a focus that's obvious. Most marketing and advertising is that way. Other art invites you to step in and explore. It might encourage an exploration of color or texture, but it has no specific point other than the color or texture.

Figure 9.37 Emphasis creates the focal point—a place where the eye is naturally drawn when encountering the image. Use this to your advantage when designing.

Think of emphasis as the main point or primary idea in a piece of art. You can move the viewer's eye to a specific point in the design by making something *different*. You can easily find examples right on the pages of this book. Chapter headings are larger than the rest of the type. Glossary terms are a different color. Even the simple process of *italicizing* words or putting them in **boldface** makes text stand out. The human eye is naturally drawn to unique things. So if you want to make something stand out, make it different.

Careful use of contrast is critical to master because a typical design newbie tries to make everything special and unique. As a result, nothing stands out. The design looks *random*, not cool. Give a piece some unity, and it will feel right. You can then emphasize what's truly important.

The Principle of Contrast

Video 9.15 *Design School: The Principle of Contrast*

Contrast generally creates visual interest and a focal point in a composition. If you think about it, a blank canvas is a canvas with no contrast. As soon as you begin to alter the surface and create contrast, you also start to create a focus. The principle of contrast can be defined as a difference in the qualities of the elements in an image. To use contrast is to create something different from the surrounding pieces of the composition.

Many artists limit their understanding of contrast by confining it to color or value. But contrast is much more than that. Any difference between one thing and another creates contrast. You can have contrast in size, texture, value, color, or any of the defining characteristics you learned about in exploring the elements.

The most important thing to remember about contrast is that all contrast creates some emphasis, and if you have too much emphasis, you will have no focal point.

The Principle of Unity

Video 9.16 *Design School: The Principle of Unity*

Unity generally communicates calm, peaceful, or cool feelings in your art. The principle of unity (also called harmony) requires that the things that go together should *look* like they belong together (**Figure 9.38**). The elements in your design should feel like a family. This doesn't necessarily mean that everything needs to be the same—just that they should share some similar traits. When you have no unity, you can have no focal point and, therefore, no emphasis.

Figure 9.38 The similar lines, colors, and even values of this image give it a unified feeling.

Note the headings of the different sections in this chapter. They make it easy to find the content you are looking for when skimming the book. Even the breaks between paragraphs help distinguish one concept from another. But all of the words in this paragraph belong together because they share a unity of typeface, spacing, color, and so on.

Unity is important in your compositions so that when you create contrast it draws the viewer's eye where you want it to go. In design, more than in art, we are interested in guiding a viewer's perceptions. Design generally tends to be much more intentional than art. Both are important, however, and beginning with design can make your experimentation with artistic elements and principles much more effective and productive.

The Principle of Variety

▶ *Video 9.17 Design School: The Principle of Variety*

Variety tends to communicate energy, heat, and high emotion in a design. When applying the principle of variety, you use different elements in an image to create visual interest. In many ways, it is the exact opposite of unity. You can think of unity and variety as being at the opposite ends of contrast. Unity is establishing a low degree of contrast in a composition. Variety does the opposite and brings a higher amount of contrast to the composition.

Variety is a principle that normally needs to be used sparingly. Too much variety quickly moves your art from interesting to chaotic and disorganized (**Figure 9.39**). Beginning artists and designers sometimes have a hard time properly using variety. They get a little bit carried away and lose all sense of focus or unity. Beware of that tendency!

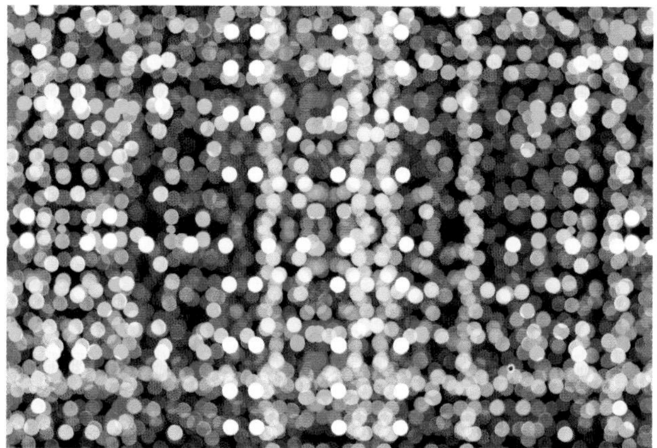

Figure 9.39 When everything is different in an image like these colored lights are, nothing stands out.

The Principle of Balance

Balance suggests the arrangement of things in an image should not be evenly distributed. This is not to say that everything should be centered, and that placing something in the top right means you should mirror it with something similar in the top left. That's how a nondesigner lays out a composition. Experienced artists learn to properly balance all of the elements—including space—in their compositions.

Video 9.18 Design School: The Principle of Balance

Balance comes in many forms: symmetrical, asymmetrical, or radial.

- **Symmetrical**: Symmetrical balance is what most students latch on to at first. It occurs when you can divide an image along its middle and the left side of the image is a mirror image of its right (or the top reflects the bottom). Using a seesaw analogy, a symmetrical balance would have two equally sized people equally distant from the fulcrum. This is the easiest balance to execute, but it conveys a very intentional, formal, and mechanical feeling.
- **Asymmetrical**: Asymmetrical balance (**Figure 9.40**) achieves balance with different elements on each side (or the top and bottom) of an image. Imagine an adult on a seesaw with a child. They can balance, but only if the adult is closer to the fulcrum and the child is farther away. To achieve asymmetrical balance, you need to use space to counterbalance the different weights on each side.

TIP

Many artists and designers characterize pieces that are out of balance as "leaning to the left," "leaning to the right," or "top-heavy." Over time, you'll develop these feelings too and be able to spot when art seems like it might physically tip over.

Figure 9.40 This image, though asymmetrical, is well balanced. The bright sun is offset by the visual weight of the rocks in the lower right.

- Radial: Radial balance (**Figure 9.41**) is a circular type of balance that radiates from the center instead of the middle of a design. Many artists get the feeling that they're viewing a radially balanced image from above. This kind of balance is almost always circular. An excellent example of radial balance is a kaleidoscopic image, which can feel balanced and unified but also typically feels more static than the other types of balance.

Figure 9.41 This image has a radial balance.

The Principle of Proportion or Scale

Proportion, sometimes called **scale**, describes the relative sizes and scale of things. If you've ever seen a drawing and observed that "the head is too small" or "the body is too fat," you're evaluating the proportion. It's simply the sense that things seem to be the proper size relative to each other.

Video 9.19 Design School: The Principle of Proportion or Scale

You can manipulate proportion and scale to create emphasis. Things that are larger than they should be appear stronger, more important, or more powerful. Take the chapter headings in this book. By making the headings disproportionately large, we've indicated importance and emphasis. You can also reduce the perceived value, strength, or importance of something by reducing its scale.

The Principles of Repetition and Pattern

The two principles of **repetition** and **pattern**—along with movement and rhythm—seem to be the most confusing and difficult to grasp. As a matter of fact, some artists and writers more readily connect pattern and repetition with rhythm than with movement. In this introductory look at these concepts, think about the simplest and most concrete uses of them here. As always, you're encouraged to explore these areas much more deeply on your own.

Video 9.20 Design School: The Principles of Repetition and Pattern

Repetition is a principle that is pretty easy to grasp: repeating an element in your design. Repetition can convey many things, but it often represents importance, movement, or energy. Think of an illustration of a ball moving or a cartoon of a bird flapping its wings. Just repeating a few lines can convey a sense of motion.

Pattern happens when different objects repeat in a sequence. The best way to think about the difference between repetition and pattern is that repetition is done with a single element (such as pinstripes on a suit), whereas pattern happens with a collection of elements (such as a floral pattern on fabric). Pattern also happens when elements are repeated consistently and, at some point, eventually move past repetition and become a pattern.

Another important way to think about repetition is to share certain traits of the elements in your design. Doing so brings some unity to those elements and lets the viewer know they're related. For example, you could repeat the colors of the logo in headers and bold type or repeat the same colors from a photo into the header text of an associated article in a magazine. Repetition of this kind conveys a sense of unity in the design.

The Principles of Movement and Rhythm

▶ *Video 9.21*
Design School: The Principles of Movement and Rhythm

Movement and **rhythm** are similar, much like repetition and pattern. They modify an image much the way an adverb modifies an adjective. They explain a feeling that the elements create, rather than making specific changes to the elements.

Movement refers to the visual movement in an image. Depending on the context, it can refer to the movement the eye naturally follows across an image as it moves from focal point to focal point, or the perceived movement or flow of the elements in the image.

Movement can also refer to the "flow" of an image, and is a critical principle to consider in your work. It's more of a feeling than a concrete visual aspect of your design. When something "doesn't feel right," it may be that the flow is uncertain or contradictory. If you haven't considered the flow of your design, analyze it and create a flow that guides the viewer through your design. The more linear your flow, the more your design will convey a sense of reliability, consistency, and calm. A more complex flow can convey a sense of creativity, freedom, or even chaos.

Rhythm refers to the visual "beat" in the design, a sense of an irregular but predictable pattern. Just as a rhythm is laid down by a drummer, a design's rhythm is creative and expressive, rather than a consistent pattern or repetition. Depending on the design you're working on, rhythm may or may not be a critical principle to consider. A predictable rhythm can convey a sense of calm and consistency, whereas an erratic or complex rhythm can convey a sense of urgency or energy.

These two principles tend to be the most subjective, so be sure to clarify anything you're unsure about when discussing these principles with a client. Because they're more of a feeling than a specific element or technique, it takes a little experience to get a handle on them. But these are just like all of the principles: once you start looking for them, you'll start to see them.

Wrapping Up the Design Concepts

As a visual designer, you must understand the elements and principles so that your work can communicate clearly to your audience. Learning the technical basics of Photoshop is fairly easy, and they can be mastered by people who will never "make it" in the industry.

Video 9.22 *Design School: Wrapping Up Design School*

Take the time to develop your design skills set and to remember that it *is* a skills set. You've got to practice and continue to develop your craft to level up those skills. Using Photoshop without having a design sense is like starting up a jet engine without the jet. It's powerful, but you won't be able to fly it to a destination. The artistic elements and principles are the wings and controls that let you harness that power and get your art to go where you want it.

Invest the time and effort to practice and refine your design sense. You'll find that your personal art not only grows more impressive over time, but that the entire world opens up and becomes much more interesting, beautiful, and detailed.

Photoshop is about learning to create visual designs with exceptionally high quality and detail, but becoming an artist and refining your skills is about learning to *see*.

Open your eyes… and enjoy the beauty you've been missing that's all around you!

> **TIP** *Connect with us at www.brainbuffet.com/design to see our ever-growing collection of design-related resources or follow us on twitter @brainbuffet for weekly resources, inspiration, and freebies to use with your design projects.*

CHAPTER OBJECTIVES

Chapter Learning Objectives

- Understand your client's needs.
- Familiarize yourself with copyright and licensing basics.
- Explore project management.
- Avoid project creep.

Chapter ACA Objectives

DOMAIN 1.0
SETTING PROJECT REQUIREMENTS

1.1 Identify the purpose, audience, and audience needs for preparing images.

1.2 Summarize how designers make decisions about the type of content to include in a project, including considerations such as copyright, project fit, permissions, and licensing.

1.3 Demonstrate knowledge of project management tasks and responsibilities.

1.4 Communicate with others (such as peers and clients) about design plans.

DOMAIN 2.0
UNDERSTANDING DIGITAL IMAGES

2.2 Demonstrate knowledge of basic design principles and best practices employed in the visual design industry.

CHAPTER 10

Working with Outsiders

As a visual designer, you're going to work with others. Being a designer and being an artist are two different careers, but most people who do creative work for a living find a need to do both. It's similar to the way a lot of photographers shoot weddings to pay the bills. It may not be their favorite type of photography, but it pays well and makes people happy. However, if you love to shoot old, crumbly walls and rusty farmhouse doors, you will find that you simply can't pay the bills with your "rusty hinge" photo collection.

Aside from the money, you will probably learn to develop an immense passion for creating designs for others. The secret to this part of the job is twofold: really listen and really care.

Video 10.1
Introduction to Project Planning

Who You're Talking For and Who You're Talking To

★ *ACA Objective 1.1*

The first step in designing for a particular project is to understand the client's needs. This is critical because, among other things, the client pays the bills. Most of all, the client is hiring you to speak for them. As a visual designer, that's a weighty responsibility. You're being trusted to communicate for an entire company or cause. First and foremost, you need to address that client's needs and goals for the project. This will be the guiding principle when answering design questions. You must constantly remember your goals and focus narrowly on them to streamline your workflow and minimize distractions.

Let's look at a few example scenarios:

- Rockin' Zombies is a metal-opera-jazz-bluegrass fusion band that wants to promote an upcoming free concert at the local farmer's market.
- Hoi Polloi Church needs a brochure for their project to solicit volunteers and donations to help orphaned children recover from Hurricane Sally.
- OfficeHome Custodial Services wants to share with businesses about their upscale, environmentally friendly office cleaning services.
- Zak's Bulldozer wants to promote their tree removal for residential homes using low-impact tools.
- The city's Health Department wants a campaign to promote healthy eating and active lifestyle changes and to inform and warn people about common bad habits.
- Pop-Lite is a new, collapsible photo light, and the inventors need a logo and image for their Kickstarter campaign.

Each project has different goals, right? Some want to give away something for free. Some want to make money. Some want to solicit help from others. It's important to help the client pin down their project goals—and that can be hard to do.

Single Voice, Single Message

Video 10.2 *Discovering Client Goals*

Here's a brainteaser. You have 20 close friends, and you can no longer understand what they say. Why? They're close enough to talk to one another. They are all speaking your language. They are all speaking loud enough for you to hear clearly. They have no health or physical impairments. What's the problem?

They're all talking at once!

If a design says too much, it says nothing. It becomes "noisy" and makes it hard for the viewer to focus on the main idea. This reality is similar to the design concept of focal point. All creative projects have a kind of focal point. It's important to clearly define and pin down the most important goals of a project. Sometimes, clients are trying to clearly define their purpose, vision, or dreams for their organization. The overall goals and dreams for the business are helpful in the design process and should be heard so that you understand your client. But to get a project done efficiently—and create a project that communicates well—you must work with the client to establish and narrow down the goals for this project.

This short version of a campaign's goals is often called the "elevator pitch" because it summarizes the project in the time that it would take for an elevator ride. It's communicating your purpose in a short, simple sentence. Normally, I push a client to shoot for seven words or less. The aim is to clearly define the goals for this particular design project.

Here are some elevator pitches related to the scenarios listed earlier:

- Come to our free concert.
- Help child victims of a disaster.
- Get safe cleaning services for your office.
- Trees removed without damaging your yard.
- Get healthy and avoid hidden dangers.
- Our little photo lights are fun and functional.

Admittedly, these pitches are not elegant or enticing. There's no "pop" to the message. But they're the very core of what you're trying to communicate. It is the reason your client is paying you to design the project. You'll need more detail than this to deliver an effective design, but focusing on this core goal can help you rein in the insidious forces of project creep (which we'll talk about later in this chapter). But first, let this sink in: Your client's goals are your number-one priority.

If the goal is unclear, the finished product will be unclear. Figure out the goal, and you can always come back to it as a "home base" when the project starts to grow or lose its focus. Sometimes the goal isn't obvious, or it turns out to be different than it first appeared. But it's always critical, and one of your first jobs is to help the client focus on the primary goal of the project. Nonetheless, at the end of the day you work for the client, so the client calls the shots, has the final say, and makes the decisions—even if you disagree.

Now we'll talk about the second-most important person on the project—the one who doesn't really exist. I'm talking about the ideal audience for the piece.

Identifying Your Client's Ideal Customer

★ *ACA Objective 1.2*

In life, we shouldn't judge people, make assumptions, and lump them together. But we do. And as creative professionals, we *must*. This means developing a demographic for the project and identifying the target audience. It's a critical step in helping your clients bridge the gap to the audience they want to reach. You do this by identifying the common characteristics of that audience and creating an image in everyone's minds of the typical customer. Some clients will say "Everybody needs my product," but those clients will still need to focus on a target demographic specific to the project at hand. As the old saying goes, "Aim at nothing and you'll hit it every time." Those are wise words, especially when identifying a target audience.

Video 10.3 *Finding the Target Audience*

Identifying a target demographic for your project is a critical step, second only to defining the client's goals. And generally, it's also a part of the client's goals. For example, when you want to create a new fishing pole, you can easily picture your target audience: fishermen. So you're probably not going to use the same graphics, words, images, or feel as you would to reach a punk rock audience. At the same time, expectant mothers probably wouldn't be drawn to those images.

Identifying a demographic helps you focus on who you want to get your message. Understand the goals of your viewer as well as the speaker, your client. Make sure you share information in a way that will connect or resonate with that audience. And if you understand what your audience needs and feels, you can show how what you're sharing meets those needs.

The easiest way to do this is to create imaginary "perfect fits" for your client's project. Here are some things to consider:

- **Income:** Determine if you want to focus on quality, exclusivity, or price.
- **Education:** Establish the vocabulary and complexity of the design.
- **Age:** Dictate the general appeal, attitude, and vocabulary.
- **Hobbies:** Help in choosing images, insider vocabulary, and attitudes.
- **Concerns, cares, and passions:** Identify core beliefs, trigger points, and so on.

It's easy to see how different audiences will need different images. You don't want images of extreme sports in an ad aimed at expectant mothers. You wouldn't use a crowded nightclub image in a design for a camping and canoe outfitter company. Inexperienced designers sometimes try to make a production to please themselves, and that isn't always what pleases the target audience.

What makes your audience unique? Who has the problems that this product solves? Have those pictures in your mind. Work these ideas over with your client and help them envision their typical customer. Then look for images that will appeal to that ideal customer, this project's target demographic.

Think of yourself as a matchmaker. You're trying to introduce your client to the perfect customer or consumer. Speak in the language that the ideal client would want to hear, and use images that will bring their lifestyle and outlook together with your client.

The Golden Rule for Client Projects

Effective design helps someone else convey their vision. It communicates a message. When you're starting a new edit, use the business version of the golden rule: He who has the gold makes the rules.

▶ ***Video 10.4*** *The Golden Rule for Client Work*

Ultimately, you work for your clients. Help them see what you regard as the most effective way and identify the right questions to ask, but don't fight with them. They might have insight or perspective about their target audience that you don't have. Even when you disagree with a client about a design decision, you still need to help them realize their vision for their project. If you don't like it, you don't have to put the final piece in your portfolio, but you'll still get to put their check in the bank. If it comes down to what the client wants versus what you think their audience will respond to, do what the client asks. It's their project, their audience, and their money.

There's one exception to this rule that you need to follow at all times. When your client asks you to skirt copyright law, you're still responsible for respecting the law and your fellow creative professionals. Often the clients are just confused and you can help them understand that you can't copy other designs or employ copyrighted materials without authorization. Along those lines, let's take a moment to talk about copyright.

Copyrights and Wrongs

★ *ACA Objective 1.2*

Copyright is an amazing set of laws designed to protect and promote artists along with their art, creativity, and learning. It's gotten a really bad rap, and you should can set aside any preconceived ideas for a bit and think through the copyright concept (**Figure 10.1**).

Figure 10.1 Copyright can be a complex issue, but the basics are straightforward.

Copyright law is generally misunderstood by the public, so understanding it is an awesome way to score high at trivia night. A solid understanding of copyright law will also enable you to help your struggling author and artist friends realize that they don't have to pay an attorney tons of money to "make sure they get their stuff copyrighted." You can do it for them or show them how to do it themselves. It's free and easy. As a matter of fact, it's probably already been done.

Keep in mind that I'm a designer and instructor, not a lawyer. This chapter does not constitute legal advice; it's just intended to help you understand the law and the reasons it exists so you can appreciate it. It's easier to obey a law that you understand and appreciate, and copyright laws protect your rights. So get on board.

Here's something to remember: **Copyright law promotes freedom and creativity**. Let's explore how.

Copyright Happens

The first thing to know about copyright in the United States is that it just happens. If something can be copied, then it's copyrighted. You needn't fill out any special forms, report to a government office, or do anything extra to put it in place. The law is written so that copyright happens as soon is something original and creative is recorded in a "fixed form." This means that as soon as you write something down, sketch it out, or click the shutter on your camera, whatever you just created is copyrighted. The only reason you might do anything additional is to establish verifiable proof of when a creation was copyrighted, because the person who can prove that she recorded it first owns the copyright.

Video 10.5 *About Copyright*

Imagine that you're in a restaurant talking with a friend. During this conversation you make up a song on the spot. A famous singer in the booth behind yours hears you and writes it down. He claims the copyright to the lyrics and melody and makes a million bucks with your spontaneous song, and there's little you can do about it. However, if you recorded it on your phone when you sang it, you recorded it in fixed form *first*. So, *you* own the copyright on the lyrics, and the artist now owes you a truckload of money.

TIP

While your original work is automatically copyrighted without registering it with the US Copyright Office, you can potentially collect much higher monetary damages from an infringer if you do register the work.

Why does the law have this quirky little rule? Because the courts have to decide who owns copyright when its ownership is contested in court. And courts rely on tangible proof. So the law makes it simple by stating that she who first records something in fixed form wins. This way, you're not going to sue someone if you have no proof that you were first. But even if you were, and you can't prove it, you're out of luck.

So why do we have a copyright notice on music, DVDs, and one of the first pages of this book? If we don't need it, why do we display it?

Simply put, it reminds people who owns this copyrighted material. When no date and copyright symbol are displayed, people may think they can legally make photocopies of this book for their friends. Most people assume if no copyright notice appears, then no copyright exists. (They're totally wrong.) The presence of a visible copyright statement discourages this conclusion and behavior.

So it certainly can't cause any harm to scratch a copyright symbol on your art when you're done with it, but it's more to remind *the public* than to protect *you*. You're already protected by law. Adding the copyright symbol to your work is like putting one of those security system signs in your front yard. It won't stop a determined thief, but it can deter less committed offenders. Still, if you think it makes your front yard look cheap, you don't need it for protection. The system already protects you.

Placing a Copyright Notice In Digital Content

▶ *Video 10.6* Digital Tools for Tracking Copyright

The beauty of digital files is that they have the ability to contain hidden information that never compromises the enjoyment of the document itself. As a result, you can add copyright information to digital content without having a visually distracting copyright notice on the artwork (**Figure 10.2**). You do this by adding information called **metadata** into your digital files.

Figure 10.2 You don't need the mark or any sort of label, but it does make sure others know your work is copyrighted.

Metadata is information that doesn't show up on the document itself but is hidden inside the file. This is a perfect way to store copyright information, contact details, and so on. On some digital cameras, metadata can record the lens information, the location via GPS, whether a flash was attached and fired, the camera settings, and more. In digital files, metadata can share the computer on which it was created, the time, and even the name of the creator. (This is how good technology teachers catch cheaters.) Be sure to make use of metadata when you're sending your work out over the web, and always check files that your clients give you to make sure that you're not violating another professional's means of making money when you're trying to make some yourself.

"But I'm not trying to make any money with their art, so it's okay, right?" Well, that's a tough question with a few interesting rules attached.

Playing Fair with Copyrighted Material

▶ *Video 10.7* Fair Use and Copyright

Can you use copyrighted material when you're practicing with Adobe Photoshop? Can you make a funny image using a movie poster by replacing the faces of the actors with the faces of your friends? What about using cool images from your favorite videogame as you're learning Photoshop?

These uses of copyrighted material are completely legit. The people who came up with our copyright laws were careful to make sure that the laws don't limit—but instead promote—creativity. They did this with a set of ideas called fair use.

Fair use policy is a set of rules that make sure copyright protection doesn't come at the cost of creativity and freedom. Copyright can't be used to limit someone's personal growth or learning, freedom of speech, or artistic expression and creative exploration. Those ideas are more important than copyright, so copyright doesn't apply when it gets in the way of these higher ideals. You're free to use copyrighted materials in the pursuit of these higher goals. Some people (mistakenly) believe that fair use doesn't apply to copyrighted materials, but in fact, it applies only to copyrighted materials. Here is a list of issues that a court would consider when making a decision about fair use:

- **Purpose: If you use the work to teach, learn, voice your own opinion, inspire you to create a new piece of art, or report news, you're probably safe.** Protected reasons include educational purposes (teaching, research), freedom of speech (commentary or criticism), news reporting, and transformative work (parody or using the work in a new way). It isn't considered fair use if you're making money from the use, using it just for entertainment, or trying to pass it off as your own work.
- **Nature: If the nature of the original work is factual, published information, or the work was critical to favoring education, you're probably safe.** Was the content already published, fact based, and important for society to know? Then you're pretty safe to use the work. But if it was unpublished, creative (such as art, music, film, novels), and fictional, you're probably not cleared to use it.
- **Amount: If you use a small amount of a copyrighted work, it's more likely that your use of the work is fair use.** If you use only a small quantity—not the main idea or focus of the work, but just enough to teach or learn from—you're probably safe. If you use a large portion of the work or basically rip off the central idea or the "heart of the work," it isn't fair use.
- **Effect: If nobody is harmed because of the action you've taken, then your action is probably fair use.** If you use a legitimate copy of the original work, it doesn't affect the sale of another copy, and you have no other way to get a copy, you're in pretty good shape. But if your copy makes it less likely that someone would buy a copy or you made a large number of copies, you're probably hurting the original creator, and that's not fair use.

As mentioned earlier, copyright law addresses a simple question: "How can we promote more freedom and creativity in the world?" This is the question that copyright laws seek to answer. Fair use makes sure that beginning artists can experiment using anything they want. Just be sure not to share anything that might be another artist's copyrighted work.

But as a beginning designer, how can you get good-quality assets to use in real-world projects? Happily, you have access to more free resources than ever before in history via the Internet and free stock photo. We'll look at some in the next section.

Uncopyrighting

Video 10.8 *Licensing Strict and Free*

You have a couple of ways in which to undo copyright. One is voluntary. An author can choose to release the copyright to her material. Believe it or not, this can be more difficult to do than you'd expect. Copyright law protects creators of their works, and it can be difficult to *not* be protected by copyright law.

The second way is to let the copyright expire. Copyrights normally expire between 50 and 100 years after the death of the original author, but exceptions to this rule and extensions can be requested. It's beyond the scope of this book to discuss copyright at length, but it's important to realize that some materials have expired copyrights. When copyright is expired or released, the work is said to be in the **public domain**. This means that copyright no longer applies to the content, and you can use the material without worrying about copyright infringement.

Licensing

Licensing is another way that you can legally use copyrighted material. For designers and artists, licensing is fairly common because it allows us to use copyrighted material for a certain time and in a certain way by paying a fee established by the copyright holder according to the use of the material.

Stock photos are popular items licensed by all sorts of designers, and you can find them from many sources at various prices. Stock photos are images for which the author retains copyright but you can purchase a license to use these images in your designs. For almost everyone, this is a much less expensive solution than hiring a photographer to go to a location and shoot, process, and sell you the rights to an image.

CREATIVE COMMONS

In the last decade or so, a lot of exploration has been done in finding alternative ways to license creative works. **Creative Commons** licensing (**Figure 10.3**) is built on copyright law but offers ways that artists can release their works for limited use and still choose the way the works are used and shared.

Creative Commons licenses include many different combinations of the following attributes, so you'll need to do some research when using Creative Commons–licensed materials and when releasing assets with Creative Commons licensing.

- **Public Domain** (CC0) licenses allow artists to release their works to the public domain. It's a bit difficult to give your materials away to the public domain, but CC0 is generally recognized as a way to do so and is respected in most parts of the world.
- **Attribution** (BY) requires that you credit the original author when using her work. You can do whatever you want with the work as long as you give that credit.
- **ShareAlike** (SA) allows you to use the item in anything you want as long as your creation is shared under the same license as the original work.
- **NoDerivs** (ND) requires that you not change the material when you incorporate it into your own work. You can use NoDerivs material freely, but you must pass it along without changing it.
- **NonCommercial** (NC) means that people can use your work in their own creative works as long as they don't charge for it. You're getting it for free, so if you want to use it, then you have to be generous and also give away your work for free.

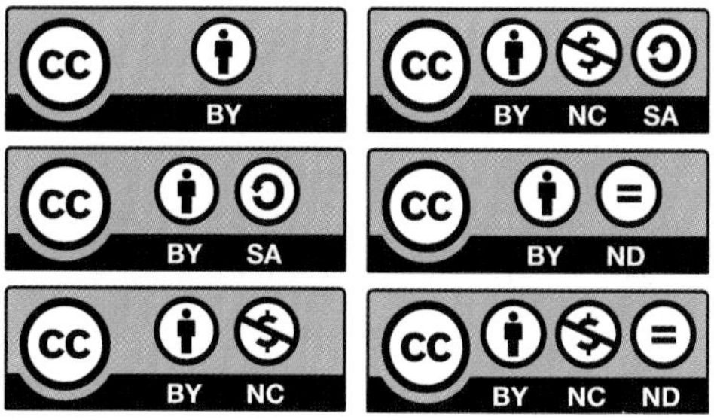

Figure 10.3 Creative Commons licenses allow for a variety of easy-to-understand licensing options.

Creative Commons licenses are widely accepted and used, and you can find a ton of amazing resources that use this licensing. If you have any questions about Creative Commons licenses, you can find out everything from a general overview to detailed legal descriptions at *www.creativecommons.org*.

PEOPLE PERMISSIONS

Because many assets we use in Photoshop include photographs, we need to talk about extra permissions such as **model releases**. This type of release is required when a person's face is identifiable in the design will be used to promote something, whether it's a product or an idea. Any work you do for a client is by definition a commercial use and will require a model release for every identifiable face.

Think Like a Boss

Some might say that the only thing you need to know to succeed in life is how to solve a problem. That's not how to solve a specific problem; that would be only an exercise in memory. A well-trained monkey can mimic a person's actions and get a similar result. But a monkey can't think with the depth of a human. My preferred way to solve problems is to work to understand things deeply and explore all the nuances of a potential solution. But for others, this process is a little outside their comfort zones and they find it faster and easier to copy someone else's solution.

In Photoshop, copying another solution or technique means following tutorials. In entry-level jobs, it's being a dutiful employee, efficient worker, and good follower who shows up on time.

But what do you do when you're the leader? What happens when you need to do something new and fresh for your job? What if the boss doesn't know how to do it and that's why she hired you? At times, your client's main request will be something as vague and daunting as "Do something that hasn't been done before."

That's where the problem-solving process comes in—the only skill you need to be successful. If you can do that, you can figure out anything.

★ *ACA Objective 1.3*

▶ ***Video 10.9** Project Management Intro*

Project Management

Project management is really just the problem-solving process in action—geared toward supervising resources, people, and team-based projects. The DNA of project management is problem solving and organizing the process so that you tackle the right issues at the right time using the right tools. Project-management systems take on many forms (as do problem-solving systems), but if you truly grasp the ideas behind the labels, you can translate them into whatever management strategy your client, team, or boss is using.

The problem-solving process is creative in itself. A good solution to a problem can be artistic in its elegance and efficient grace. If you can grasp problem solving, you can learn whatever you need to learn now and in the future.

The following procedure will help when you need to solve a technical problem on hardware or equipment, handle an editing issue within your visual design project, or figure out how to get your hand out of that jar you got it stuck in. It will help you translate a tutorial written for Photoshop CS6 into your current version (things change fast these days!). And it boils down to three simple steps: learn, think, and do.

Learn

The first step of a problem-solving process is to learn. It includes two important steps: learning what the problem is and learning how others have solved similar problems (research and investigate). It seems simple, but the process can be confusing. Most projects with major problems get stuck at this initial step because they didn't learn well—or at all. Let's talk about them.

▶ ***Video 10.10*** *Project Management—Understand the Problem*

UNDERSTAND THE PROBLEM

As we discussed earlier in this chapter, the first step of every project is to understand the problem. For most design projects, you must figure out how to most effectively help your client share their goals with the target audience. If the client is yourself, then it's about getting to the essence of what you want to communicate and communicating it so that your target audience can act on it.

Understanding the problem is the most difficult part of the problem-solving process. Mess it up here, and by definition, you're not solving the problem. You haven't properly identified the problem, so how can you solve it? Sometimes you can make the problem worse by implementing a plan that creates a new problem without solving the real one.

You can avoid trouble down the road by clearly understanding and defining the problem at the start. "I want to sell a million widgets" is not a problem you can solve; it's a desire the client has. So what's the problem you can help with? He hasn't sold as many as he wants? That's not it either. How do you get to the bottom of the problem?

Start with good questions: Do people need a widget? If so, do people know widgets are a thing? If so, do they choose a competing widget? If so, why do they choose this other widget? Why do you think they should use your widget instead? Who would be most likely to buy your widget? What is your budget for widget advertising? What do you want to spend on this particular project? What are your expectations?

Many clients become frustrated with this set of questions. They just want action to be taken so that they can feel like they're doing something. But let me repeat that old saying: "Aim at nothing, and you'll hit it every time." This is when you sharpen your axe so you don't have to chop at the tree all day.

This part of the project can be fairly informal on smaller projects but can be huge on large projects. Here's a list of critical questions to answer:

- **Purpose:** Why are you doing this creative project? What result would you consider a success?
- **Target:** Who needs this message or product? Describe your typical customer.
- **Limits:** What are the limits for the project? Budget and time are most necessary to nail down.
- **Preferences:** Aside from the results we've already discussed, are there any other results you'd like or expect from this project?

These examples are intended to show how quickly you can determine a client's expectations. The answers to these questions define the size of the job and how you'll best be able to work with the client.

Sketches and written notes from this initial step will help. Gather as much information as you can to make the rest of the project go smoothly. The more you find out now, the less you'll have to redesign later, because the client hates the color, the layout, or the general direction you took the project. Invest the time now, or pay it back with interest later. With a clear idea of what the problem is, you'll get the information you need to solve it in the next step.

RESEARCH AND INVESTIGATE

After you understand exactly what your client is expecting, you can start doing the research to arrive at the answers you need. Let's take a quick look at that word: *re-search*. It literally means "search again." Lots of people fail to research; they just search. They look at the most obvious places and approaches, and if things don't immediately click, they settle for a poor but quick and easy solution.

Depending on the job, researching can be a relatively quick process. Find out about the competitive products, learn about the problem you're trying to solve, and understand the demographic you're going to target. The more research you do, the better information you'll have about the problem you're trying to solve, which will help you with the next step.

Think

The next couple of steps represent the "thinking" phase. You can do this quickly using a pen and napkin, or you can do it in depth and generate tons of documentation along the way, particularly on large projects (**Figure 10.4**). But thinking is the part that most of us often mistake as the beginning. Remember that if the learning step isn't done well, your thinking step might be headed in the wrong direction.

Video 10.11 *Project Management—Think it Through*

Figure 10.4 As a designer, you'll often do much of your thinking on paper, even if you're not producing traditional or formal storyboards. Sketch out your sequence first and have that reference to show the customer and to come back to for clarity.

BRAINSTORM

The next step is to brainstorm. As with research, you need to really grasp the meaning. It's a brain**storm**. Not a brain *drizzle*. A full-on typhoon of ideas. At this point, it's important to stop thinking analytically and start thinking creatively. If you start thinking critically instead of creatively, you'll change direction and you'll lose ground on your brainstorming task. If you start moving in the critical direction, that's the opposite of creative. Stop that! Don't try to work hard on brainstorming. Work relaxed instead.

At times, analysis will need to happen. You start analyzing how to complete your ideas when you should be creating them. Here are some things *not* to do when brainstorming and directions that trigger the critical mode of thinking:

- Judging your ideas
- Trying to finish an idea when you should still be brainstorming

- Getting stuck on a particular idea
- Planning out the project
- Thinking about how much time you have
- Thinking about the budget
- Thinking about numbers
- Grouping or sorting your ideas
- Developing the idea that you think is best

Here are things you should be doing to get into creative mode:

- Listen to music.
- Look at cool art online.
- Call a friend.
- Doodle on something.
- Read a poem.
- Take a break.
- Go for a walk.
- Watch a movie.
- Write a haiku.
- Meditate for five minutes.
- Exercise.
- Sleep on it.

When you're in brainstorming mode, don't edit your ideas. Let them flow. If a crummy idea pops into your head, put it on paper. If you don't, it will keep popping up until it's been given a little respect. Give the weak ideas respect; they open doors for the great ones. Brainstorming is a matter of quantity, not quality.

PICK AND PLAN

Video 10.12 *Project Management—Get it in Writing*

After brainstorming, you need to pick a solution that you generated in your brainstorming session and plan things out. You'll find that the plan you go with is rarely your first idea. Through the process of brainstorming, the idea will go through several **iterations**. A common mistake for beginners is to fall in love with an early idea—beware of this pitfall! Your best idea is lurking in the background of your mind, and you have to get rid of all the simple ideas that pop up first. For a small project or a one-person team, you might quickly hammer out a contract and get to work, but in larger projects, the planning needs to be detailed and focused.

The larger the project, the more formal this process will be. Small projects with just one person working on it will have little planning necessary for moving forward. However, larger projects will need a project plan to set the project requirements for the team.

SETTING PROJECT REQUIREMENTS

★ ACA Objective 2.2

This is where the action happens. Look through the ideas you've generated and pick the one that seems best and plan how to make it happen. This is where you determine exactly what has to be done, establish some direction, and identify a clear target. This planning stage (which most creative types naturally tend to resist, myself included) is where you clarify what needs to be done; it establishes your direction and identifies a clear target. We resist it because it seems to limit us. It ropes in our creative freedom, and it gives us a checklist—all things that many creatives hate. These things are creative kryptonite—or at least we *think* they are. But let's consider this for a moment.

If you don't perform this admittedly tedious step, what won't you have? You won't have a definition of what needs to be done, a direction to head in, or a target to hit. Everyone will be in the dark. Although this step doesn't seem creative in itself, creativity isn't the priority at this particular juncture. You're at a journey-versus-destination moment. Creativity without limits is a journey, which is great for your own work, but a disaster for a client-driven job. A client-driven project requires clearly defined goals—a destination. You need to arrive somewhere specific.

Two critical points that must be a part of every project plan are the project scope and project deadline. Every contract needs to have these critical components defined to focus the project:

- **Project scope** is the amount of work to be done. On the designer's side, this is the most important thing to establish. If the scope isn't clear, you're subject to the Achilles heel of editing and production work: **project creep**. This is a pervasive problem in our industry (you'll learn more later in this chapter), but simply writing down a defined scope can prevent the problem. Get in writing *exactly* what you need to do and make sure specific numbers are attached.
- **Project deadlines** dictate when the work needs to be done. This is the client's most important element. The deadline often affects the price. If the client needs ten animated banner ads in six months, you can probably offer a discount. If they need a draft by tomorrow morning, then they'll have to pay an

additional "rush" fee. Deadlines on large projects also can be broken down into phases, each with its own fee. This division of tasks helps you pay the bills by generating cash flow during a large and lengthy project. It also limits the impact—for you—of payment delay.

I strongly encourage you to include the following additional items in your creative project plans. These items, when shared and discussed with your client, will save time, money, and disagreements. These additional **deliverables** are the raw materials of project planning and help convey the exact target of the project. The following two deliverables are critical for every production project:

- **Sketches** are helpful to show the client how your project and edit will flow. It's even better when the client has an idea of what they're looking for and can give you their own storyboard, however crude. Does this limit your creative freedom? Yes, and it also saves you a ton of time. The goal of a client job is to get a project done to their satisfaction. If they're very particular and know what they want, you're not going to convince them otherwise. Sketches save time because they limit your direction to one that the client will accept, and they help you get to that acceptance faster. That means you get finished and paid sooner. The better the storyboards are before you get into actual editing, the fewer changes and revisions you'll need. You don't have to be a master sketch artist; just convey the idea. Sometimes sketches may just be **wireframes**—very rough representative sketches of how to lay out the project—especially in regard to interactive media projects.
- **Specifications**, or specs, are detailed, clear written goals and limits for a project. Many times, the specifications themselves will be referred to as the "project plan" and become part of the contract. This will involve the target platform and feature set of the interactive project. All project plans should include two critical pieces of information: the scope of the project and the deadlines that need to be met. Be sure to always include both of these items in your project specifications.

AVOIDING PROJECT CREEP

Video 10.13 Project Management—Avoiding Creep

Project creep occurs when a project starts to lose its focus and spin out of control, eating up more and more time and effort. It is important to be aware of this phenomenon. It happens all the time, and the main culprit in every case is a poorly designed project plan that lacks clear specifications and deadlines.

Here's how it happens: Joe Client creates a product and wants to sell it. He comes to you for marketing materials. You determine that he wants a logo, a flyer, and a three-page informational website. You've settled on a price of $4,500 and you've got a month to get it done. You go to work.

Then Joe realizes that he also wants some images for social media. Could you just make a few? He also realizes that he needs to put his new logo on new business cards. Could you just design a card with the logo on it? Oh, and he can't figure out how to get his product onto his favorite online marketplace. Could you just help him set that up? And he changed his launch date. He doesn't need it next month, he needs it next week because he just reserved a booth at a large convention. By the way, do you know anything about designing booths?

This is why it's critical to create a detailed project plan with task definitions and deadlines attached. Sometimes the client asks for something and it takes you 30 seconds. It's a good idea to always happily deliver on these little items. A favor is any job that takes you five minutes or less. After that, the favor turns into work. And your only defense is your contract defining a clearly stated scope.

Just make sure that the project's scope is clearly stated. If the contract says that you'll provide *any* images for the company's web presence, you're in trouble. If it says that you'll specifically provide up to nine images for the client's website, you're in great shape. Taking the hour it requires to specify your project and its deadlines in detail will save you from many hours of work and contract revisions.

If the client has approved your project parameters and then asks for something different, you need to charge them for the change if it's going to take more than 5 to 10 minutes. Sticking to this policy helps the client think about changes before sending them to you. If you fail to charge when addressing impromptu changes, the client has no reason to think about the requests in advance. Charging your customer for additional changes focuses them on what they really want.

Of course, if the client asks for something that makes the job easier and faster, then make the change and do it for free. The bottom line is this: Establish goodwill whenever it's good for both you and your client. But when an 11th-hour alteration serves only one side of the relationship, the requesting side has to pay for the service. This arrangement ensures that everyone ends up winning.

Do

Video 10.14 *Project Management—Make It So*

The last phase of the project plan is to knock it out! This is the "two snaps and a twist" phase because it generally happens quickly when you have a good plan—unless there's a hitch. But at this point, on most design projects you're pretty much wrapping things up.

BUILD IT

This step is obvious: Make it happen. This phase is where most people think all the action is...but honestly, if you've done the prior steps well, this can be the fastest part of the process. You already know what to do—now just do it. The design decisions and feature specifications have been made and you can get to work. Of course, when doing this step, it's best to regularly refer to the specifications and keep the client informed. The best way to do so is to have a feedback loop in place.

FEEDBACK LOOP

ACA Objective 1.4

A **feedback loop** is a system set up to constantly encourage and require input and approvals on the project direction. Keeping your client informed is the best way to speed through the process. For an interactive media project, **iterative work** establishes effective guideposts to send to the client for review and input. Iterative work is work you're sharing as it's done. Doing so performs a couple of critical functions. First, it lets the client see that work's being done and helps reassure them that the process has momentum. Second, it lets the client chime in on anything that they don't like while it's still easy to make a change.

Establishing this open communication channel encourages and enforces a healthy exchange of opinions and can enable you to most efficiently adjust and fine-tune your project to suit your client.

TEST AND EVALUATE

This very last step can also be fast if you've had a good feedback loop in place. For visual design projects, it's essentially checking the work against your project plan and making sure that you met all the specifications to satisfy you and your client. If not, you should essentially start the problem-solving process again to understand the current problem. Find out exactly what the client believes doesn't meet the requirements.

Assuming a good project plan with storyboards and a good feedback loop, the test-and-evaluation phase should require only minor tweaks—no different from any other iterative work resolution. If you don't have a good feedback loop and the first time the client sees your work is upon delivery, that client could become unhappy and demand innumerable changes. Avoid this migraine headache with an effective and well-defined feedback loop as part of your plan. Those two tools are your weapons against project creep and unreasonable clients.

WORKING FOR "THE MAN"

Video 10.15 *The Advantages of Working at a Firm*

Many visual designers begin their careers working at larger firms, which can be a much easier way to get started than freelancing with your own business. If you're exclusively an artist, this type of job may require you only to do the tasks you're best at doing. In a large firm, someone else does the sales, manages client relationships and projects, and creates technical specifications.

As an artist at a larger firm, you're responsible only for working with footage and editing it. Everything else is handled by someone else, which is a good trade-off for artists who don't like the detail-oriented checklist work of project management and bookkeeping.

Working within an experienced company can also be an amazing education. You can develop your strengths, learn about the industry, and slowly increase your involvement in the other aspects of this career beyond Photoshop proficiency.

Conclusion

Video 10.16 *Wrapping Up Project Planning*

Much of this chapter digressed from the hands-on Photoshop work that similar books cover. But starting their careers without the information presented in this chapter can pose a problem for many beginning artists. You need to master a lot of industry information, creative knowledge, and business skills to be successful. We're stoked that you read this far. Many of us creative people have a hard time with the business side of the career, but it's best to understand these ideas and concepts now before a lack of understanding becomes a problem. The tips and techniques that you've read in this chapter will eliminate a lot of the inherent frustration in the complexity of working with and for other people.

Photoshop is an intensely creative and varied application that tends to attract adventurous individuals. The qualities that make us great at thinking outside the box and designing new and beautiful images are the same qualities that may make us less skilled at the organized detail work of business and client management.

ACA Objectives Covered

DOMAIN OBJECTIVES	CHAPTER	VIDEO
DOMAIN 1.0 Setting Project Requirements		
1.1 Identify the purpose, audience, and audience needs for preparing images.	**Ch 10** Who You're Talking For and Who You're Talking To, 236	**10.2** Discovering Client Goals **10.3** Finding the Target Audience **10.4** The Golden Rule for Client Work
1.2 Summarize how designers make decisions about the type of content to include in a project, including considerations such as copyright, project fit, permissions, and licensing.	**Ch 10** Identifying Your Client's Ideal Customer, 238 **Ch 10** Copyrights and Wrongs, 240	**10.5** About Copyright **10.6** Digital Tools for Tracking Copyright **10.7** Fair Use and Copyright **10.8** Licensing Strict and Free
1.3 Demonstrate knowledge of project management tasks and responsibilities.	**Ch 10** Project Management, 246	**6.22** Layer Comps **10.9** Project Management Intro **10.10** Project Management—Understand the Problem **10.11** Project Management—Think it Through
1.4 Communicate with others (such as peers and clients) about design plans.	**Ch 10** Feedback Loop, 254	**4.24** Client Review Prep **10.12** Project Management—Get it in Writing **10.13** Project Management—Avoiding Creep **10.14** Project Management—Make It So

DOMAIN OBJECTIVES	CHAPTER	VIDEO
DOMAIN 2.0 Understanding Digital Images		
2.1 Understand key terminology related to digital images.	**Ch 8** Insider Terminology, 182	**8.2** Industry Terms for Digital Images **8.3** Industry Terms in Photography
2.2 Demonstrate knowledge of basic design principles and best practices employed in the visual design industry.	**Ch 9** Leveling Up with Design, 191 **Ch 9** The Elements of Art, 197	**3.2** See Like an Artist **3.20** Designing in Photoshop **4.17** Seeing Like an Artist **9.2** Design School: Creativity Is a Skill **9.3** Design School: The Design Hierarchy **9.4** Design School The Elements of Art **9.5** Design School: The Element of Space **9.6** Design School: The Element of Line **9.7** Design School: The Element of Shape **9.8** Design School: The Element of Form **9.9** Design School: The Element of Pattern and Texture **9.13** Design School: The Principles of Design **9.14** Design School: The Principle of Emphasis **9.15** Design School: The Principle of Contrast **9.16** Design School: The Principle of Unity **9.17** Design School: The Principle of Variety **9.18** Design School: The Principle of Balance **9.19** Design School: The Principle of Proportion or Scale **9.20** Design School: The Principles of Repetition and Pattern **9.21** Design School: The Principles of Movement and Rhythm
2.3 Demonstrate knowledge of typography and its use in visual design.	**Ch 4** Tweak Character Settings, 90 **Ch 9** The Element of Type, 217	**4.14** Tweaking Type **9.12** Design School The Element of Type
2.4 Demonstrate knowledge of color and its use in digital images.	**Ch 9** The Element of Color, 211	**9.10** Design School: The Element of Value **9.11** Design School: The Element of Color
2.5 Demonstrate knowledge of image resolution, image size, and image file format for web, video, and print.	**Ch 8** Images and Industries, 184	**8.4** Print Industry Standards **8.5** Web Design Industry Standards **8.6** Video Industry Standards

continues on next page

continued from previous page

DOMAIN OBJECTIVES	CHAPTER	VIDEO
DOMAIN 3.0 Understanding Adobe Photoshop		
3.1 Identify elements of the Photoshop CC user interface and demonstrate knowledge of their functions.	**Ch 1** The Photoshop Interface, 8	**1.4** Tour the Photoshop Workspace **1.5** Changing and Resetting Workspaces
3.2 Identify and define the functions of commonly used Panels, including the Properties, Layers, Brushes, Adjustments, and Type panels.	**Ch 3** Name Layers, 57 **Ch 4** Master Text, 88	**3.14** Naming Layers **4.10** Solid Fill Review **4.13** Designing with Type
3.3 Define the functions of commonly used tools, including selection, drawing, painting, type, and vector shape tools.	**Ch 3** Brush Color on an Image, 52 **Ch 3** Erase Mistakes, 55 **Ch 4** Master Text, 88	**3.10** Brushing Color on an Image **3.12** Erase Mistakes **4.9** Smart Objects **4.13** Designing with Type **4.15** Adding Event Info **4.16** Adding Vertical Text
3.4 Navigate, organize, and customize the workspace.	**Ch 1** Creating Custom Workspaces, 10	**1.6** Creating Custom Workspaces **1.7** Organizing Your Data **6.23** Close Up, Clean Up
3.5 Use non-printing design tools in the interface, such as rulers and guides.	**Ch 4** Work with Rulers and Guides, 80	**4.5** Guides and Rulers **6.3** Artboards **6.29** Adding an Artboard
3.6 Demonstrate knowledge of layers and masks.	**Ch 3** Work with Layers, 50 **Ch 3** Tweak Layer Settings and Color for a Natural Look, 54 **Ch 3** Name Layers, 57 **Ch 3** Add More Layers and Colors, 58 **Ch 4** Create a Layer Mask, 87 **Ch 4** Fade the Image Using a Mask, 87 **Ch 4** Smart Filter Masks, 103 **Ch 5** Perfect Masks and Selections, 119	**3.9** Work with Layers **3.11** Tweaking Layer Settings for a Natural Look **3.14** Naming Layers **3.15** Adding Layers for New Colors **4.11** Layer Masks **4.12** Gradients to Blend with Masks **5.7** Quick Mask Mastery **6.11** Masking Models

DOMAIN OBJECTIVES	CHAPTER	VIDEO
3.7 Manage colors, swatches, and gradients.	**Ch 6** Replace Colors in an Image, 147 **Ch 6** Gradient Goodness, 164	**6.16** Replace Colors in an Image **6.17** Get Clipped **6.27** Gradient Goodness
3.8 Manage brushes, symbols, graphic styles, and patterns.	**Ch 4** Solve Design Problems with Styles, 95 **Ch 6** Brush Mastery, 136 **Ch 6** Brush Bling, 153 **Ch 6** Shatter the Heroine, 162	**4.18** Using Styles **6.9** Brush Mastery **6.10** Reuse and Save Brushes **6.20** Brush Bling **6.21** Brush Better **6.26** Shatter Selections
DOMAIN 4.0 Creating Digital Images Using Adobe Photoshop		
4.1 Create a new project.	**Ch 4** Create a Print Document, 79 **Ch 4** Soft Proof Colors, 80 **Ch 6** Create a New Document, 128	**4.2** Designing for Print **4.3** Create a New Print Document **6.2** Set the Stage **6.3** Artboards
4.2 Import assets into a project.	**Ch 2** Opening Images, 18 **Ch 3** Restore Damaged Photos, 38 **Ch 4** Import Images, 83 **Ch 5** Create a Mystical Animal, 114 **Ch 6** Smart Is as Smart Does, 129	**2.2** Opening Images in Photoshop **3.1** Restore Damaged Photos **4.6** About Opening and Placing Images **4.8** Raw Images **5.2** Gather Your Images
4.3 Make, manage, and manipulate selections.	**Ch 4** Smart Filter Masks, 103 **Ch 5** Grab the Bull by the Horns, 114 **Ch 5** Perfect Masks and Selections, 119 **Ch 6** Mask Mastery, 133 **Ch 6** Copy and Paste the Loaded Mask, 143 **Ch 6** Selection Perfection, 158	**5.3** Grab the Bull by the Horns **5.7** Quick Mask Mastery **6.4** Import Linked Smart Object **6.5** Raster Effects on Smart Objects **6.7** Mask Mastery **6.8** Refine Your Masks **6.13** Load, Copy, and Paste a Selection **6.24** Selection Perfection **6.25** Striped Selections
4.4 Transform images.	**Ch 2** Resize Images, 20 **Ch 2** Flip or Rotate the Image, 26 **Ch 3** Rotate and Straighten the Image, 39 **Ch 3** Expand the Canvas, 63 **Ch 5** Tweak the Horns, 116 **Ch 5** Extend the Canvas, 116 **Ch 6** Warp Tour, 145	**2.4** Resize Images **3.3** Rotate, Crop and Straighten an Image **3.21** Expand the Canvas **5.4** Transform Tricks **5.5** Open Up the Canvas **6.15** Warp Tour

continues on next page

continued from previous page

DOMAIN OBJECTIVES	CHAPTER	VIDEO
4.5 Create and manage layers and masks.	**Ch 3** Organize Layers, 58 **Ch 3** Add a Solid Color Fill Layer, 65 **Ch 3** Merge and Flatten Layers, 71 **Ch 4** Fade the Image Using a Mask, 87 **Ch 4** Solve Design Problems with Styles, 95 **Ch 5** Perfect Masks and Selections, 119 **Ch 6** Mask Mastery, 133	**3.17** Organize Layers **3.18** Unlock and Reorder Layers **3.22** Add Solid Fill Layer **3.26** Merge and Flatten Layers **3.27** Duplicating Layers **4.12** Gradients to Blend with Masks **4.18** Using Styles **5.7** Quick Mask Mastery **6.7** Mask Mastery **6.8** Refine Your Masks
4.6 Use basic retouching techniques—including color correction, blending, cloning, and filters—to manipulate a digital image.	**Ch 2** Fixing Redeye, 19 **Ch 2** Fix Color Balance, 24 **Ch 2** Fix Color in Aged Photos, 28 **Ch 3** Adjust Levels Manually, 41 **Ch 3** Shift Colors, 56 **Ch 4** Adjust Smart Filters, 103 **Ch 4** Making Adjustments for the Client, 107 **Ch 5** Believable Blending, 117 **Ch 5** Content-Aware Move and Extend, 121 **Ch 6** Attack of the Clones, 130	**2.3** Remove Redeye from Your Photos **2.7** Correct Color Balance **2.8** When the Redeye Tool Won't Work **2.9** Basic Photo Restoration **2.10** Restoring Color in Aged Photos **2.11** Convert Images to Black and White **2.12** Removing Dust and Scratches **2.13** Perfecting a Great Image **2.14** Fix On Your Own **3.4** Manual Levels Adjustments **3.5** Content-Aware Fill **3.6** The Spot Healing Brush **3.7** Sharpen and Save **3.8** Color Modes and Color **3.13** Shifting Colors **3.16** Ballerina Mission **4.22** Adjusting Filters **4.25** Making Adjustments **5.6** Smart Color Blending **5.8** Content-Aware Move **5.9** Patching Things Up **5.10** Chernobyl Zoo **6.6** Attack of the Clones **6.12** Blending Selection Tools
4.7 Create a vector drawing, such as an icon, button, or layout.	**Ch 6** Shape Layers, 151	**6.19** Shape Layers

DOMAIN OBJECTIVES	CHAPTER	VIDEO
4.8 Add and manipulate type.	**Ch 3** Add Text, 67 **Ch 4** Master Text, 88	**3.23** Add Text **3.24** Advanced Character Settings **4.13** Designing with Type **4.20** The Title Styles
4.9 Add filters.	**Ch 2** Sharpen Using Unsharp Mask, 21 **Ch 4** Solve Design Problems with Styles, 95 **Ch 4** Working with Filters, 100	**2.5** Sharpen Using Unsharp Mask **4.18** Using Styles **4.19** Managing Layer Styles **4.20** The Title Styles **4.22** Working with Filters **4.23** Explore Filters Further
DOMAIN 5.0 Publishing Digital Images Using Adobe Photoshop		
5.1 Prepare images for export to web, print, and video.	**Ch 2** Save Images for the Web, 22 **Ch 3** Save as a PSD Document, 70 **Ch 3** Save for Social Media Use, 74 **Ch 4** Give Proof, 107 **Ch 4** Making It Final, 109 **Ch 7** Print at Home or Work, 169 **Ch 7** Design for Commercial Printing, 177 **Ch 7** Create Images for Use in Other Applications, 178	**2.6** Save Images for the Web **3.29** Save for Social Media Use **4.4** Soft Proof Colors **4.26** Making It Final **7.2** Quick Prints **7.6** Designing for Commercial Printing **7.7** Designing for Use in Other Adobe Applications
5.2 Export or save digital images to various file formats.	**Ch 3** Save as PSD, 48 **Ch 3** Save Your Work, 62 **Ch 3** Export Layers as Separate Files, 73 **Ch 4** Browse with Bridge, 83 **Ch 4** Making It Final, 109 **Ch 5** Save Your Progress, 118 **Ch 6** Save the Masked Model as a PSD File, 143 **Ch 7** Save for the Web, 171	**3.19** Save Color Version **3.25** Save for Multiple Purposes **3.28** Export Single Layers **4.7** Browsing with Bridge **4.21** Safer Saving **4.26** Making It Final **7.3** Prepping Web Ready Images **7.4** Saving Photos for the Web **7.5** Saving Graphic Images for the Web

Glossary

additive color Created by combining light.

adjustment layers Adjust all the layers below them with effects or image adjustments.

alignment Indicates how elements are aligned, such as by left edges, centered, or right edges.

all caps Uses only uppercase letterforms for each letter.

analogous (colors) Colors that are side by side on the color wheel. They create gentle and relaxing color schemes.

asymmetrical Achieves balance using elements with different weights or values on each side (or the top and bottom) of an image.

attribution Written acknowledgment provided with the name of the original copyright holder of the work. Creative Commons and other licenses feature different kinds of attribution requirements.

Auto Tone Automatically sets the black and white points in an image to make the blacks truly black and the whites truly white.

balance Evenly distributed, but not necessarily centered or mirrored.

baseline An imaginary line used to organize text along a horizontal plane.

bitmap An image created by a grid of pixels with each pixel assigned a color and, in some file formats, a transparency value.

Blackletter fonts Also known as Old English or Gothic. Feature an overly ornate style.

bleed The part of the image extending past the cut edge to ensure an edge-to-edge print.

blending mode Determines how a layer blends with the layers beneath it, such as Darken, Soft Light, or Difference.

blown-out Images that have no detail in the brightest (pure white) areas due to overexposure.

bokeh An out-of-focus effect created by lenses and apertures, especially when referring to the circular blur from lights that are out of focus.

Bridge An Adobe product that helps you stay organized and simplify your workflows. It gives you centralized access to all the media assets you need for creative projects.

canvas The image area in Photoshop.

cast shadow The shadow cast on the ground and on any objects that are in the shadow of the form. Shadows fade as they get farther from the form casting the shadow.

chaotic A description of lines or shapes that appear disorganized and messy. Convey a sense of urgency, fear, or explosive energy.

Clone Stamp Tool that paints by copying pixels from a defined target area elsewhere in the image.

color The perceived hue, lightness, and saturation of an object or light.

color cast Unwanted tint in an image from incorrect camera settings. Performing a white balance can prevent or fix this issue.

color harmonies Color rules that are named for their relative locations on the color wheel.

color mode Determines the color model that Photoshop uses to create the image, such as RGB or CYMK.

complementary (colors) Colors that are opposite each other on the color wheel. They are high in contrast and vibrant.

compositing Combining two or more images into one.

Content-Aware fill Feature that analyzes the area surrounding pixels selected to be deleted, and then fills the area with similar pixels.

Content-Aware Move Allows you to reposition a selection and automatically fill in the hole left behind based on the pixels that surround the hole.

contrast Creates visual interest and a focal point in a composition. It is what draws the eye to the focal point.

Creative Commons Ways that artists can release their works for limited use and still choose the way the works are used and shared: Public Domain, Attribution, ShareAlike, NoDerivs, and NonCommercial.

crop sensor A term to describe cameras with a sensor smaller than the 35mm standard; these cameras will appear to have a zoomed-in effect with standard lenses.

cropping Reframing an image, deleting unwanted portions and adjusting its focal point and compositional balance.

curved (line or shape) Expresses fluidity, beauty, and grace.

decorative fonts Also known as ornamental, novelty, or display fonts. They don't fall into any of the other categories of fonts. Convey a specific feeling.

deliverables A predetermined list of items that will be delivered to the client.

depth of field (DoF) Describes the depth of the focal plane of a camera within an image. A shallow DoF will show only a small part of the image in focus whereas a deep DoF will show the whole image in focus.

desaturate Removing the amount of color in an image.

design principles The verbs of design, such as emphasis, contrast, unity, variety, alignment, balance, rhythm, movement, and proportion.

destructive editing Where you change the image information without reserving the ability to undo or modify the changes later.

diagonal (line) Traveling neither on a vertical nor a horizontal path. Expresses growth or decline and implies movement or change.

dingbat fonts Also known as wingdings. They are a collection of objects and shapes instead of letters.

direction A common way to describe lines, such as vertical, horizontal, diagonal.

document window This area contains your work area and canvas.

dpi Stands for dots per inch and refers to the resolution of an image when printed.

elements of art The building blocks of creative works. They are the nouns of design, such as space, line, shape, form, texture, value, color, and type.

emphasis The focal point to which the eye is naturally and initially drawn in a design.

fair use A set of rules that specify how and when copyrighted material can be used and that make sure copyright protection doesn't come at the cost of creativity and freedom.

feedback loop A system set up to continually encourage and require input and approval on a project's direction.

fill light A light used on the darker side of a subject in a photo to make it appear more dimensional.

filter Filters apply effects that can to clean up or retouch photos, create unique transformations using distortions and lighting effects, or even make a photo appear like a sketch or painting.

flattening Combining and rasterizing all of the layers in the document.

flow A category related to the energy conveyed by lines and shapes.

focal point What the design is all about. The call to action or the primary message you are trying to get across.

fonts The whole collection of a typeface in each of its sizes and styles.

form Describes three-dimensional objects, such as spheres, cubes, and pyramids.

gamut The range of colors a device can capture or display

geometric (line or shape) Tends to be straight and have sharp angles. Looks manmade and intentional. Communicates strength, power, and precision.

glyph Each character of a font, whether it is a letter, number, symbol, or swash.

grain The term used to describe sensor noise (a stippled look) in images shot with low light.

hand-drawn (line or shape) Appears as though created using traditional techniques, such as paints, charcoal, or chalk.

handwritten fonts Also known as hand fonts, they simulate handwriting.

hardness Determines how much a brush fades from its center point. A brush with a hardness of 100 has no fade, and a hardness of 0 has the maximum fade.

high key An image that has very few dark pixels, resulting in a light and bright image; this can be a desirable artistic effect.

highlight The area of a form that is directly facing the light and that appears lightest.

horizontal Moving from left to right; for example, the horizontal line in an "H." Expresses calmness and balance.

hue The actual color of an element (such as red, blue, or green).

hyphenation Determines if and when words should be split with hyphens when wrapping to the next line.

ideographs (ideograms) Images that represent an idea, such as a heart representing love.

image mode See color mode.

implied (line) Doesn't really exist but is implied by shapes, such as dotted or dashed lines, people waiting in a line, or the margin of a block of text.

indent Settings that determine how far an entire paragraph is indented from the rest of the text on each side or in just its first line.

iterations New versions of a design that successively become closer to the desired result.

iterative work Work that is shared as it is completed, allowing the customer to chime in with comments while it is still easy to make a change.

justified Aligns text to a straight edge on both the right and left edges of a paragraph.

kerning The space between specific letter pairs.

Layer Comp A snapshot of the document and all of its layers in its current state.

layers A way to put some elements in front of, or behind, others. When items are on separate layers you can manipulate one item without affecting another, even if the two are in exactly the same area of the image.

leading The amount of space between the baselines of two lines of text, as in double-spaced text in a word processor.

licensing A way to legally use copyrighted material for a certain time and in a certain way, usually associated with paying a fee established by the copyright holder.

ligatures Special characters used to represent letter combinations, such as "fi."

light source The perceived location of the lighting in relation to the form.

lightness A color setting affecting tone, from darker to lighter.

line A mark with a beginning and an end point.

low key An image that has very few light pixels, resulting in a very dark and moody image; this can be a desirable artistic effect for some images.

mask Used to hide portions of a layer by painting black, and reveal portions of the layers below by painting white.

megapixels Describes the number of pixels in millions that a device can capture. Among devices with the similar image sensors, megapixels provide higher image detail.

menu bar This is the standard application menu bar that displays all the menus for Photoshop.

merging Combines and rasterizes selected layers.

metadata Information that is included in a document but is hidden, such as copyright, lens information, location via GPS, camera settings, and more.

model releases The permission that is required when a person's face is identifiable in a photo and the image will be used to promote something—whether it's a product or an idea.

monochromatic Different shades and tints of the same color. Communicates a relaxed and peaceful feeling.

monospaced fonts Fixed-width or non-proportional fonts that use the same amount of horizontal space for each letter.

movement Visual movement within an image, such as the natural tracking of the eye across an image as the eye moves from focal point to focal point.

negative space Blank areas in a design. Also known as white space.

NoDerivs Creative Commons licensing. Requires that you not change material when you incorporate it into your own work. It can be used freely, but you must pass it along without change.

NonCommercial Creative Commons licensing. Means you can use work in your own creative work as long as you don't charge for it.

nondestructively Making changes in a way that allows you to revert to the original image, even after the document is saved (no loss of pixels).

object shadow The area of the form that is facing away from the light source and appears darkest.

opacity The opposite of transparency, a measure of visibility. If a Photoshop layer has an opacity of 100%, it is completely visible (opaque). An opacity of 0 would make all of the elements on that layer transparent.

Options bar The part of the Photoshop interface that contains tool options that is context-sensitive; meaning it changes depending on the selected tool.

organic Describes lines, shapes, or forms that are irregular and imperfect, as those found in nature.

panel group A tabbed grouping of multiple panels.

panels This highly customizable area containing common tools in the interface that can be easily moved, rearranged, or resized.

paragraph settings Affect an entire paragraph rather than selected words. These settings include alignment, hyphenation, and so on.

paragraph spacing Similar to leading, but applies to an entire paragraph instead of lines of type within them defining the spacing above or below paragraphs.

Patch tool A tool that allows you to repair a damaged area by bringing in pixels from an undamaged part of the image.

path Often related to vector images, a specific path created by a vector to define a shape or line. Paths technically have no dimension, so a stroke must be added to make it visible.

pattern A repetitive sequence of different colors, shapes, or values.

pictograph (pictogram) Graphic symbol that represents something in the real world. Computer icons are pictographs that suggest the function they represent, such as a trash can icon to delete a file.

pixel A single dot that makes up a raster image. Pixel is short for "picture element."

points Used to measure type, approximately 1/72 of an inch.

ppi Stands for pixels per inch and is a setting that affects only printed images. Higher ppi affords more detail in printed images.

primary colors Colors that cannot be created by combining other colors, and can be combined to create every other color in the visible spectrum. Additive color systems such, as a computer, use the primary colors of red, blue, and green (not red, blue, and yellow as in painting).

project creep Unplanned changes that increase the amount of work, or scope, that a project requires. When the project loses focus and spins out of control, eating up more and more time and effort.

project deadlines Dictates when work needs to be completed.

project scope Outlines the amount and type of work to be completed.

proportion (scale) Describes the relative size and scale of elements.

public domain Creative Commons licensing. When copyright is expired or released and no longer applies to the content or when an artist releases their work. It can be used without worrying about infringement.

Puppet Warp Allows you to reposition objects like you would a puppet by setting pivot points and altering from there.

radial Circular type of balance that radiates from the center instead of the middle of a design.

raster Originally described an image created by scan lines on CRT monitors, but today it is basically synonymous with bitmap.

rasterize To convert an image of another type into a raster/bitmap image.

reflected highlight Area of a form that is lit by reflections from the ground or other objects in a scene.

render To convert a nonraster image or effect into a raster image.

repetition Intentionally repeating an element in a design.

Replace Color An adjustment that allows you to change the hue and saturation of a specific color range within your image.

resolution A measurement of the number of pixels in a given space—either in an inch (ppi) or total pixels (such as 1920x1080).

rhythm Creative and expressive, rather than a consistent pattern or repetition in a design.

rule of thirds A technique for laying out the space of your page to provide a focal point. Two vertical and two horizontal lines evenly divide the space into nine equal boxes, as in a tic-tac-toe board.

sans serif fonts Text without serifs. Often used for headlines and titles for their strong, stable, modern feel.

saturation The level of black or white in a color: less black or white means a more vivid, or saturated, color.

scale See proportion.

script fonts Mimic calligraphy. They convey a feeling of beauty, grace, or feminine dignity.

secondary colors Created when you combine primary colors.

serif fonts Fonts with serifs: the little "feet" on character ends, created by typewriters. They convey tradition, intelligence, and class.

shape Area enclosed or defined by an outline, such as circles, squares, triangles, or even clouds.

ShareAlike Creative Commons licensing. Allows you to use an item (design) in any way you want as long as your creation is shared under the same license as the original work.

sharpen Add contrast to the fuzzy details to make an image look crisper.

sketches Representative drawings of how to lay out a document or web page. These are sometimes one of the deliverables of a project.

slab serif fonts Squared-off versions of a typical serif font. Also known as Egyptian, block serif, or square serif. Convey a machine-built feel.

small caps Uses only uppercase letterforms for each letter and appears in a smaller size.

smart filters Filters applied to a smart object. These can be edited after they are applied.

smart object Nondestructive layers that can be linked and used across Adobe applications. Filters applied to smart objects become smart filters.

Solid Color fill layers Essentially an infinite plane of color. You cannot paint on these layers, but you can still edit layer settings—such as opacity, blending mode, and masks.

space The canvas, or working area. Its dimensions are determined by the resolution of the page you are creating.

specifications Detailed written goals and limits for a project. These are sometimes one of the deliverables of a project.

Spot Healing brush A Photoshop tool that enables you to paint away image imperfections quickly and easily.

stock photos Images for which the author retains copyright but for which a license for use is available.

stroke The thickness of the visual representation of a path.

Style A category of descriptors for lines, forms, or shapes, often describing the "feeling" of the element.

subtractive color The familiar model from childhood, mixing red, yellow, and blue to make colors. We see the colors because of subtracted light.

swashes Special characters with flowing and elegant endings for the ascenders and descenders.

symmetrical Occurs when you can divide an image along its middle, and the left side of the image is a mirror image of the right (or the top reflects the bottom). Conveys an intentional, formal, and mechanical feeling.

tertiary colors Created by mixing primary and secondary colors.

texture Describes the actual tactile texture in real objects or the appearance of texture in a two-dimensional image.

Tools panel Contains all the tools that you can use in Photoshop. It's important to know that each icon on the toolbar represents a stack of tools that you can access by clicking and holding down the mouse button over the tool's icon.

tracking The overall space between all the letters in a block of text. It allows you to compress or expand the space between the letters as a whole rather than just between specific pairs, as you do with kerning.

transparency An area of an image that is not visible. When exporting a file, transparency is only supported by certain file formats.

Type layers Vector layers in Photoshop specifically for text.

type size A font's height from the highest ascender to the lowest descender.

typeface Specific letterform set, such as Helvetica, Arial, Garamond, and so on. It is the "look" of letters.

unity Also known as harmony and sharing similar traits. Low contrast. Things that go together should look like they belong together. The opposite of variety.

Unsharp Mask A Photoshop filter that sharpens only the edges within the subject of the photo while retaining the overall smooth textures of skin, clothing, and sky.

value Lightness or darkness of an object. Together with color, value represents the visible spectrum, such as a gradient.

variety High contrast. The opposite of unity.

varying-width (line) Expresses flow and grace.

vector A series of points connected by lines and curves determined by mathematical equations. Vector images built from these points are resolution independent. This means they can scale infinitely with no loss of quality.

vector layers Layers consisting of data that can be manipulated with no loss of quality (rather than an arrangement of pixels).

vertical Moving from top to bottom. Vertical lines tend to express power and elevation.

vertical and horizontal scale Describes the function of stretching letters and distorting the typeface geometry.

vibrance A way of adjusting saturation so that clipping is minimized in very saturated colors and preventing muted colors, such as skintone, from becoming over saturated.

warp Distort an object's shape using a grid.

weight (line) The thickness of a line.

white balance Adjusting a device to capture or display white properly by removing color created by the lighting. See also color cast.

wireframe A schematic sketch of a project, commonly used for interactive projects.

Workspace switcher This menu on the Options bar enables you to choose preset workspaces and save the layout of your customized Photoshop interface.

workspaces Specific arrangements of the panels on the screen for easy access to features you use often. There are built-in workspaces or you can design a custom workspace that suits your needs.

zoom A function of the camera lens that enlarges image elements on the sensor of a camera—digital zoom simulates this effect.

Index

D

E

F

G

T

U

V

W

Z

+ Express your creative vision

= Adobe Press + Adobe Creative Cloud Photography Plan

Adobe Press and Adobe invite you to become a Creative Cloud Photography plan member today and **SAVE UP TO 20%** on your first year!

Visit **adobepress.com/register** and follow the instructions to receive this offer!

Adobe, the Adobe logo, Creative Cloud, and the Creative Cloud logo are either registered trademarks or trademarks of Adobe Systems Incorporated in the United States and/or other countries.

The save up to 20% Creative Cloud Photography plan special offer is a limited time offer, expires 12/31/2016.